W9-CMK-650

Praise for David Bornstein's *The Price of a Dream*

"It so greatly transcends research and reporting because of [Bornstein's] common sense, good judgment, and sympathy, which infuses the whole thing. The information on experiences, puzzles, and possibilities will be wonderfully useful in North America."

—Jane Jacobs, author of
The Death and Life of Great American Cities

"Conscientious [and] carefully researched. Bornstein brings his subject to life."

—*Los Angeles Times*

"[*The Price of a Dream*] makes it dramatically clear that the Grameen Bank has pioneered a far better way to help the poor than the massive top-down schemes so long favored by the World Bank and other international development agencies. Bornstein's account [is] superb."

—*Wilson Quarterly*

"If there is one man who has achieved stardom of sorts at the United Nations Fourth World Conference on Women [September 1995], it is [Muhammad Yunus] who wandered into a desperately poor village and got an idea that is changing the face of banking."

—*New York Times*

DISCARDED
FROM
UNIVERSITY OF DAYTON
ROESCH LIBRARY

The Price of a Dream

The Story of the Grameen Bank

DAVID BORNSTEIN

OXFORD

UNIVERSITY PRESS

OXFORD

UNIVERSITY PRESS

Oxford University Press, Inc., publishes works that further
Oxford University's objective of excellence
in research, scholarship, and education.

Oxford New York
Auckland   Cape Town   Dar es Salaam   Hong Kong   Karachi
Kuala Lumpur   Madrid   Melbourne   Mexico City   Nairobi
New Delhi   Shanghai   Taipei   Toronto

With offices in
Argentina   Austria   Brazil   Chile   Czech Republic   France   Greece
Guatemala   Hungary   Italy   Japan   Poland   Portugal   Singapore
South Korea   Switzerland   Thailand   Turkey   Ukraine   Vietnam

Copyright © 1996 by David Bornstein
Afterword © 1997 by David Bornstein

First published by Simon & Schuster, Inc., 1996

First issued as an Oxford University Press paperback, 2005

Oxford is a registered trademark of Oxford University Press

All rights reserved. No part of this publication may be reproduced,
stored in a retrieval system, or transmitted, in any form or by any means,
electronic, mechanical, photocopying, recording, or otherwise,
without the prior permission of Oxford University Press.

Library of Congress Cataloging-in-Publication Data
Bornstein, David.
The price of a dream : the story of the Grameen Bank / David Bornstein.
p. cm.
Originally published: University of Chicago Press ed. Chicago, Ill., 1997.
Includes index.
ISBN-13: 978-0-19-518749-6
1. Grameen Bank.
2. Banks and banking—Bangladesh.
3. Rural poor—Bangladesh—Economic conditions.
4. Women—Bangladesh—Economic conditions. I. Title.
HG3290.6.A8G7278 2005   332.2'8'095492—dc22   2005015493

3 5 7 9 8 6 4 2
Printed in the United States of America
on acid-free paper

HG
329 .6
A9
G 278
2005
COMMUNITY

For my parents

and Selma,
still fighting the good fight
in her ninth decade

Preface

Over the past year, since the publication of my second book, *How To Change The World: Social Entrepreneurs and The Power of New Ideas,* I've spoken with more than a hundred audiences across the United States and Canada about microcredit and social entrepreneurship. When addressing groups, I often ask people to consider the question: "Is the world getting better or worse?" There is no simple answer, of course, but like the pollster's pre-election staple "Is the country headed in the right direction?" it sheds light on people's outlook. And these days, I have found that most people say the world is getting worse.

But when I ask people if they have heard about the Grameen Bank, or microcredit, among general audiences less than a third raise their hands. To me, this is a sign of a serious deficiency in our media. The global spread of microcredit over the past ten years is one of the most positive developments in human history, and it is largely unknown. Without minimizing other problems we face, we should be celebrating the fact that major gains are being made in the area of poverty alleviation. Thousands of institutions, many of which did not exist or had only a fraction of their capacity ten years ago, are extending opportunities to poor people around the globe and demonstrating a viable path toward the eradication of abject poverty.

Most of these institutions are still small, but a few hundred have achieved major scale. Collectively, the microcredit "industry" has demonstrated that poor people are credit-worthy and resourceful. Not long ago, banking with the poor was considered a radical notion; now it is seen as a good business. This shift in perception about the poor—from dependent beneficiaries to competent clients—may be the greatest legacy of microcredit. It opens up a world of possibilities that are just beginning to be seen.

How far have we come? By the end of 2005, the Grameen Bank will have more than 5 million borrowers. In Bangladesh, the epicenter of microcredit, there are some 700 microcredit institutions reaching 14 million families, more than half the nation's total. Today, the odds are better than 3 to 1 that a poor women in Bangladesh is being served by a microcredit program. Microcredit is often cited as an explanation for the fact that, in Bangladesh's past two national elections, more women voted than men.

In 1997, practitioners and supporters of microcredit gathered in Washington, D.C. for the first "Microcredit Summit"— a meeting not organized by any government body, but by citizens. The goal was to extend microcredit (and other financial services) to 100 million of the world's poorest families, especially the women in those families, by 2005. In 1997, the 618 institutions that reported to the campaign were extending credit to 13.5 million clients, of whom 7.6 million were among the "poorest" (meaning that they fell within the bottom half of people living below the poverty line in their countries). By 2003, the campaign reported that close to 3,000 institutions were reaching 81 million clients, 55 million of whom were among the poorest (and 83 percent of whom were women). Sam Daley-Harris, the summit's director, expects that by December 2005 microfinance institutions will be reaching 100 million families, and that by 2007, they will surpass the summit's goal of 100 million "poorest" families. This represents one of the few times that a major development promise is going to be fulfilled—and remarkably close to schedule.

What does it mean that 100 million poor families enjoy access to credit at a fair price? Consider what credit means in your life. In the United States and Canada, how do we buy our cars and houses, our college educations, our business assets? Most of us could never afford them if we had to pay in advance. But we have the option of buying these things in installments. This is, in fact, a big part of our freedom: it allows us to move beyond the circumstances of our births. This option is now being extended to villagers, slum dwellers, excluded people around the globe.

Installment buying enables radical changes, quietly, without the sloganeering of revolutions. For example, the Grameen Bank has extended 620,000 home mortgages to Bangladeshi families, who pay off their houses over five years for less than $1.50 a week. Grameen Phone now leases cell phones to more than 120,000 "village phone ladies" who earn a living selling calls to other villages. In Brazil, a social entrepreneur named Fabio Rosa rents solar electric systems to poor villagers for a fee based on what villagers typically pay for candles, batteries, and kerosene (about $15 per month). There are two billion people in the world who are without electricity—and a billion of them could afford solar energy if they could rent it or pay it off in installments.

Historically, much of the start-up and growth financing for microfinance has come from governments and philanthropy in the form of grants and low-interest loans. These funds—currently under $1 billion a year—continue to play an essential role helping young organizations grow and professionalize, but they are nowhere near adequate to meet the long-term credit needs of the poor, which are estimated in the hundreds of billions of dollars. Today, the trend that promises to transform the sector is the commercialization of microcredit. The big opportunity is to tap into the ocean-deep pockets of the world's capital markets.

This process is just getting underway. Major banks, including Citibank and ICICI Bank, in India, are now looking at microcredit not as a channel for philanthropy, but as a core business opportunity. They are facilitating investments in microfinance institutions, underwriting bond issues, providing loan guarantees, and securitizing portions of microfinance loan portfolios—a process that dramatically increases the availability of funds for lending. And they are beginning to gather data—hard, boring banking data—about the loan performance of poor people.

Although it is obvious to insiders that microfinance is a sound business, because of the dearth of historical data, among bankers there remains a big gap between *perceived* and *actual* risk. This is a classic example of a market inefficiency, one that facilities such as the Microfinance Information Exchange (The Mix), are seeking to address by making standardized data from hundreds of microfinance institutions available online.

Another approach to the "capital access" problem has been the creation of "apex" or intermediary bodies, such as the Grameen Trust and Grameen Foundation, USA, which identify, vet, support, and occasionally help create microfinance organizations. These networks link capital markets to microfinance institutions by aggregating demand and providing credibility and oversight. The Grameen Trust provides support to more than 130 programs serving more than 2 million clients. Under the direction of Alex Counts, the Grameen Foundation, has grown dramatically: it now works with 47 partners serving 1.2 million clients and is embarking on an aggressive expansion to add 5 million new borrowers by 2008.

Governments also have a critical role to play in microfinance, not by providing services directly to the poor, but by creating supportive regulatory environments and allocating financing through politically insulated funding mechanisms.

Looking ahead, the Microcredit Summit campaign has set a "Phase II" goal of reaching 175 million poor families by 2015, while ensuring that half of those families are moved out of abject poverty. If successful, it would go a long way towards achieving the Millennium Development Goals, the commitment by governments to cut worldwide abject poverty in half by 2015.

Grameen Bank founder Muhammad Yunus is already working towards "Phase III" of microcredit, with the goal of creating a "poverty-free world" by 2030. Yunus envisions microcredit institutions gradually converting themselves into a new breed of banks, financed through local deposits, with their own legal frameworks and regulatory authorities. He envisions these Microcredit Banks providing a range of services like those that Grameen has already instituted, including: a variety of savings and loan products, investment opportunities, remittance facilities, student loans and scholarship programs, pension funds, life, health and loan-repayment insurance, home mortgages and access to technology for solar energy, telecommunications, data processing and conversion of waste to fuel.

"Microcredit will become an integral part of the national and global financial systems," Yunus says. "It will make the financial system stronger and inclusive. Microcredit may be the path that will connect the poorest people to the mainstream economy and give the first taste of social-business entrepreneurship to many whom will later dominate the business world. In that sense microcredit may make a contribution far beyond its own territory."

Bringing together the worlds of high finance and microfinance could present some exciting new alignments. What happens, for example, when the interests of wealthy banks coincide with the interest of millions of poor people? Will bank lobbyists start pressuring governments to enact policies supportive of the poor— to ensure that their microloan portfolios stay healthy?

Of course, commercialization comes with risks, the biggest one being a potential loss of focus on the very poor and on women. Although research has shown that microfinance institutions committed to serving customers below the poverty line are among the most cost-efficient and best managed organizations in the industry, many lenders remain wary of the very poor, preferring to serve the "moderate" or "upscale" poor who can manage larger loans. There will probably always be a pressure to turn "microcredit" into "minicredit"— and so there will always be a corresponding need for vigilance on the part of committed funders, advocates, managers, and government agencies to ensure that microfinance's social mission does not get too diluted. To this end, the Grameen Bank has redoubled its efforts to reach out to the poorest of the poor through its "Struggling Members" program, which has extended loans for as little as $3 per year to 42,000 beggars.

Microcredit has always been more than banking. In the words of Susan Davis, the chair of the Grameen Foundation, it is a strategy that was "crafted by the hands of poor women." At a point when the industry is gearing up for major expansion into new terrain, it is important to remember its initial purpose. Loans are a means; profit is a means; scale is a means. The goal is to decrease suffering: to build a framework of social and economic supports that free people from the captivity of poverty and allow them to fulfill their dreams.

David Bornstein
New York, June 28, 2005

Contents

PART V   THE WORLD

PART VI   THE FUTURE

A NOTE ON THE NAMING

Throughout this book, characters are referred to by the names their colleagues and neighbors usually use. Thus, Muhammad Yunus is Yunus and Sabina Yasmin is Sabina. All the characters in this book go by their real names, except for a few villagers whose names I have changed at their request.

The Price of a Dream

This Business of Bangles

Inside, the mud walls were smooth to the touch. A light scent of burning straw came from the kitchen. Above a wooden table hung a framed birth certificate and a political campaign poster featuring the party's logo—a river boat. Another wall was decorated with yellow pages from *USA Today*. Suspended from the ceiling was a pot of fresh flowers.

Oirashibala Dhor set her basket on the ground beside my translator. She appeared to be constructed entirely of angles—knees and elbows jutting sharply from beneath her plain white sari. Her hair was silver, her brow deeply creased, and she had only half her teeth. She was born, as she put it, "before the British-Japanese war of 1943."

The woman who lived in the house served us eggs, sweet noodles, and tea with cardamom. Oirashi, as everyone calls her, didn't usually receive such hospitality on her daily peddling rounds, but this day she had arrived with guests.

Whispers could be heard from behind a bamboo screen, where two girls of marrying age were hidden. Two young sisters and an older woman emerged, and were joined by several neighbors and their children. By the time Oirashi finished her tea, a dozen people surrounded her basket. She took up a red capsule. "Lip gloss," she announced. "You put this over lipstick, your lips shine."

An older woman moved closer. "Can I try?"

"How old are you?" said another woman. "Are you young?"

"How much is the lip gloss?" a young girl asked. "Give it to me for 6 takas."

Another girl, browsing through Oirashi's basket, inquired, "How much is this hair clip?"

"Don't be so extravagant," her mother said.

Oirashibala Dhor

The girl dropped the hair clip and picked up a jar of Fair and Lovely beauty cream, which promised "noticeably fairer" skin in six to eight weeks.

"That's for older people," Oirashi said. She selected a bangle, polished it with her sari, and asked the girl if she liked the color. The girl nodded. Oirashi requested soap and water. She wet the girl's tiny wrist and then squeezed and twisted until the bangle slid on. The girl extended her arm to show her mother. Children at the door pressed forward to see.

"Stop blocking the door," an older woman yelled. "Let the breeze in."

"Nowadays, children are so disrespectful."

"Please give me the lip gloss for 3 takas less," the first girl said, her final plea.

"Don't kill me," Oirashi replied.

Outside, twenty minutes later, the women waved good-bye. "You have a basket full of money," one called. "The *dakoits* [bandits] will get you."

"I hide my money inside my clothes," Oirashi said. "One peddler had her earrings stolen a few days ago. But I'm careful."

. . .

Oirashi has been supporting herself since the death of her husband, twenty-five years ago. "He died of Frozen Satan's Gout," she told me. "Nowadays, the doctors call it pneumonia." Every morning, except Sunday, when her Grameen Bank meeting is scheduled, she gets up with the sun, offers a prayer, places her basket on her head, and sets out to sell her wares. She walks for miles. Though she sells sandals, she never wears them. I asked her why.

"I'm just a simple peddler," she replied. "How can I be seen wearing sandals?"

As Oirashi walked along the narrow partitions separating rice plots, she drummed on her thighs. I asked about the basket balanced on her head. "It's not heavy," she replied. Sparrowlike, she gestured left and right, pointing out the Muslims, the Hindus, the well-to-do villagers and the very poor ones. We approached a cluster of huts situated on a mud plateau that rose four feet above the bristling green field. "Those are all Grameen Bank house loans," Oirashi said. "All the old houses were washed away in the [1991] cyclone."

Several women waved. "These women have become a lot braver because of the Grameen Bank," Oirashi said. "Previously, if any strange man came, they would go into their houses and sit behind the purdah" (literally, "veil"; figuratively, the Muslim code of conduct that confines women to their homesteads). "Now they come out and they talk."

Oirashi passed by one woman who called her over. "I'll only come if you cook me a hen," Oirashi joked. She had no time to waste with nonbuyers, she said. "People take a lot of time picking and choosing from my basket. If I could go to more places, I'd be rich."

Oirashi set her basket of bangles, earrings, and cosmetics on the ground in front of a house where a woman was squatting on a cane mat, spreading unhusked rice to dry in the sun. "Do you need anything?" she called. "I have special things for Eid [the Muslim festival at the end of the month of Ramadan]."

"Do you have Indian things?" the woman inquired.

"I'm a Bangladeshi," Oirashi replied, feigning indignation. In fact, her basket was full of costume jewelry manufactured in India.

The woman came over and sifted through the basket. Nothing caught her eye.

"This is only the first of the moon," Oirashi said. "I'll have better things soon."

Another woman, eyeing us from a distance of fifteen feet, would not come closer because of me.

"You're a member of the Grameen Bank," Oirashi said. "Why are you feeling shy?"

The woman said nothing.

"Aren't you going to look?"

"No, I'm feeling sad," the woman said.

A young girl darted out of a hut and was instantly called back by her mother. She turned and pleaded for a bangle.

"I don't have the money for such things," her mother said. She turned to Oirashi. "Why is she being so unreasonable?"

Oirashi made a face and picked up her basket. "People won't buy, won't buy," she said, "then somebody will spend 20 or 50 takas. That's how this business of bangles goes. I can't complain. Things are easier for me than they used to be. Today's girls like their jewelry and they wear a lot of makeup."

"Why did that woman say she was feeling sad?" I asked, after we had left.

"Because they barely get by."

We crossed a bamboo bridge over a creek and followed a sun-bleached path lined with bamboo fences that enclosed mud huts; coconut, mango, and papaya trees; and haystacks shaped like giant turnips. We passed an old man struggling to peddle a rickshaw loaded with several large sacks of rice. At each bump or incline, he had to get down and push. The bazaar was three miles away. At a tiny, immaculate hut Oirashi paused to exchange a few words with a woman who would not come outside. Afterward, she explained: "The man of this house has two wives. One wife owes me 20 takas. She was supposed to pay me today but she went somewhere—so my money went with her."

By a much larger house, a woman in a bright red sari greeted us with a smile. "You always come to make us buy things," she said. These were good customers. "They're fond of me and they understand my sorrows," Oirashi explained. "If I sell 10 takas' worth of merchandise, then I'll give them a one-taka discount because they buy only from me."

"Does it increase your sales to do business this way?" I asked.

"It increases the love," Oirashi said.

"Do people know your buying price?"

"No," Oirashi said, laughing. "I always lie."

To the women inside the villages, Oirashi brings news and gossip; occasionally, she arranges a marriage. Her overriding concern, however, is finding a husband for her second daughter, who is in her mid-twenties and still unmarried. In Bangladesh, daughters usually move in with the families of their husbands after marriage, but Oirashi doesn't want to be left alone in her old age. So she is looking for a *ghor jamai,* a son-in-law who agrees to live in his mother-in-law's house. Finding one is not easy; most men look down on the idea. Oirashi knows that if her plan has a hope, she must sweeten the pot. She will have to come up with a sizable dowry and expand her house.

"When I have all the jewelry and money," she explained, "then I will tell my eldest daughter's husband to find a boy. After he has found one, I will go and see for myself. If I like him, then the wedding will take place."

"Will you ask your daughter's consent?" I asked.

"If my daughter doesn't like him," Oirashi said, "my liking him won't help. Is this my marriage?"

The wedding (dowry included) will cost more than 15,000 takas (about $375). For many villagers such a sum represents two or three years' income. Oirashi has been working to save it for the better part of a decade. Fortunately, in the past few years, her peddling sales have increased. Oirashi often sells on credit, but when she buys merchandise in the bazaars, she does better to pay cash. Cash flow had always been her major business constraint. To overcome it, Oirashi joined the Grameen Bank. In six years her annual borrowings increased from about $60 to about $260. Like all retailers, with cash in hand she found herself in a stronger position. She could haggle with vendors over price, stock higher-quality merchandise, and take advantage of volume discounts.

Before the Grameen Bank came along, Oirashi borrowed from moneylenders, whose interest rates ranged from 10 to 20 percent a month. "Now I always buy with cash," she explained. "Look—I do my business for profit."

Introduction

As cold waters to a thirsty soul, so is good news from a far country.

PROVERBS 25:25

Buses and trucks barrel down Mirpur Road, in Dhaka, Bangladesh, blasting their horns and leaving trails of black smoke to settle on rickshaws and oxcarts. By the side of the road a high brick wall encircles four buildings in a compound, one of which is dominated by a tropical garden that opens to the sky. On many afternoons rain falls into the garden, and at their desks accountants can pause to listen to the sound of water slapping leaves. This is the head office of a bank that does its work in the countryside.

Thousands of visitors have traveled to Bangladesh to learn from this bank, and many arrive carrying tape recorders and note pads. When they enter the office, they find no receptionist, no carpets, no elevators, and few telephones. The rooms are equipped with ceiling fans, manual typewriters, paperweights, and stacks of ledgers. Despite the heat, only the computer room on the fifth floor is air-conditioned. Here, programmers monitor operations and prepare reports, which they love to spice up with wild-looking graphs depicting their organization's growth. The programmers like to alternate colors and switch between bars, cylinders, and lines, but their graphs all look basically the same: like ski hills, rising slowly at first, and then shooting up at impossibly steep angles toward the sky.

Over the past two decades, the Grameen Bank has extended loans in excess of $1.5 billion for self-employment purposes to some of the poorest people in the world—landless villagers in Bangladesh. It has lent half that amount in just the past two years. Today, through a network of more than 1,050 branch offices, the bank serves more than 2 million clients, 94 percent of them women. Each month, it adds thousands more. Each month, it extends new loans totaling $30 to $40 million. The proportion of its loans that are repaid, 97 percent, is comparable to the repayment rate at Chase Manhattan Bank.

"Grameen" comes from the Bangla word *gram,* or village, and true to its name, the Grameen Bank works only in villages, which is one of many ways it has reimagined the idea of a bank—turned it on its head, so to speak. Another is that it lends money mainly to women in small amounts for short periods of time. Yet another is its method of screening borrowers: To qualify for a loan, a villager must show that her family's assets fall *below* the bank's threshold. She will not be required to furnish collateral, demonstrate a credit history, or produce a guarantor; instead, she must join a five-member group and a forty-member center, and attend a meeting every week, and she must assume responsibility for the loans of her group's members. This is crucial, because it is the group—not the bank —that initially evaluates loan proposals. Defaulters spoil things for everybody else, so group members choose their partners wisely. If all five repay their loans promptly, each is guaranteed access to credit for the rest of her life—or as long as she elects to remain a customer. In this fashion Grameen is faithful to the Latin from which "credit" derives: *credere*—"to believe."

"The myth that credit is the privilege of a few fortunate people needs to be exploded," explains Muhammad Yunus, the founder of the Grameen Bank. "You look at the tiniest village and the tiniest person in that village: a very capable person, a very intelligent person. You have only to create the proper environment to support these people so that they can change their own lives."

Pure idealism? Well, yes. Nonetheless, these words come from a man who has designed a bank that forces its borrowers to save money for emergencies, provides them with benefits in the event of death, and is in the process of instituting a village-based health-care and insurance program, which will be self-financing. Today, against the backdrop of two and a half decades of often-wasted international aid, Grameen's entrepreneurial approach stands out as singularly effective and sustainable. Up to 1994, the bank had revolved its loan capital more than five times. Along the way, it helped millions of villagers to move from one or two meals a day to three, from one or two sets of clothing to three or four. Grameen members have borrowed money to pay for their children's education, to buy medicine, to build houses, to accumulate assets for old age, and, like Oirashi, to pay for their daughters' weddings.

It was in 1991, shortly after completing a master's in journalism, that I first heard about the Grameen Bank from a friend who was directing a documentary film about it. Before journalism, I had studied commerce and worked for four years writing computer systems for business applications. I had always been interested in innovative businesses. So I asked my friend to lend me some literature—a book and several articles—on this bank in Bangladesh.

The book I borrowed said nothing about business as I had studied it. It was a compilation of case studies entitled *Jorimon and Others: Faces of Poverty,* edited by Muhammad Yunus. The book told of poor villagers who had taken loans from the bank and improved their lives. It was while reading the third story, entitled "Sakhina's New Identity," about a woman who once had to beg for food, who took a loan and began supporting herself by selling sweet potatoes, that I thought: If these stories are true, then the Grameen Bank is the most beautiful business I have ever heard of.

A newspaper article dating from the fall of 1990 said that it had financed 800,000 "microentrepreneurs." How did they all turn a profit? The bank charged the commercial interest rate, then 16 percent. This seemed awfully high. Was it necessary to charge poor people so much? Of course, the cost of managing such small loans had to be high. But was this rate low enough to allow them a fair return on investment? It had to be, I guessed, because, as the article pointed out, each year the villagers took larger loans, and each year they repaid them, and according to the bank they repaid them on time.

Yunus, an economist, had founded the bank while teaching at a university in southern Bangladesh. One day, walking in a village near his campus in 1976, he met a woman trying to earn a living by constructing bamboo stools. The woman had no money to purchase materials and so she barely earned enough to feed herself. Yunus related the story to his graduate students and together they designed an experimental credit program to assist her and others.

From there, the story unfolded like a fable. The experiment spread from a half dozen' villagers to a few hundred, and the system held. It spread from a few hundred to a few thousand, and it still held. Yunus quit teaching. A cadre of graduate students abandoned their career plans to join him. At 50,000 clients, things were still working. Yunus raised millions of dollars and set out to franchise his operation. At a certain point, for reasons the articles I had did not make clear, the bank switched from banking with men to banking almost exclusively with women.

After several years, similar banks had sprouted up in Malaysia, in the Philippines, in Malawi, and in dozens of locales in Africa, South

America, and even North America. Yunus had won international awards and was touted as a candidate for the Nobel Prize.

For peace or economics? I wondered.

He said his target market was the poorest half of Bangladesh, some 10 million families. Was he serious? Surely his system would break down before it reached that point. The market would become saturated. Bureaucratic torpor would set in. How far could it go?

He took it even further, estimating that a billion poor people around the world could improve their lives relatively quickly with support from institutions like the Grameen Bank. In the foreword to *Jorimon,* apparently surprised by his own success, he wrote that the villagers' stories illustrated how easy it is "to change a person's life for the better; which seems unbelievable at times."

It did seem unbelievable. Better than cold fusion—if it were true.

As Yunus saw it, poverty was not the complex, insuperable problem it had been made out to be. The process of impoverishment was quite predictable, and the way to arrest it was also quite predictable.

The Grameen Bank was an attempt to prove this thesis.

Bangladesh was certainly an appropriate place to try. Stricken by floods, droughts, and cyclones, Bangladesh was a country so poor it had been dubbed the *Fifth* World and labeled by diplomats an "international basketcase." To many observers, Bangladesh was not just a troubled nation, it was a disturbing *notion.* From afar, this little country seemed proof of the randomness of the universe, proof that some people are just plain unlucky and there's not much that can be done about it.

The Grameen Bank was the first organization I'd read about that appeared to dispel this notion.

It had its work cut out. The numbers were staggering. Imagine almost half the population of the United States packed into an area the size of Wisconsin, and the vast majority of them malnourished, illiterate, and desperate for work.

Each day, thousands of villagers flooded into Dhaka, Bangladesh's choking and wheezing capital city, seeking employment. Millions were poised to follow in the coming years. But this problem wasn't unique to Bangladesh. Throughout Asia, Africa, and Latin America, urban populations were skyrocketing as cultivable land grew ever more scarce and tens of millions could no longer survive in their villages.

"By the end of this decade," wrote Richard Critchfield in his 1994 book *The Villagers,* "more people will live in towns and cities than in villages, a great milestone in human history." It was a milestone he feared would be accompanied by "drastic cultural disruption." Robert Kaplan, writing in *The Atlantic Monthly* the same year, envisioned, in the coming decades, "an increasingly large number of people . . . living in shanty-towns where attempts to rise above poverty, cultural dysfunction, and ethnic strife will be doomed by a lack of water to drink, soil to till, and space to survive in."

Did development along the lines of the Grameen Bank offer an alternative to this grim scenario, a means of helping people by providing them with opportunities for self-employment where they lived? How many of the Grameen Bank's borrowers would have moved to a slum in Dhaka had the bank not granted them a loan?

The questions prompted a broader inquiry: Did helping people stay in their villages represent economic progress? Two centuries ago, hadn't Adam Smith written that the "greatest improvements in the productive powers" of mankind were attributable to the division of labor? And hadn't this led to industrialization, urbanization, factories, assembly lines, and, in the end, greater wealth for all? Look at postwar Japan, look at the Asian "tigers."

Yet here was a twentieth-century economist, one of the most highly respected voices in world development, arguing that the best (in fact, the only) way to combat the world's most entrenched poverty was to create the conditions whereby millions of tiny entrepreneurs scattered in hundreds of thousands of villages and small towns could support themselves through self-chosen pursuits. Not wage-employment, but self-employment; not giantism, but gradualism; not cities, but villages; not men, but women.

Was this the vision of a modern-day Luddite, a machine-smasher? To the contrary. Yunus had been schooled in the tradition of the renowned growth economist Joseph Schumpeter. Schumpeter viewed the entrepreneur as the dynamic factor in the economy, a force that issued a "gale of creative destruction," exploiting new technologies and exploring "uncharted sea[s]." But Yunus had also grown up in Bangladesh and seen the effects of technology thrust haphazardly upon a preindustrial society. When villagers left the countryside in droves to become factory laborers, he didn't call it progress.

"Unless designed properly, wage employment may mean being condemned to a life in squalid city slums or working for two meals a day for one's life," he wrote. "Wage employment is not a happy road to the reduction of poverty. The removal or reduction of poverty must be a continuous process of creation of assets, so that the asset base of a poor person becomes stronger at each economic cycle, enabling him or her to earn more and more."

In fact, Yunus doubted that the developing world was *capable* of creating wage employment for the estimated 38 million people who, each year, entered the labor forces in Asia, Africa, and Latin America.

What interested him were advancements that helped societies reorganize themselves along more intimate lines. In the age of the Internet, why did people have to leave the countryside for cities? Because that's where the factory jobs were! So, rather than move the villagers to the capitalists, move the capital to the villagers. That was the general idea.

The Grameen Bank was the first step in this process. By placing resources directly into the hands of poor people, it got them involved in myriad businesses—providing services, trading, processing, manufacturing, and shopkeeping—while gradually expanding the economic role of women. In time, many village-based entrepreneurs would upgrade their skills and management abilities. It might take decades or generations, but, Yunus felt, eventually they would be able to carve out profitable niches in the world economy. In the meantime, although they remained extremely poor by international standards, they would enjoy more options and hopefully lead more satisfying lives.

(In the late 1980s, the Grameen Bank began helping villagers with intermediate-level technology in agriculture and fisheries. In the early 1990s, the bank began helping thousands of weavers market millions of yards of cloth to manufacturers producing shirts for the American and French markets. In 1995, Yunus submitted a proposal to the government to implement a cellular phone network in Bangladesh to be run by thousands of his borrowers [business name: Grameen Telecom]; and began exploring the commercial possibilities of borrowers generating and selling solar power in villages [business name: Grameen Energy].)

Oddly enough, one could think of the Grameen Bank as a version of supply-side economics: Reaganomics, with a twist. Rather than injecting capital into the economy at the altitude of corporate investors, as tax cuts or special incentives, it was injected at ground level, as loans to the poor. Call it trickle-*up*—or better, *bubble-up*—economics.

What did bubble-up economics promise? In the short run, modest but measurable improvements for the poorest segment of society: better food, shelter, and clothing; some basic health care; opportunities for education; more control, less anxiety; and the ability to plan, within a limited range, for the future.

Here was the kicker: In the long run, Yunus believed that everyone, including the wealthy, would benefit. These small-business people would eventually reach a point where they had more spending power, where they could each afford a few more bars of soap each year, a few tubes of toothpaste, an extra sari for special occasions.

Across Bangladesh, this would translate into a demand for millions of bars of soap, millions of tubes of toothpaste, and millions of saris. And then, although they may have no idea why soap or sari demand is up, those in the business of producing these items would experience the pleasant sensation of bubbles nudging them from below. All those small loans finally reaching the surface.

Bubble-up seemed infinitely more attractive than trickle-down for the simple reason that it started with, rather than ended with, the people who needed assistance most. But could it really change a national economy? Or would it remain, as some predicted, mired in low productivity and ever-diminishing returns? And what was the alternative for Bangladesh? Since its birth in 1971, the country had absorbed more than $25 billion in foreign aid and the majority of its citizens had grown *poorer.* Here was an organization producing results where so many others had come up empty.

In 1991, the Grameen Bank surpassed one million borrowers; in 1994, it surpassed 2 million. (Since each borrower represents one family, its loans have an impact on roughly 10 million people.) In the four years since my first visit to Bangladesh in 1992, the bank's annual disbursements have increased 400 percent. Microenterprise banks and programs have since opened shop throughout the world, with hundreds in the United States and Canada. Their systems vary according to context and culture, but their objectives are the same. Like Grameen, they view poor people as clients, not beneficiaries, and they seek to provide them with the means to support themselves through dignified self-employment.

Typically, Americans are reluctant to look to other countries for guidance with their social problems. However, as the current political debate rages over how big government should be, Grameen's experiences are more relevant to the United States than ever before. The Grameen Bank has received praise from U.S. commentators and policy makers on both the left and the right. Being Bangladeshi, it has the advantage of being seen as a perennial underdog: a one-armed pitcher throwing a no-hitter. And, no doubt, the bank speaks to something at the core of the American ideal: what Ralph Waldo Emerson called "the heroism and grandeur which belong to acts of self-reliance."

Grameen is a pure meritocracy, providing opportunities for self-advancement based not on class or race or inherited privilege but on character, imagination, and hard work. Only those who belong to the poorest 50 percent of the population are eligible to join. But Grameen does not demand less of its clients because of their circumstances; it demands *more* of them. While wealthy Bangladeshis often get away with defaulting on their bank loans, Grameen clients are not permitted to miss a single installment. Only those who repay their loans promptly are granted subsequent loans, and only those judged trustworthy by their neighbors are accepted into borrowing groups in the first place.

Grameen is also a political chameleon. It has the ability to affirm beliefs that both conservatives and liberals hold dear. From the right, Grameen can be seen as an entrepreneurial institution that makes the case for less government; from the left, it appears to be an enlightened social welfare program that argues for the value of government involvement. Some see Grameen as an example of reinvented government. Muhammad Yunus disagrees. He sees his bank as an example of reinvented capitalism. In fact, he calls it a "socially conscious capitalist enterprise."

In the end, Grameen resists all attempts to reduce it to an ideology. As an institution, the bank has few precedents; it is a business that scrupulously controls costs and aims at profitability *and* a social program whose mandate is to end poverty and hunger.

Consider: The Grameen Bank charges interest four points above the commercial rate. It never forgives loans, not even after a flood or a cyclone, although it restructures them when necessary. It provides no free services to its borrowers, charging fees even when it distributes such essential items as water-purification crystals, vegetable seeds, and iodized salt. Although the bank has received tens of millions of dollars in grants and low-cost loans from foreign governments, it remains a private enterprise, with 90 percent of its shares controlled by its 2 million borrowers. For all its efforts to contain costs, Grameen remains committed to a clientele that is inherently expensive to serve—a clientele that in the absence of an ethical imperative would probably never have been discovered by the free market.

Laissez-faire or interventionist? Either way, Grameen is a performer —which is why, in July 1995, the World Bank broke with its tradition of financing primarily large-scale infrastructure-development projects by launching a drive to raise more than $200 million for Grameen-style lending, and why, over the past few years, many Americans have attempted to tackle poverty in the United States in similar ways. Part of a movement some call the "first Third World technology transfer," the

Association for Enterprise Opportunity, a network of microenterprise development organizations established in 1991, listed, by 1995, four hundred members across the United States and Canada. Yunus is excited by the spread of these programs. "If the United States becomes convinced that poverty can be eliminated," he told me, "then it can be done."

But given the canyon of cultural and economic differences separating the two countries, the "technology transfer" poses difficulties. To begin with, Bangladesh has a long tradition of self-employment. By contrast, very few Americans—not even one in ten—work for themselves full-time, and low-income Americans who wish to be self-employed require training, technical assistance, and, perhaps most important, access to business networks along with credit.

Confronting these obstacles, American microbankers who have borrowed from Grameen have had to innovate and adapt the model to diverse economic and social conditions across the country. Many have impressive repayment rates—about 95 percent—and excellent training programs. Most remain quite small and, at present, none comes close to breaking even. But their program costs continue to drop and their borrowers continue to draw larger loans. One banker for the poor has recently franchised his operation and is currently working with more than 1,800 small businesses in New England, Delaware, and South Miami.

In the meantime, in Bangladesh, Grameen's money continues to revolve—going out as loans, coming back as installments. Along the way, in the steady rhythm of their weekly meetings, Grameen bankers provide bits of useful information to millions of villagers, chipping away at old habits and attitudes, slowly turning the ship of one of the world's poorest nations.

Some have called Grameen a development "miracle," but this just misses the point. Miracles by definition occur once. Grameen has extended its services to 35,000 villages. Yunus likes to compare it to McDonald's. "People know the quality of our service," he says. "Our job is to make sure it doesn't deteriorate in any corner of the country."

Indeed, the Grameen Bank has marketed small loans like burgers and fries. With millions served.

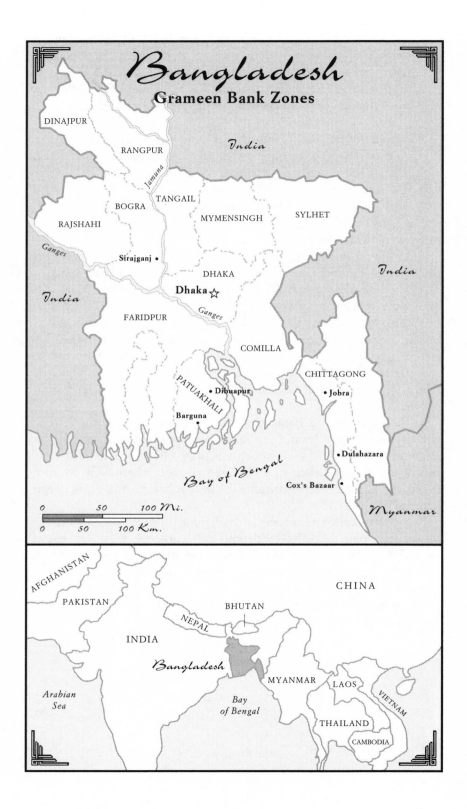

PART I

The Idea

The reasonable man adapts himself to the world: the unreasonable one persists in trying to adapt the world to himself. Therefore all progress depends on the unreasonable man.

GEORGE BERNARD SHAW

1

Fairy Tales

In 1972, after the War of Independence, Muhammad Yunus returned to Bangladesh to help rebuild his country.

The War of Independence was the culmination of an untenable political arrangement dating back to 1947, when India and Pakistan were partitioned and Pakistan found itself split into two "wings" separated by a thousand miles of hostile territory. Except for Islam, the Eastern Wing and the Western Wing had little in common. The West had a stronger industrial base and its language was Urdu. The East was poorer and more populous and its economy was almost totally dependent on agriculture. The language spoken was Bangla. The government was located in the West.

Within a few years, the Bengalis in the East began to resent the government in West Pakistan, which exploited their resources while directing a disproportionate share of the country's wealth to its own people. When the government went so far as to declare Urdu the only national language, the Bengalis were enraged. The move sparked riots and gave birth to a political movement grounded in Bengali national identity. At the heart of this movement was the Bengali's pride in their language—Bangla—with its rich heritage of poetry and song.

In 1971, the Awami League, a political party representing the Bengali majority, won power in a national election. After the government in the West refused to accept the result, Sheik Mujibar Rahman, the leader of the Awami League, declared independence. West Pakistan sent in troops and a nine-month civil war ensued in which more than a million Bengalis were killed. In December 1971, India entered the war on the side of Bangladesh and helped bring about the surrender of Pakistan. By February, most of Asia and Europe had recognized a new nation: Bangladesh —the land of the Bangla speakers.

In his seven years in the United States, Yunus had completed a doctorate in economics at Vanderbilt University in Nashville, Tennessee; taught at Tennessee State University and in Colorado; and lived for a short period in Washington, D.C., where, in 1971, he lobbied Congress to stop military aid to Pakistan. Yunus had married an American woman. After the war, they returned to live in Bangladesh.

Back home, Yunus found himself caught up in the euphoria of liberation. No longer under British or Pakistani rule, Bangladesh could shape its own destiny. So much was possible. So much work remained to be done.

At the urging of a former teacher, he accepted a job with the government planning commission as deputy chief of the General Economics Division. However, within weeks, his enthusiasm waned. The new government seemed every bit as bureaucratic, corrupt, and ineffectual as previous regimes. After two months, convinced that he could accomplish little of value, he left a letter of resignation on his desk and walked out.

He applied for a teaching position with Dhaka University but was turned down. So he joined Chittagong University as chairman of the Department of Economics. Chittagong was Bangladesh's second university. It lacked the prestige of Dhaka University, but something far more important recommended it: location. Chittagong University was situated in the hills north of the city, set back off the main road and surrounded by villages. One road to the university passed right through the heart of a village called Jobra.

For the thousands of men and women who staff the Grameen Bank, the story of their organization's birth has the resonance of myth. Colleagues who were around at the beginning relate Yunus's experiences in Jobra the same way an old friend might describe Bill Gates's first attempts at writing his famous computer operating system.

Immediately, he began changing the way things were done at Chittagong University. His experiences in the United States had shown him new possibilities for teacher-student relationships. "In Bangladesh, you would never just talk to your teacher," he recalled. "You were always bowing to him."

When he arrived in Nashville in 1965, at the age of twenty-five, Yunus found himself surrounded by young people intent on overturning all authority. "Flower children, Woodstock, the Vietnam War—don't trust anybody over thirty." The message he carried home was that young people were capable of transforming their society. Eager to translate his ideas into action, he established the Rural Economics Program with a grant from the Ford Foundation, and encouraged his students to get involved with local villagers as part of their course work.

"A public mourning raises the price of black cloth," wrote Adam Smith. But how did the monsoon affect the price of straw? How did the price fluctuate throughout the year? How much food did local farmers grow?

Before he could begin talking meaningfully about economics in the classroom, Yunus felt that he and his students needed to know the answers to these questions. So he joined them in Jobra, conducting interviews and surveys. He organized an immunization program. And when it came time for local farmers to transplant rice crops, he and his students stood with them knee-deep in mud.

Before long, students from other departments were crowding into Yunus's classes to hear him speak. One former student recalled: "He had wide shoulders and he carried a big canvas bag over one shoulder. He had a car with no muffler. He also had a foreign wife.

"He was seen as a very extraordinary man."

Chittagong University was located a half hour from the city, and many professors commuted to work. Most classes were scheduled in the morning and, by 3:00 P.M., the faculty offices were empty. Yunus lived on campus, so in the late afternoons he was free to explore Jobra. He would stop and chat with villagers by the roadside, in the shade of a tree, or join groups of men in tea stalls, sharing biscuits and gossip. "He would spend hours listening to the villagers," a colleague recalled. "Their problems, their ideas, their experiences."

In 1974, flooding caused widespread crop failure throughout Bangladesh. Bangladesh had an emergency food distribution system in place, set up after the haunting famine of 1943, in which 3 to 5 million people died. It saved the country from a similar nightmare in 1974. But when distributors hoarded rice, causing the price to double that autumn, tens of thousands of villagers starved.

In the wake of the famine, Yunus all but lost interest in the abstractions of classroom economics. While villagers went hungry outside, within the halls of Chittagong University classes and exams proceeded on schedule, undisturbed. When he referred to his texts, he envisioned himself gazing down upon the world from a great altitude "totally blinded by the height," thinking he was "seeing" the world when in fact he was only "imagining" it. And he asked himself and his students if, for all their knowledge of equations and formulas, they really understood how 90 percent of the people in their country lived?

Muhammad Yunus

"It was all fairy tales," he recalled. "All make believe. How could I teach something that I was disenchanted with myself? I was trying to look for some relevance to what I saw around me."

Before the famine, Yunus had spent the better part of a year running from one government agency to another trying to get a Deep Tubewell (DTW) installed in Jobra so that locals could irrigate their land and grow a high-yielding rice crop during the dry winter season.

When he finally succeeded, the results were disappointing. Farmers fought among themselves over water distribution and how much each had to contribute for fuel. Just as the rice was at its flowering stage, the farmers ran out of money, and to save the crop, Yunus had to pay for diesel fuel from his own pocket.

The following season, he got the farmers together. "You have so many resources," he told them. "You have land, you have water, you have people. Yet you are going without food, without rice."

"We're fed up," he was told. "We tried. We can't do it."

Yunus listened to the villagers' stories of infighting, and he saw that what was needed was an independent party to manage the well. This was the story of life in Bangladesh: Poverty created a climate of such intense competition, villagers found it difficult to work together. Yunus proposed that he and his students take it over. They would pay for the fuel and provide the farmers with all necessary farm inputs; in exchange, they would receive one third of the crop. The remainder would be split evenly between farmers and landlords. If the farm operated at a profit, the villagers would keep the surplus; if not, Yunus would pay the loss out of his own pocket. He named it the New Era Three Share Farm.

Most of the villagers remembered Yunus's generosity from the previous year and trusted him, but others worried that his plan was a trick to socialize their land. In the week following the meeting, however, several villagers who had been reluctant to join came forward. They could not afford to plant a winter crop on their own; if they didn't join the Three Share Farm, their land would simply lie fallow.

Four students were given chief responsibility for the New Era Three Share Farm. One of them, an economics major named Dipal Chandra Barua, had grown up in Jobra. Dipal had long, thick hair, a baby face, and an easy way about him. In another life, his photograph might have adorned the lockers of junior high school girls. He had a keen loyalty to Yunus. A few years earlier, his father, Pulim Bihari Barua, a local farmer, had ventured to the university to inquire about the possibility of enrolling his son in economics. Rather than seek advice at the admissions office, he elected to approach Yunus directly at home. Pulim, who had a third-grade education, felt uneasy as he passed by the circles of well-dressed students waiting for the train back to the city.

When he arrived at Yunus's house, located at the top of a hill, and knocked on the door, he was almost overwhelmed by the appearance of the man who answered. He had seen Yunus before, but up close and in his own home, the professor seemed powerful and imperious. "He was a handsome figure," Pulim recalled, adding that Yunus's hair, even longer than his son's, made him look fierce. "He looked like a *dakoit,*" he said with a laugh.

Yunus invited Pulim in and listened to him. After he finished, he asked only one question. "Can you afford to send your son to university for all four years?"

"I think so."

"He'll have to pass the exam first," Yunus said. "Even if Sheik Mujib sent his son here to me, he'd still have to pass the exam."

The day of his exam, Dipal returned home depressed. He told his father that every time he answered a question, Yunus had broken out in laughter. He was certain he failed. But Yunus was delighted with the youth's plain speaking style and intelligence, and he encouraged him to get involved with the Rural Economics Program. Since Dipal was from Jobra, he would have a natural advantage.

While Dipal and three other students organized the villagers into four blocks to distribute water for the Three Share Farm, Yunus approached the manager of the Janata Bank, a nationalized bank with a branch on campus, to inquire about a loan. Here he ran into a problem: The branch had never extended a loan to a group of villagers; in fact, it had never extended a loan at all. It merely accepted deposits, which were used to finance businesses in urban areas. However, because Yunus was a well-known figure in the area, the manager accepted him as personal guarantor and granted him a loan of 40,000 takas (about $1,250).

As water began to flow, more and more villagers joined the farm. Soon the acreage jumped from forty to eighty and then, problematically, to eighty-five acres. Since the DTW had the capacity to irrigate only eighty acres, Yunus warned the villagers that there might not be enough water to go around. The villagers said that for a little extra money they could dam a local stream and supply the additional water—an option always available but never tried.

The dam worked, and when the crop was harvested, the farmers were thrilled to discover that the average yield per acre was double the national average. However, when Yunus collected the management share, the amount fell well short of the promised one third, and he was left owing 13,000 takas to the bank. Because the landlords had supervised the harvest, they received full shares, but Yunus hadn't been present and the villagers had shortchanged him.

The next year the villagers approached him to manage the farm again but Yunus refused. He wasn't angry about the money, he said. He was interested in seeing the villagers run it themselves. He helped them secure another loan and suggested a method for supervising the harvest to prevent theft, and again the farmers turned a profit.

At the annual convention of the Bangladesh Economic Association in 1976, Yunus presented a paper entitled "Institutional Framework for a Self-Reliant Bangladesh," in which he argued against the favored development approach of the time: massive donor-financed projects implemented by the national government. He suggested that emphasis be placed, instead, on developing local-based institutions so that villagers could make better use of the resources at their fingertips.

A colleague named H. I. Latifee recalled Yunus's speech: "He said that, although Bangladesh is a small country, it is for any particular person something very big—well beyond his imagination. But if we consider a single village, a neighborhood, or a family, and direct our attention to the resources available there, I think that even if we cannot solve the problems of the country as a whole, we can solve the problems at that level. So why do we only talk? Why not try it ourselves, in the village, and see what we can do?"

The economists argued that the poor would never be able to acquire real power through village-based institutions because wealthier villagers would seize control of them. Yunus countered that the poor were in the majority and could not be overlooked. In any event, he added, at this stage it was just talk. Somebody had to try it out.

The following year, the Three Share Farm model was picked up by the national government, which renamed it the Package Input Program and proceeded to turn out a series of programs that didn't take. The programs failed, Yunus felt, because the government had shut the villagers out of the decision-making process. For his effort, Yunus was awarded the prestigious President's Award, but by then he was already deeply involved in another experiment in Jobra.

2

856 Takas

The Three Share Farm had been a success, but for whom? The villagers who benefited most were farmers or landlords, and in Bangladesh both of these groups are comparatively well off.

This was an old development story. The technological advances in plant genetics that became known as the Green Revolution made it possible for farmers to grow vastly greater quantities of food than ever before. Throughout the developing world in the 1970s, agricultural production soared. However, in the absence of land reform and minimum farm-wage policies, the benefits of the Green Revolution accrued to wealthier villagers, while millions still did not eat three meals a day. In Bangladesh, this problem was particularly acute. Here the "hard-core" poor, the "landless," made up roughly half the population.

Yunus could not forget the women who had turned up at harvesttime earlier in the year, threshing the newly cut rice with their feet. The work had lasted a few days for some, a few weeks for others. How did they get by the rest of the year? Most were not begging or stealing, so they had to have other skills. And what about landless men? How did they support themselves when there was no agricultural work?

A quick survey was conducted. How many families had food stocks for a year, for six months, for one month? How many lived day-to-day? Of those who lived day-to-day, what sort of work did they do and how much did they earn?

For men, rickshaw driving was a common occupation. Rickshaws were the principal source of transportation in the country. Pedaling or "pulling" one, as Bangladeshis say, is arduous but not dishonorable work, and a man who owns a rickshaw owns an important asset. Most drivers are renters not owners, however, and Dipal discovered that the fee they paid each day to the owner left them only a slim margin to live on. "Some rickshaw pullers had been pulling for twenty years, but they still hadn't become the owner of the rickshaw," he told me. "The owner would become old; the puller would become weak." For women, a common occupation in Jobra was bamboo weaving. This was what Sufiya Khatun was doing when Yunus met her in the spring of 1976.

Sufiya was a beggar. A second wife of a man who died in the 1950s, she had given birth to seven children. Only two daughters had survived. Sufiya was trapped between the contradictions of Bangladeshi society. On one hand, many villagers in Jobra treated her with kindness, giving her food and clothing when she came around. On the other hand, when Sufiya tried to earn money by weaving bamboo stools for sale, she was virtually strangled by local business practices.

Sufiya told Yunus that when she needed to buy bamboo, the only person who would give her a loan was the trader who purchased her final product. But the price he set barely covered the cost of her materials. She ended up earning two pennies a day.

"It was a form of bonded labor, of slavery," Yunus recalled.

His instinct was just to give Sufiya the money. But first he wanted to see how many other villagers were in the same circumstances. With a few students, he canvassed Jobra. How many others were missing out on a fair income?

A week had passed. Yunus examined the findings before him, a list compiled by his students containing the names of forty-two people, whose initial capital requirements, in order to purchase materials and work freely, added up to 856 takas, about $26. He was stunned.

Through the years, Yunus would recount the story hundreds of times, for reporters, for colleagues, and for audiences around the world. A decade later, testifying before the U.S. Congress Select Committee on Hunger in a hearing devoted to microenterprise credit, he recalled what went through his mind: "I felt extremely ashamed of myself being part of a society which could not provide $26 to forty-two able, skilled human beings who were trying to make a living."

The moment was as much disturbing as revealing. Yunus felt disgust toward his profession and toward a society that spent a great deal of time and money "teaching fancy 'development' theories in the classroom" while permitting this sort of exploitation to go on down the road.

He gave his students the 856 takas and instructed them to distribute it as loans to the villagers, explaining that they had to pay him back but with no interest, since he was not a bank. He told the students to tell the villagers that they should feel free to sell their products to the highest bidder. The villagers accepted the money and Yunus arranged for the loans to be repaid in small, daily installments at a local tea stall. Soon he began feeling dissatisfied. "This was not a solution," he said. "Every time they needed money they couldn't come to me."

Where should the villagers be able to go when they needed money?

Yunus decided to pay another visit to the manager of the Janata Bank, which continued to finance the Three Share Farm. He had an idea.

"Ten taka loans?" the manager exclaimed. "That's not even worth the paperwork they have to fill out."

"To them this is really important," Yunus said.

"Well, we can't give loans to poor people."

"Why not?"

"They don't have any collateral."

"So what? You don't *eat* collateral. You want your money back."

"Of course we want our money back, but at the same time we need collateral."

Yunus explained that the villagers were repaying his loans. Why wouldn't they repay the bank's loans? "To me, it doesn't make sense," he added. "If somebody can be sure that the money will come back, why do you need collateral?"

"That's our rule," the manager said.

As Latifee recalled: "Yunus kept pursuing it until finally the manager said, 'Okay, I can't help you, but if you're so serious, I suggest you see whether my boss in the city can do something for you.'"

Shortly thereafter, Yunus met with a more senior manager. "This is my idea," he told him. "I've already taken some money from the bank and I've repaid it. Now I need this small amount of money for an experiment, to see what can be done for these people."

The man listened and then told Yunus that governments, not banks, existed to help the poor. Seeing that Yunus was not dissuaded, the banker added that if he were to sanction the loans, he would require a well-to-do villager to stand as guarantor for each and every loan.

"I can't do that because then the guarantor would become a tyrant," Yunus said.

After some thought, the manager said, "Okay, I can give you some money on your personal guarantee because you are a professor at the university."

Lending money to Yunus entailed no risk, the manager knew. Yunus's father was a wealthy businessman in Chittagong and his family name was well respected. In Yunus's mind, this detracted from what he was trying to accomplish.

"Professor Yunus is a very bold person," explained Latifee. "He said, 'Okay, I'll stand guarantee for the money, but I'll tell you I am going to try an experiment and I'm convinced of the villagers' ability and their sincerity. I hope that they'll use the money, earn something, and repay it. But in the event that they fail to make repayment, although I stand guarantee for the money, I tell you I will *not* repay you from my own pocket. So you can do what you have to. If they do not repay the money, I will not repay you."

Latifee smiled with delight. "You see, Professor Yunus was trying to break the bank's rule. He was saying, 'If you can believe me, why can you not believe him? Why do you require that he have land, assets, and education? Why don't you just see what he can do?' "

Yunus requested 10,000 takas, about $300. The manager agreed on condition that the loan not exceed that amount.

"Okay," Yunus said. "That will be enough for me."

After six months, the head office authorized the loan. That December, the Jobra Landless Association was launched. It had no formal structure, no members, no paid staff, and no operational procedures. "I didn't even know what I was doing," Yunus recalled. "I certainly had no intention of starting a bank."

3

Social Collateral

Yunus soon encountered a problem. Chittagong was one of the most conservative areas of Bangladesh and all his students were male. When they visited the village, women would disappear from view.

Dipal had a cousin in her early twenties, Priti Rani Barua, who had been widowed at seventeen in the first month of the War of Independence. Dipal told Priti that Yunus needed a woman to act as a liaison with the Muslim women in Jobra. As a widow, Priti had the freedom to accept such a job, and as a Buddhist, she did not worry about purdah.

Yunus offered to pay her 50 takas a month, and with that Priti became the first paid employee of the then-unnamed Grameen Bank—a distinction that would confer upon her a special status after thousands had followed.

Initially, Priti was mainly interested in earning extra money. Her daughter needed clothes for school, the work took up only a few afternoons each week, and she enjoyed spending time with Yunus. At thirty-six, he was ten years her senior, but she recalled, "For a professor, he was so youthful and fit. And his words were so sweet. He really knew how to get you motivated." As weeks passed, however, Priti found herself looking forward to her visits with the village women. "I enjoyed hearing their stories," she told me, "all the ins and outs of their families."

While Yunus waited for the loan from the Janata Bank, he set out to gauge the number of villagers who would be interested in borrowing money. While walking around Jobra, he found that suspicions were often aroused. Villagers asked, skeptically, Why are you offering to lend us money at so little interest?

He learned to keep his pitch simple. This was an experiment, he

Priti Rani Barua

explained. All he had to do was lay it out. If a man was "pulling" a rickshaw and paying 8 takas per day rent, that meant that he was paying more than 50 takas rent per week, or about 2,500 per year. But a second-hand rickshaw could be *purchased* for about 2,500 takas.

So, to the puller, he would say: "Instead of paying the rent everyday to the owner why don't you take a loan and pay me back at the end of each day. Then, at the end of the year, you will be the owner of the rickshaw."

For women, Priti acted as his voice. She would sit inside houses while Yunus remained outside, occasionally directing the conversation through a bamboo screen. How are you managing? What problems are you encountering? If you took a loan, could you do better?

Priti had to gain the trust of the women. It was not easy for a villager to speak openly about her poverty. If a woman could not afford proper rice she might purchase for her family pieces of half broken rice (called *khud*). If a woman owned only one sari, when she washed it she might hide naked or wrapped in a threadbare cloth inside her hut while it dried on the line outside. Such stories were deeply embarrassing. But

Yunus felt it was essential that he and his students understand exactly who they were dealing with. A bank requires collateral primarily because it has imperfect information about its borrowers. The more specific the questions the better. At each visit, Priti would ask: What did you eat today? What did your children eat today?

Soon she began to notice a change in herself. "We often talk about our hardship," she told me. "But when I would talk to these women, my troubles seemed like nothing. They would disappear."

Yunus was wary of repeating the experience of credit cooperatives in Bangladesh, where money out the door was rarely seen again. Even the nationalized commercial banks like the Janata Bank, for all their demands of guarantors and collateral, had abysmal repayment records. Yunus dubbed them "charity outfits for the rich."

He was determined to be different on three counts: First, the loans would be repaid and repaid on time. Second, only landless villagers would be eligible. Third, as far as possible, they would try to work with women, who were largely confined to their homesteads and, thus, were excluded from most commercial activity. This wouldn't be easy: Chittagong was a hotbed of fundamentalist activity.

He reflected on his earlier experiences. Projects imposed on villagers failed to have the desired impact; however, when villagers determined the structure and rules, their local organizations had flourished. The lesson? Ask, don't tell.

So Yunus assembled groups of villagers and asked them how the loans should be administered. From one of these discussions emerged the decision to form groups to facilitate collection. The groups would be based on loan activity and would comprise five to ten villagers. There would be rickshaw groups, milch-cow groups, chili-trading groups, bamboo stool–weaving groups, and so on.

Poor villagers are wary of institutions such as the police, military, and courts, because they are often used by wealthier individuals to exploit them, particularly to usurp their land. Though somewhat less threatening, banks fall into a similar category: The landless are not welcome.

Yunus saw banks as "antipoor, antilandless, anti-illiterate, and anti-women," and he felt it was vital that the villagers be made to feel comfortable. There would be no secrecy and no confidentiality. All banking transactions were to take place within the village itself, and to be handled in as transparent a fashion as possible. The rule was: the more eyes the better.

To minimize the trauma of parting with a lump sum, the loans were

to be repaid bit-by-bit over the course of a year. Initially, daily installments were tried, but they proved unmanageable; later, Yunus switched
to weekly payments, and to further simplify things, spread payments
over fifty weeks so that each installment represented exactly 2 percent
of the loan principal. Interest, charged at the bank rate (then 13 percent),
was due at year end. All payments were to be made at compulsory
weekly meetings held in various huts in Jobra.

Yunus remembered how he had been shortchanged by the farmers in
the Three Share Farm. The only way to prevent similar abuses in the
credit project was through vigilant supervision. But a formal approach
would alienate villagers.

Essentially, he needed a substitute for collateral, the banker's traditional security. The villagers had already decided to form groups to
facilitate collection. Why not add a few rules to make the groups serve a
double function: provide support to the villagers and security to the
bankers? Make the group a self-supervising unit, with each member
jointly responsible for everyone else's loan. One of the strongest forces
in a Bangladeshi village is social pressure. What if this force could
be harnessed? One way to implement this would be to stagger loan
disbursements within a group, say, two at a time, so that if the first two
recipients failed to repay their installments promptly, the next two would
not receive loans, and so on. The following year, group members would
receive subsequent loans only if everybody remained in good standing.
If a borrower was feeling lazy or began entertaining dishonorable
thoughts, at the first sign of trouble her group mates would remind her
that she was not in this alone. The warning signs would come early;
villages afford little privacy. In rural Bangladesh, villagers can smell what
their neighbors are cooking for dinner.

And the peer pressure wouldn't kick in only when a member was
acting in bad faith. If someone was experiencing difficulties due to illness
or poor management or bad luck, the group would be obliged to pull
her through. Call it social collateral.

Yunus added another rule: Each borrower had to save at least one
taka per week. This was mandatory.

To his students, he instructed: "Whatever rules we make must be
followed up religiously: the weekly meetings, the one-taka savings, the
follow-up visits."

To the villagers, he explained: "Nobody has ever trusted you with any
amount of money, whether 10, 100, or 1,000 takas. The door has been
opened. We trust you and we know that you have a survival scheme, but
you have no capital. We are here with the money. You don't have to

offer us any security provided you abide by our rules. We will go with you as far as you can go.

"If you do not abide by the rules, if you do not come to the meetings, if you do not pay the installments or savings, you will be closing the door not only on yourself but also on others who enjoy these benefits."

"People accepted this," he recalled.

On January 3, 1977, the first loans totaling 16,050 takas—about $500—were disbursed to seven individuals. Yunus was already exhibiting expansionist tendencies. He had promised the bank manager that 10,000 takas would be sufficient for his experiment.

A few of the villagers purchased rickshaws, a few cows. Sufiya, the very first borrower, decided to forgo bamboo weaving and try sales. For years, she had spent her days moving from house to house begging for rice. Now she borrowed 50 takas, loaded up a basket with bangles and sweets, and set out to call on the same people, this time as a peddler.

In the weeks that followed, the bookkeeping began to grow complicated. One afternoon, a student, Shaikh Abdud Daiyan dropped by Yunus's office. He wanted to get involved with the other students. Daiyan had an intensity to his personality. He radiated self-confidence, occasionally to the point of arrogance. His family had a motor-parts business in Chittagong. Daiyan enjoyed business but at university he had found himself drawn to politics, and on campus the only fun politics were leftist politics. "I didn't have any particular philosophy at the time," he told me. "I liked to gossip and go around in groups. My friends did politics so I did politics."

But when Yunus talked about his ideas, Daiyan felt frivolous. What were these student leftists really accomplishing? Here was an individual from a wealthy family who had given up a teaching position in the United States to help rebuild his country. What did he think of student politics? He had no use for it. He preferred to spend his time talking with villagers.

Yunus gave Daiyan an assignment to draw a map of Jobra. Shortly thereafter, Daiyan took over the statistical analysis for the Rural Economics Program. His job in the credit program was to develop a system to track disbursements and collections, and analyze cash flows. The system had to accommodate many small, intermittent transactions. The mathematics were not terribly challenging, but Daiyan enjoyed coming up with elegant solutions to potentially messy problems. Yunus stressed the importance of keeping things simple so that, as the program grew—and he was certain it would grow—Daiyan could move on and new recruits could take over his responsibilities.

In the meantime, demand for credit was increasing. Between April and December, 94,800 takas were disbursed to fifty-eight villagers, with Yunus cosigning each loan. The project was becoming a source of irritation for the Janata Bank, which had not anticipated a steady stream of business from Jobra. The head office began delaying loan approvals and occasionally declining them. Early in the year, villagers waited six weeks to receive their money; by December, it was taking three months.

The students tried to maintain borrowers' confidence, but the delays led to disappointments that confirmed to the villagers that this was yet another short-lived development experiment. Attendance dropped off at the meetings. Taking advantage of the situation, one borrower sold a cow he had purchased with a loan, and pocketed the money. His group members in turn confiscated another cow he owned, sold it, and repaid the loan. Everyone in Jobra heard about the affair. If the group had not acted quickly, others may have done the same. If villagers thought that the program was dying out, why would they continue repaying their loans?

4

It Cannot Be Done

A few months later, Yunus was in the Dhaka office of the Ford Foundation when a Ford representative invited him to a meeting with the managing director of one of Bangladesh's nationalized banks, the Krishi Bank.

The director of the Krishi Bank, A. M. Anisuzzaman, was having a bad day when Yunus walked into his office. And as soon as he sat down, the banker seized the opportunity to vent his frustrations about intellectuals and "academicians" and all of Yunus's colleagues who were continually complaining about the terrible job he was doing. What were they contributing to Bangladesh? "They talk, they don't do any work," he said. "They complain about everything that we do. Nobody helps me to get this bank cleaned up but everybody complains about all the inefficiency and the malpractice."

It was a sunny afternoon in 1994 when Yunus related the story to me in his office. He sat behind a desk piled high with files. He appeared stylish in a well-pressed, short-sleeve shirt, trousers, and sandals. His dark wavy hair was combed back and to the side. His hands moved lightly in the air as he spoke. He had long, graceful fingers. I had seen a few of his drawings—colorful village scenes—painted on cards that he had sent to branches to commemorate the end of Ramadan.

A representative of the Ford Foundation interviewed on *60 Minutes,* in 1990, had compared Yunus to Gandhi, J.F.K., and Martin Luther King, Jr. My friend who had worked on the documentary film about the Grameen Bank had mentioned that when she first met Yunus she said to him, "So you *are* mortal," and he replied, "Don't be too sure." And months before I left for Bangladesh, a Canadian aid official had told me: "Yunus has a real presence, and it is the presence of a *president."* (Indeed, rumors were circulating in late 1995 to the effect that due to political unrest, Yunus might soon be appointed Bangladesh's caretaker prime minister until an election could be held.)

Now I understood what they meant. I could feel his magnetism. His face was marvelously expressive. He laughed heartily and generously. When he smiled, he squinted, his cheeks grew round and his shoulders dropped. But when his emotion or indignation took hold, his face grew commanding, even leonine. His eyes pressed out as in a caricature; at times they seemed about to bulge out of their sockets.

Shortly into the interview I forgot that I was in the presence of an economist. The man before me would have been bored silly by calculus or statistics or staple theory. He certainly was not the same person who authored the Vanderbilt University Ph.D. dissertation entitled: "Optimal Allocation of Multi-purpose Reservoir Water: A Dynamic Programming Model."

No, this man was a storyteller, and like one who is practiced in the art of telling children's tales, he was acutely aware of his listener's limitations. Nothing he said was the least bit complicated; everything was kept simple, at times deceptively simple. He came off as surprisingly accessible for someone running an organization with more than 12,000 employees. Many people more influential than I had interviewed Yunus; nevertheless, he granted my first request for an interview the same day. He never asked, nor did he seem to care a whit, about my credentials. I had come to Bangladesh to write about his bank; that was my qualification.

And yet, although I felt disarmed by Yunus, I did not feel at ease in his presence. He spoke humorously of human absurdity, but beneath the surface it was clear that he was dead serious and quite adamant about his ideas. Einstein's words on Gandhi seemed to fit: "[A] man of wisdom and humility, armed with resolve and inflexible consistency."

Yunus's central theme was that a great many people suffered terribly and unnecessarily because of human inaction and folly. So, of course, it couldn't really be called folly; in truth, it was gross negligence. And here he demanded, *insisted* on full attention. I found it difficult to pull my eyes away from his when he spoke, even just to jot down a note or check my tape recorder. And although I felt pulled in, I was conscious of being somehow pushed away. Perhaps I anticipated this. I had been told that very few people got close to Yunus. In a culture that is compulsively social, not even his most intimate colleagues felt free to drop by his apartment or invite him to a dinner party. As head of the Grameen Bank, Yunus welcomed visitors from around the world and made himself available for their questions. But if he had the power to charm, he also had the power, and it seemed the desire, to remain distant. As an individual apart from the Grameen Bank, he seemed unapproachable.

The office window was open. Outside, the air was filled with clanking sounds—construction workers putting the finishing touches on Grameen's new office building.

"So he loves talking," Yunus said. "And he kept on talking for hours. So when I get a chance, I try to say a few words, but he brushes me off and goes on.

"So finally I said, 'Look, would you please stop and listen to what I have to say.'

"He says, 'Go on, say it.'

"I say, 'I cannot clean up your whole mess—it's too much. But this is what I'm doing in Chittagong through the Janata Bank. Why don't you give me a branch of the Krishi Bank in Jobra and give the responsibility of running that branch to me? I'll make the rules. And I'll demonstrate what can be done. And give me one year's time and one million takas that I can use as loans. And after one year if you don't like it, throw me out. It can't be any worse than what's going on in the rest of the country. But something good might come out of it. And if something good comes out of it and you like it, and you don't like the other parts, just pick up that one good piece and use it in other ways. Forget about the rest of it. And if you'd like me to continue, give me another year. I'll continue. If you don't like it, throw me out.' "

Anisuzzaman immediately accepted Yunus's proposal. "It will be done," he said. "You will have a branch. Do you need anything more?"

"Now that I have become the managing director of one branch," Yunus replied, "I don't need anything more. Whatever I need, I can solve myself."

Anisuzzaman called his regional director in Chittagong and told him: "Doctor Yunus will be coming back to Chittagong tomorrow"—and he asked Yunus his flight time and continued over the telephone—"you be at his house in the campus before he arrives, and from then on you take orders from him so far as the project that he is talking about is concerned."

"This is the kind of guy he is," explained Yunus. "He just said I could do it. I thought everything was resolved. So when I went back, sure enough the poor guy is waiting for me. Because after all the big guy told him to."

"What is it that I'm supposed to do?" the banker asked.

"I'm not sure myself," Yunus replied. "Why don't we sit down and I'll tell you what I told him and you tell me how to get it done."

"I explained that there will be a branch in Jobra and that branch will be run by me."

"That cannot be done," the man replied.

"But he said it could be done."

"The first thing is that you have to submit a proposal for a project, write out the details, give the budget, and so on. And I will offer my opinion on this project and it will be sent to my immediate boss; he will give his comments and it will go up the ladder to the managing director —because I cannot write to the managing director myself. And then he will decide which way to go.

"Even the managing director cannot give away his authority just like that," the banker explained. "He has to take it to the board and the board has to decide. And there are certain things even the board cannot change, because they have to do with fundamental principles of the bank. So you have to go back to the Parliament or whoever made the law for that. And your suggestion involves that kind of change."

"Well, I don't know anything about *that*," said Yunus. "He didn't say anything about a proposal. But if you need a proposal, why don't you ask me questions and I'll answer them, and we'll put it down and that will be my proposal?"

"So this fellow became very scared," he recalled. "He said, 'I better not ask you questions. Why don't I come back on another convenient day and bring my colleagues so that we can all write it down together and try to develop a project proposal.' "

"Good enough," Yunus said.

A date was arranged. When the bankers finished the first draft, Yunus rewrote it, giving himself more autonomy. The bankers objected.

"This is what I want," declared Yunus. "You cannot change it."

"It cannot be done," replied the bankers.

"So a compromise was made," Yunus recalled. "It became not quite a branch; it became a booth, a window. I named it the Experimental Grameen Branch. It didn't say that I took it over. It said there would be some experimental things going on but the manager is still the final authority—with the understanding that he would allow me to do certain things."

The Experimental Grameen Branch opened the following spring in a thatch hut with bamboo walls and a tin roof. On its first day in business, it disbursed 52,000 takas to twenty-four villagers. That summer, it signed up another 341 customers. By September, the bank had spread to three villages and disbursed more than a half million takas—about $15,000—

to four hundred villagers, one quarter of whom were women. The default rate was less than one percent.

With the increased workload, Yunus took a closer look at procedures. At the rate things were growing, even a small oversight could develop into a crisis. One problem the students discovered was that grouping by activity made little sense, because it failed to ensure that group members shared close personal ties, and in any event, people often switched businesses. If the group was to be the basis of loan security, it had to be a stable unit. So the students decided to form groups of villagers who knew each other well.

Then there was the issue of group size. If the group was too large, those with weaker personalities would get lost in the crowd, while everybody's sense of accountability would be diminished. If it was too small, it wouldn't allow for a range of pursuits and opinions. After trial and error, Yunus settled on the number five. Part of this was intuitive: A working hand has five fingers; there are five pillars of faith in Islam, and each day, five calls to prayer.

Each group elected a "chairman" and "secretary," positions that rotated annually; and two new funds were introduced: the Group Fund and the Emergency Fund. The Group Fund was a collective savings from which villagers could borrow when they needed a short-term loan. Initially, each borrower was to deposit one taka per week into this fund, but as it became clear how critical the Group Fund was to long-term security, Yunus introduced a 5 percent "group tax" to be levied on each loan.

The Emergency Fund was a reserve into which borrowers had to contribute a fee at the end of the year. In case of default, accident, or theft, the group could make use of this money however it saw fit. All appropriations from the Group and Emergency Funds required the consent of all five members. (In later years, the Emergency Fund would evolve into a form of life insurance. When a Grameen borrower dies, her beneficiary today receives a payment of up to 5,000 takas—about one year's income for a poor villager.)

To appreciate the importance of these two funds, one has to look closely at the roots of poverty in Bangladesh. Most foreign observers see Bangladesh's troubles as a combination of ignorance and bad luck— often with the legacy of colonialism thrown in as an afterthought. When Bangladesh declared independence, its wealth had been largely depleted, its cotton and textile industries long destroyed, and international observers looked at this tiny country with its tens of millions of villagers, with its floods and droughts and cyclones, with a literacy rate of 25 percent, and they shook their heads gravely. Bangladesh, the diplomats agreed, would be an "international basket case."

Who could argue with them? And yet the way Yunus saw it, he didn't have to worry about Bangladesh's problems; he only had to worry about the problems of a few hundred villagers. He had little use for the diplomats' pronouncements. Such views of national poverty were counterproductive, he felt. They only obscured the reality of individual poverty, and individual poverty was the result of social processes that could be readily understood and addressed.

Shortly after his arrival at Chittagong University, Yunus had directed his students to survey the landless of Jobra and record each family's history, focusing on their changes in fortune over three generations. He was particularly interested in land, by far the most important asset to a villager. The rise in landlessness was well documented in Bangladesh: Since World War II, the proportion of landless had jumped from 20 percent to more than 50 percent of the population. Of the landless villagers surveyed, Yunus discovered that 252 had lost their land in their own lifetimes, 89 in their fathers', and 18 in their grandfathers'.

The population surge in recent decades, due in part to improvements in sanitation and the spread of medical services and immunization programs, was often cited as the prime reason for the increase in landlessness, and some even argued that medical advances had exacerbated the situation in Bangladesh. Yunus was not interested in debating whether technological advancements made matters better or worse. Technology wasn't going away. For him the more relevant question was, With so much land changing hands, which villagers lost and which ones gained? And why?

The pattern was fairly predictable, as he discovered. A family with some land would start to fall behind for any of a number of reasons: illness, a poor crop, theft, dowry, the death of a father, or a natural disaster, such as a flood. Until they could recover, they would have to borrow money for food, perhaps for a few months, perhaps only for a few weeks. There is perhaps no country in the world in which the "time value" of money is as great as in Bangladesh, with its cycles of dearth and plenty. A family whose food stocks are depleted, say, six weeks before harvest can borrow forty kilograms of rice on the condition that they repay eighty kilograms two months later—an effective annual interest rate of 600 percent. If a villager needs a fast loan to purchase medicine, his only recourse may be to mortgage or sell his land, doing so in the vain hope that he might one day recover it.

In the end, wealth flows in one direction: steadily and inexorably,

Ferrying passengers from a river launch to shore

from poor to rich. Despite Bangladesh's problems with floods and cyclones and droughts, its most oppressive poverty is not the result of
natural disasters but of social processes; and in Jobra, Yunus discovered
that the first step is often the establishment of a credit relationship with
a moneylender.

The Group Fund was designed to bring this process to a halt by
providing a pool of short-term, inexpensive credit so that villagers would
not have to resort to moneylenders or dig into their productive capital
each time they encountered difficulties. Withdrawals were not permitted
from this fund. If a member needed money, the group had to sanction a
loan; the other four dictated the terms. (Usually, villagers grant
interest-free loans to one another.) When explaining the rationale
for the group tax, the students would compare it to a women's tradition in Bangladesh of setting aside a handful of rice before each meal.
"You don't miss it but soon you accumulate a sizable amount," they
would say.

Some villagers protested but Yunus retained the tax because he believed that the only hope poor people had of gaining control over their lives was through saving and asset accumulation.

Two other changes were introduced: The definition of a "landless" person was expanded to include villagers whose families were "functionally landless," which meant they did not own enough land to live off for most of the year. (A local unit of measurement, one *kani,* equal to .4 acres, was initially set as the upper limit.)

An organizational hierarchy was established. Up to six groups formed a center—with men and women kept separate. Each center elected a center chief and deputy center chief. All loans were to be collected at weekly center meetings.

The system seemed capable of managing a growing clientele, so after the new procedures were finalized, Yunus encoded them in a set of bylaws and statements of principle called the *Bidhimala:* the constitution. Dipal served as his amanuensis. "I had the best handwriting," he explained.

Section 1.0 read: "The objective of the Grameen Bank Project is to introduce and institutionalize a non-traditional banking system in rural areas which would provide credit facilities under special terms and conditions. This project attempts to serve those rural people who are not covered by the traditional banking system. The success of this project entirely depends on the sincere efforts to follow the rules and regulations prescribed below."

The *Bidhimala* covered the formation of groups and centers; the duties of group chairmen and secretaries, center chiefs and deputy center chiefs; the procedures for disbursements and collections; the administration of the group and emergency funds; the protocol for forming and dissolving groups; and provisions for amendments to the constitution.

5

He Found You Under a Tree?

Yunus had put out the word that the project needed more women students. One of the first to come forward was Nurjahan Begum ("Begum," akin to "Missus," is usually appended to women's names in Bangladesh). Nurjahan had grown up in a conservative family. Her mother observed purdah so stringently that she wore gloves and socks to conceal her hands and ankles from public view. Although her father shared her mother's views about propriety, he nevertheless believed in the importance of education for women. After his death, however, Nurjahan's mother decided to pull her daughter out of school to marry her off. Nurjahan fought her. "I had no intention of getting married," she recalled. "I wanted to finish my education and get a job. I was determined—but so was my mother."

By invoking her father's wishes, Nurjahan was permitted to continue her studies, but not on her terms. Her brother would not allow her to attend Chittagong University, so she enrolled in the women's college. She had wanted to study history, but in the women's college there was only one subject: Bengali literature.

When Nurjahan met Yunus, she had just completed a master's degree and was in another battle with her mother over a job she'd been offered by a Canadian development organization. Unfortunately, the day the Canadian official came to interview her, Nurjahan was out. Her mother explained that Nurjahan would be getting married soon, so she could not accept the job. Nurjahan was infuriated. "I managed to get it through to my mother that I was adamantly opposed to marriage," she recalled. She contacted the Canadians and told them she needed two more weeks to "work on" her mother, but the Canadian woman had already described the nature of development work to Nurjahan's mother, and there was no hope of moving her. No daughter of hers was going to be seen "wandering around the countryside."

When Yunus asked Nurjahan if her family would permit her to work for the Grameen Bank Project, she responded yes immediately. Did she know anything about banking? he asked. Had she ever worked closely with villagers? Nurjahan responded no to both questions.

"Then you can try it out," Yunus said. "See if you like it."

Nurjahan liked this attitude. It was the first time anybody had ever made a decision easy for her. Yunus also mentioned that he could arrange for Nurjahan to stay in a room in the women's dormitory, if she liked. Nurjahan said she would have to speak to her mother first. Back home, she explained that she'd been offered a job with a government bank. "It's a desk job," she said. "I'll be sitting all day in an office not talking to anyone and staying at a hostel just like when I was at college."

Nurjahan laughed. A ray of sunlight poked through the venetian blinds in her office on the fourth floor of the Grameen Bank's training institute, and cut diagonally across her purple sari. She sat upright across from me, leaning against her desk with her elbows resting on the surface and her hands clasped together. Her large glasses made her features seem delicate. She reminded me of a dance instructor: poised and exacting and a little impatient. Her phone rang every few minutes and she dispatched each caller with a half dozen words.

For more than a decade Nurjahan had served as the highest ranking woman in the Grameen Bank, as principal of its training institute and the administrator of several other programs. Nurjahan made sure that the thousands of recruits the bank posted throughout the country were prepared for the rigors of the job. She weeded out the less motivated, the less dependable, and the less competent. And when the staff slackened or broke the rules, she dispatched operatives—she called them "spies"—to gather intelligence.

Nurjahan knew that her performance reflected on all the women who worked for the bank. "A woman in competition with men—not only in Bangladesh but throughout the world—is looked upon first as a woman, then as a human being," she told me. "No matter how well she works, people will look for deficiencies."

It was known that to get ahead in Grameen you had to dedicate yourself to the job, you had to be, as Daiyan put it, "one hundred percent Grameen." Which is one reason why, after Nurjahan was married (to a man of her own choosing), she and her husband elected to have only one child, an unusual decision in Bangladesh. "If I set a proper example

I can open up opportunities for other women," Nurjahan explained. "If I do not, I will create problems for them."

She resumed her story. One day, a short time after she joined the Grameen Bank Project, Nurjahan's mother sent her uncle to the office with a message. When he arrived, he was told that Nurjahan was not around; she was "somewhere in the field."

"My uncle discovered me under a tree surrounded by a group of men," Nurjahan said. "I was collecting money. He was aghast."

Nurjahan pleaded with her uncle to remain silent, but on her visit home the next Friday, her mother was waiting. "He found you under a tree?" she exclaimed.

"This was a highly unusual situation," Nurjahan said. "We had some problems so I had to visit the field. But this is very rare—once in a blue moon."

"For two years," she added, "my mother had no clue what I was doing."

When Nurjahan first joined the project she didn't have much of an idea about what she would be doing either. For one thing, she didn't realize she would be spending virtually all her time walking around villages. It was the rainy season. "There was cow dung mixed in with the mud," Nurjahan recalled. After a week, she told Yunus that she wasn't sure she was cut out for the job.

"Give it fifteen days," he said.

Before Nurjahan had a chance to make up her mind, Yunus came to her with a special assignment: to interview a woman named Ammajan, who had recently taken a loan, and to write up a case study. "Take as much time as you need," he said.

Nurjahan spent four days interviewing Ammajan. She wrote up the study, identified some gaps and inconsistencies, and interviewed her for two more days. When she showed her paper to Yunus, he commented: "This is beautiful." Then he suggested she ask a few more questions.

Ammajan's father had died penniless. Ammajan had married twice. Nurjahan recalled: "One time she told me, 'My first husband beat me with everything but the *dekhi*' " (a heavy wooden beam used to husk rice). Ammajan lost one daughter to illness, and after her second husband abandoned her, she moved from place to place begging. "She was attractive so men gave her problems," Nurjahan said. "At the time I interviewed her, she had just started with the Grameen Bank. She used to go to the bazaar and buy things and bring them back to Jobra to sell. After she took a loan she could do more business. The case study changed how I thought. I had never touched poverty like this woman's."

None of Yunus's students had explored the life of a villager so thoroughly, and Yunus asked Nurjahan to interview a few other women and develop a methodology for the case studies. In the following weeks, she interviewed several women. Sitting on cane mats on the ground, she would talk with them for hours, while helping them grind chilis, weave baskets, and cut vegetables. Children were everywhere; six- or seven-year-old girls took care of babies, carrying them on their hips, one-armed, the same way their mothers carried jugs of water from the well. Young boys were often contracted out as household servants. Occasionally they attended school, but often, for a lack of proper clothing, they did not.

On one occasion Nurjahan was trying to convince a widow with five children to consider taking a loan when the woman's brother-in-law burst in on the interview and demanded that she leave immediately. The next day she returned dressed more conservatively and explained to the brother-in-law: "I want to learn about her situation to see if it can be improved or not. If a loan will bring no improvement, then what's the use of doing this? But if it works, there are opportunities for her and a lot of other people."

To Nurjahan's surprise, the man responded by telling his sister-in-law, "Come sit for the interview."

The students had identified dozens of village women who were ideal candidates for loans; they urged them to form groups, but many retreated out of fear for their reputations. Yunus hoped to increase their numbers, but Jobra was extremely conservative. "Progress on the women front is slow," he wrote in a 1978 report.

In the project office, the atmosphere remained informal. "It was not officelike at all," Nurjahan recalled. "Professor Yunus used to ask for our advice. He had the ability to mix with anyone. He would even sit on the ground with villagers."

An incident stuck in her mind involving a villager named Muriam. Muriam had requested a loan of 1,000 takas, but Nurjahan authorized only half that amount. On the disbursement day, she visited the hut accompanied by Yunus. "In those days, men could not enter and talk with women," she recalled. "If a man did enter, a sari had to be hung down the center of the hut, so the man could not see them. Professor Yunus was standing outside and I was inside trying to convince Muriam to take the 500 takas, but she wanted 1,000 and said that 500 was no favor.

"I was ready to give up when Professor Yunus stepped inside—totally breaking all the rules. There were about twenty women in the hut and as soon as he entered they all turned to face away from him. But Professor Yunus persisted with his questions and kept explaining himself. He spoke on, and as he did, it became apparent that the women were listening. And then something remarkable happened: They started turning toward him.

"This was a tremendous moment for me. It was the first time I saw that it was possible to get through to people."

6

If You Want to Convince Us

Six months after the Experimental Grameen Branch opened, Yunus attended a conference on rural credit. Development bankers hadn't had much success in this area. Almost every credit program ran into the same problem: People stopped repaying their loans. Yunus listened while the experts explained that the new thinking was to charge extremely high interest rates, so that villagers would seriously consider before borrowing money and would therefore take their obligations seriously. Everybody spoke about landowners and farmers; nobody mentioned the landless.

Yunus had prepared a summary of the Grameen Bank Project. "It was a funny paper," he recalled. "It had a two-page description and ten pages of data. Everyone said, 'What kind of paper is that?'

"I said, 'I don't have to speak. The data says everything: who took what, how much was paid back, what savings they had, how many groups there were.' I put down everything. I said, 'Here is the data. This can be done.' And that annoyed the hell out of all the senior bank officials."

The paper detailed how 463 villagers had borrowed 604,950 takas and amassed more than 80,000 takas in savings. It tabulated loans to men and women separately and divided them into activity types. Above each disbursement date was a column headed: "Amount defaulted." The first number was 1.47 percent. The rest of the column read: "Nil. Nil. Nil . . ."

Dipal once said of Yunus: "When he speaks, he is able to change the minds of 80 percent of the people he meets." This time he let the evidence speak for itself. The Janata and Krishi bank officials had said, "This cannot be done," yet the villagers had been repaying their loans for eighteen months. It wasn't just in Jobra; it was in three villages, and plans were under way to open a second office ten kilometers away.

Yunus's presentation drew fire. Some saw it as presumptuous. Who was this professor telling the bankers how to run their shows? Some dismissed his data saying, "One village is a very tiny place." Yunus was surprised by the passions his paper generated. He was telling the bankers that an enormous market awaited them, and if anything, it was easier to reach than they had imagined. He had developed a methodology for extending banking services to people who had always been ignored. Wouldn't the bankers like to experiment with this model? Think of the potential, he said. Bringing the banking system within reach of half of the population would release vast idle energy for productive use through self-employment, and protect the landless from pauperization at the hands of moneylenders.

Those who listened thoughtfully to Yunus's argument, ironically, found its weakness in his reputation for boldness and success. A decade earlier, with a one-million-taka loan from an industrial bank, Yunus had established the first high-tech packaging business in then–East Pakistan. Within a few years, the business was turning a profit and Yunus's bankers were urging him to borrow 10 million takas to expand. About the same time, Yunus was awarded a Fulbright Scholarship, and he opted to study economics in the United States. He turned the business over to his brothers, who decided not to take the risk. "If he had stayed in business," commented Muzammel Huq, a colleague, "he could have become one of the biggest industrialists in the subcontinent."

This reputation now proved a liability. If Yunus had succeeded in Jobra, it was not because the villagers were inherently bankable, it was because of his own particular brand of magic. He was admired and trusted in the village and his students worked hard to impress him. The Grameen Bank Project was a "one-man, one-place" phenomenon. Without Yunus's personal supervision, it could not be replicated.

"If you want to convince us," he was told, "do it over a whole district."

"If you ask me to do it, I'll do it for you," he replied.

By good fortune, the individual who was most impressed by Yunus's presentation happened to be one of the top banking officials in the country, the deputy governor of the Bangladesh Bank, a man named A. K. Gangopadhyay. After the seminar, he approached Yunus, and "took pity" on him.

"Are you really serious?" Gangopadhyay asked. "You want to do that over a whole district?"

"Yes, because it can be done."

Shortly thereafter, Gangopadhyay called a meeting of the managing directors of the seven nationalized banks to give Yunus the opportunity to outline his plan. Gangopadhyay shared Yunus's vision of a bank that was an active force rather than a passive institution waiting for its customers to walk in the door, a bank that would encourage villagers to pursue new opportunities to increase their productivity and incomes. "If I had to pick one person who was responsible for the Grameen Bank coming into being," Yunus told me, "it would be Mr. Gangopadhyay."

The managing directors rejected Yunus's initial proposal, but Gangopadhyay urged them to put off the vote until the next meeting, which was to be held in Chittagong, so the bankers could take a look at the Grameen Bank Project. At that meeting his support proved decisive and Yunus's proposal was approved. But the bankers had a few conditions. "You must resign from Chittagong University and become a full-time banker," one said. Another told Yunus, "It cannot be done in Chittagong because you have special advantages as a local university professor."

Yunus had not planned to become a full-time banker, but he agreed to take a leave of absence from teaching. "I said I'd go to any district they wanted me to and do it for two years. And I was sure that within two years it would be obvious whether things were going right or going wrong. If they were going wrong, I'd have to ask for an apology and go back to the university and never talk about it again. If they were going right, then the banks would take it up and carry it to the whole country. That was the general idea. Nobody said yes to it."

The bankers decided to launch the project in a district in central Bangladesh called Tangail. Yunus took his leave, signed on as an official employee of the Bangladesh Bank, and moved to Tangail, where he was unknown. His plan called for each of the nationalized banks to provide a window for the Grameen Bank Project in three or four branches. Gangopadhyay urged the bank directors to cooperate with Yunus, but he remained skeptical about how they would respond. "He liked what I was trying to do," Yunus recalled. "But he felt that it could not be done by the existing banks. He thought that this was one way to find out. Maybe there was a chance."

From his prior dealings with banks, Yunus understood how frustrating it could be dealing with low-level officials even after senior managers had theoretically freed his hands. In Bangladesh, bureaucratic lethargy is more prevalent than in wealthier countries. The tendency toward inaction is easy to understand in a country where a lucky few land civil service jobs while virtually everybody else ekes out a meager subsistence. In a competitive environment where everyone keeps his head low, a bold decision can easily cause offense. Better to go by the book—no matter how poorly it is written.

This attitude exasperated Yunus. "When you try to do something new and push your colleagues, they get very nervous," he told me. "And I don't understand that. There's so much opportunity."

But Yunus had grown up in a large, prosperous family and he had never lacked for opportunity. His father was a well-to-do gold trader and the sort of individual who occasionally made a pretense of being strict but in fact allowed his children a great deal of autonomy. "My father never put restrictions on us," Yunus recalled. "He would tell us to be home by sunset, but if I showed up at sunset and then disappeared for the whole night, he wouldn't notice it. And my father was the kind of person who couldn't keep track of his money. He would say, 'I thought I had some money in my pocket—maybe I didn't,' and then forget about it."

"My mother was attentive," he added. "But she also had a lot of trust in us."

By the time he was in grade school, Yunus had as much independence as boys years older. He usually had plenty of money in his pocket, too—carefully removed from his father's—with which he purchased detective books and adventure stories and took himself to movies. "I saw every movie released from Bombay at that time at least once, and some five or six times."

His childhood reads like a list of adventures and triumphs. In the fourth grade, he placed first in the city in his exams, and throughout elementary and high school continued to win scholarships and awards. He joined the Boy Scouts, and at twelve visited West Pakistan and India. In 1955, at fifteen, he participated in the World Jamboree in Canada, where he met dozens of fellow scouts who had never heard of East Pakistan.

On the way home, Yunus led the group on an odyssey: They visited Washington and New York, traveled by ship to England, made their way to Germany, where they bought three Volkswagen microbuses—cheaper than airfare back home—and proceeded to tour Europe and the Middle East. "Looking at the map, deciding where to go next," Yunus recalled, "it was all happening like a movie." In Yugoslavia, the scouts wrecked one of the buses and packed into the other two. They drove to Iraq and caught a boat to Karachi. Yunus and a friend split from the group to take a detour through Bombay, Delhi, and Calcutta before returning to Chittagong.

After high school, Yunus won a government scholarship to study in England, but turned it down. "I thought, 'If I went, I wouldn't know anything about my own country.' When I look back, I still feel surprised I made that decision." He enrolled in a local college, and although he excelled in the sciences, he opted for an arts program. He tried his hand as an actor and won praise for his portrayal of a mad scientist. In college, he published a small newspaper called *Do Pata* ("Two Pages"), for which he wrote articles and drew cartoons. Still deciding on a career, he considered becoming a barrister. "Gandhi was a barrister, Jinnah was a barrister, Suhrawardy was a barrister—so naturally that was very sexy."

By the time he entered university, he had switched to economics, although he continued to publish a nationally circulated literary magazine called *Uttaran* ("Progress"). After graduating, he accepted a post as a lecturer at his former college. While teaching, his interest in publishing led him to a factory in West Pakistan where he first caught sight of the new generation of "offset" printers, then unavailable in the Eastern Wing.

He prepared a business plan to start a packaging business and approached an industrial bank. "My family had no problems with money, so they gave us a million takas. Then, a million takas was a lot of takas."

By the time Yunus was informed that he had been awarded a Fulbright Scholarship, the packaging business was growing steadily. "But, obviously, going to the United States was a very exciting thing," he said. He accepted the scholarship, turned the business over to his brothers, and moved to Nashville, Tennessee. "There, my life changed completely," he recalled. "In the United States, I realized that people could do their own thing. That was a fantastic revelation. And people could say whatever they felt. In Bangladesh, you try to fit into the slot people design for you."

In the slot that had been designed for him in the Bangladesh Bank, Yunus soon saw that every decision had to go through official channels. He could not issue an order and quickly change his mind, or respond to problems as they emerged. In Jobra, he and his students had changed tacks weekly; in the Bangladesh Bank, everything took at least six weeks to get done.

The bankers had also directed Yunus to draw his staff from their own banks. His project soon became a "dumping ground" for anyone "unusable." Most of the senior officials had predicted a quick demise for the Grameen Bank Project. Now Yunus felt they were ensuring it. Finally, he insisted on recruiting some of his own personnel. "So I recruited the students who had been working with me in Jobra."

Dipal and Daiyan had become friends in university and the two often spoke about setting up a consulting firm as a sideline after graduation. Although the Grameen Bank Project was an important part of their lives, neither expected it to turn into a career. Daiyan's parents had higher hopes for their son, especially as he was soon to be married. "I was the first master's in the family," he told me.

Today, in his early forties, Daiyan still looks as if he could be a graduate student. His wavy hair often appears hastily combed, as though he had jumped out of bed and run over to the office without checking the mirror; and his intensity hasn't diminished. "I love to dream," he told me. "And if I tell my dreams to Professor Yunus, tomorrow they will come to be reality. This is what happens in Grameen. That's why I work so hard. You might say that I'm an *addict*.

"But I love Grameen more than I can express. I love it not to please anybody—not to please Professor Yunus." Daiyan paused to reconsider his statement. "Working with a man like him is such an experience. We didn't know that he would gain an international reputation, but we knew that he was a creative man. Yes, at first, when I started with Professor Yunus, I worked to please him. But not anymore."

For Dipal the attachment to his teacher was unambiguous. It was Yunus who had given his father the encouragement to enroll him in university. Early on, Dipal had helped Yunus design and manage the Three Share Farm, and later the two had worked together encoding the *Bidhimala*. But the financial side weighed heavily on him. Dipal's father owned land in Jobra, but Dipal knew that his parents would come to rely more on his earnings as they grew older. He was committed to the Grameen Bank Project, but he also knew that development experiments in Bangladesh are a dime a dozen. Besides, Yunus planned to leave after two years. Then what? Could he afford to take such a chance with his family's future?

His father thought so. When Dipal told him that Yunus had asked him to come to Tangail, he replied: "It is because of Professor Yunus that you have come so far. You should stay with him."

Daiyan's family advised otherwise. "Joining some crazy idea, such an unreliable future, taking such a small salary."

Worse, shortly after that, Yunus was told that his budget had been cut and he had to inform his students that he couldn't pay them the full salaries he'd promised. "It almost looked as if it would be nipped in the bud," recalled Dipal.

These days Dipal's main concern is keeping the bud in good health, now that it has grown into a jungle. As head of the administration department, he is responsible for coordinating the efforts of more than 12,000 employees. The challenge, as he puts it, is simply to "maintain quality." In a decade and a half, Grameen's once-youthful staff have matured; they have married and had children; their legs have grown tired; and in many cases, their enthusiasm has waned.

Dipal is continually recruiting, promoting, and transferring staff. "We're thinking of reducing the voluntary retirement from twenty-five years to twenty," he told me in 1994. "We're even considering fifteen years. Younger people are more effective. Not only physically. They're not overburdened by their families. After retirement, they'd get some money and do something else. You need fresh blood."

Nurjahan's worry was informing her mother that she planned to move to Tangail, two hundred miles from Chittagong, ten hours by bus and train. "I was not permitted to live alone," Nurjahan recalled. "But my mother didn't know where Tangail was. So I lied. At the time, my brother was attending Dhaka University. I told my mother that Tangail and Dhaka were very close." (In fact, the bus journey takes a few hours.) "I told my mother that I would live in Tangail, and at night my brother would come stay with me.

" 'So, don't worry,' I said."

The day after Dipal completed his master's, he left for Tangail. Daiyan left two months later, accompanied by his wife; and Nurjahan soon followed—only to discover that nobody in Tangail would rent a house to an unmarried woman. After a long search, she met an older woman working for CARE who offered to rent her a room. It was far from the office, however, and with meetings ending late in the evening, Nurjahan found herself returning home alone in the dark. A few months later, she found a house closer to work. "But it was expensive—and I had to tie bamboo to the door to secure it."

PART II

The Villagers

This is the pathway trodden by many feet. Through a forest it reaches a meadow, through the meadow it reaches a riverbank. Beyond the waterway it starts again on the other bank, and creeps into a sleepy village. Passing through yellow corn-fields and the shades of a mango grove, it rounds a pond and pierces the village waste. Then on the far skyline it has reached a place the name of which I do not know. . . . Wanderers have come and gone. The life-story of each lingers on the pathway as a footprint on dust. And the long trail of such prints stretches from horizon to horizon, from the golden gates of the East to the golden gates of the West.

RABINDRANATH TAGORE

7

Water Upon Land

Aleya Begum was walking along a path by a pond carrying a clay water jug when she caught sight of me. With the jug cradled in her left arm, she stopped and stood motionless. From twenty yards, she looked like a teenager striking a cool pose. "So who is this?" she seemed to be saying. And in that instant, conscious of my freshly laundered shirt and brand-new sandals, I felt slightly ridiculous to find myself in a village in Bangladesh.

Aleya had reason to be curious. Her district, Patuakhali, is decidedly off the beaten track, even within Bangladesh, which, except for an army of development workers in Dhaka, receives only a tiny number of foreign visitors.

As I approached, two other women and a half dozen children appeared on the path. In the pond behind them a young boy slapped a ball of soapy clothes against a stone. When he saw me, he froze, too. Up close, Aleya appeared smaller but older, probably in her thirties. Her manner was pleasant although she didn't smile. After she and my translator exchanged preliminaries, Aleya inquired about my business. When I mentioned that I had come to learn about the Grameen Bank, she explained that she had been a member for six years.

"In six years," she declared, "I've never had any red ink in my book."

On my arrival in Dhaka, two weeks before, I had been assigned to the bank's International Training Unit, located in the office adjacent to Yunus's personal secretary. Since the late 1980s, Grameen had been receiving hundreds of international visitors each year—scholars, foreign dignitaries, representatives of foundations, journalists, and those looking to start microenterprise programs in their own countries. Many of these visitors arrive in Bangladesh with a good deal of apprehension. A West-

Transporting rice on the Padma River

erner planning to explore the countryside for months usually receives vaccinations or carries prophylactics for malaria, dysentery, cholera, typhoid, hepatitis, tuberculosis, and meningitis. Rural Bangladesh is full of leeches and ticks, bedbugs and lice. The traveler under the hot sun and moving in the sticky air is susceptible to heat exhaustion, heat strokes, prickly heat, and plain old sunburn. Of course, by following a few basic precautions, a visitor can eliminate most of the danger.

The staff in the International Training Unit, sought to eliminate *all* of it. The unit was staffed with employees who had distinguished themselves in the field; they coordinated bus, train, and boat travel, arranged accommodations, helped find translators, negotiated visas, and looked out for visitors' personal safety. Hospitality is a cultural imperative in Bangladesh, so it is natural that the bank would take excellent care of its guests. But Yunus also has a clear understanding of the power of the media, particularly the Western media. He is aware of the vital importance of generating good public relations for a cause, and he sees the direct links between academic papers, newspaper feature articles, and donor financing for his ideas. Which is why a visitor's time was managed like a new recruit's. Sleep off your jet lag, spend a few days in the office orienting yourself, and then off to a village.

The district of Patuakhali (pronounced Poe-too-ah-kalee), situated on the Bay of Bengal, is dominated by an extensive system of rivers, feeders, and distributaries that carry the Ganges to the sea. Patuakhali is a relatively new piece of the world: Parts of it have been settled only in the past fifty years as rivers have changed course, receding in some places, advancing in others. In 1970, the area was decimated by a cyclone that killed 225,000 people. This was the disaster that spawned George Harrison's Concert for Bangladesh, in New York. In twenty-five years, the government has planted thousands of trees to protect the shoreline, but with most of Bangladesh sitting only a few feet above sea level, global warming remains a dire threat.

I had traveled south in the company of a Bangladeshi woman who was to act as a translator and a go-between with village women. The staff in Grameen's head office had told me that the easiest way to get to Patuakhali from Dhaka was by riverboat. Indeed, river travel was the way to go in a country that often appeared less land upon water than water upon land. Rivers had created the lush alluvial delta that is Bangladesh, and occasionally, they behaved in the manner of the tyrannical father who informs his child that because he brought him into the world, he's entitled to take him out of it.

One way to trace the history of East Bengal would be to follow the movements of its rivers over the decades, as they have changed course, silted up, flooded, displaced thousands, and then enticed them back with the promise of bountiful harvests. Thanks to the fresh deposits of silt left behind by floods each year, Bangladeshi soil is possibly the most fertile on earth. The national anthem, composed by the Nobel Prize–winning poet Rabindranath Tagore, is a tribute to the golden rice fields of Bengal. When the Apollo 11 astronauts traveled to the moon, so the story goes, the soil they carried in their command module came from Bangladesh.

My launch had departed from Dhaka at sunset. The boat was itself something of a metaphor for Bangladesh. On one side, two dozen passengers relaxed in air-conditioned cabins, equipped with video screens featuring new movies from Bombay. On the other side, hundreds of villagers camped head-to-foot on the steel decks. Such a separation between first class and steerage is not unique to boats in Bangladesh.

What was striking was simply the ratio of passengers on either side: In Bangladesh, not more than 5 to 10 percent of the population can afford to travel cabin class; nevertheless, the boat was split fifty-fifty.

Within an hour, the orange glow of the city was replaced by the flicker of fishermen's lanterns dotting the black water like glowworms. Nobody really knows, but it is said that 10 million Bangladeshis live like these men, in boats. My translator delighted in the stillness of the scene. Dhaka, her home, is racked with traffic congestion and pollution.

Over the past two decades, the city has grown from 2 to 7.5 million inhabitants, and the population is projected to soar, in the next two decades, to 18 million. Sprawling networks of shantytowns have sprung up everywhere, where families live next to open sewage canals and garbage dumps and children play alongside active train lines. Like Calcutta and Jakarta, Dhaka is well on its way to becoming another Asian megacity—or "megashantytown"—with the associated crime and health hazards, unless something can be done to stem the influx of villagers.

At 6:00 A.M., we made port in Barisal. The river was strewn with branches and leaves. It appeared as if large clumps of Bangladesh had simply broken off during the night. Boatsmen were scattered about, perched on gunwales like falcons or standing at the stern of their scullers, throwing their body weight back and forth against huge oars. As the boat docked, a mass of bodies pressed toward a ramp made of two ten-inch-wide wooden boards. Women carried toddlers across the span. Young boys crossed over, staggering under the weight of enormous burlap sacks. A single misstep would have sent them into the water fifteen feet below.

Descending the ramp, I dreaded what was to come next. Though the worst poverty in Bangladesh goes easily unnoticed—it exists in the deceptively peaceful settings of villages where people do not beg but suffer in silence—the most visible misery inhabits transit stations. Here are the children intentionally maimed to be more effective beggars, the skeletal mothers with the bloated babies, the gaunt old men with the stumps and tumors.

I caught sight of one woman whose chest appeared to have been crushed by a heavy weight. She supported herself against a cement partition; her left arm lay in the dirt, palm open; her right arm rested behind an infant. When she saw a foreigner descend the ramp, her face came alive with a great effort of supplication; she raised her palm an inch off the ground and, with her eyes, implored me to help her child.

Taking advantage of my temporary loss of self-possession, an eight-year-old boy immediately wrested away my backpack. Successful, he beamed, and hustled me and my translator in the direction of jingling bells, where he placed our bags in a rickshaw belonging to another boy, who, toes barely touching pedals, transported us to the bus depot.

In Bangladesh, you often hear foreign aid workers musing about how the locals seem to lack an "entrepreneurial" temperament. Bangladeshis are attracted to business in theory, they say, but not in practice. Clearly, these people have never been on a bus in Bangladesh.

Here you find economic man in his rawest form. Unencumbered by timetables and safety regulations, the bus operator crams his passengers into tiny seats three or four abreast. He places passengers on the hot transmission box, squeezes the standing ones like linguini, so close together they are unable to raise their arms, and adds two dozen more on the roof, where they hunch and hold tight. Then he waits. He waits and he waits for more passengers until it is no longer mathematically possible to squeeze in one more paying customer. And all the while, he will not consider entertaining a single complaint, because it is universally understood that a bus in Bangladesh will never depart until it is chock full, until it has reached the very peak of its profitability curve.

Our bus driver was no exception. Inside, the air was stifling. Sweat passed from body to body. My translator squeezed next to the window so I would be the only man in contact with her. (In Bangladesh, foreigners are treated as such oddities that normal rules of conduct are suspended for them. A foreign man traveling with a young Bangladeshi woman certainly draws many curious, and a few malevolent, stares; however, in all the time my translator and I traveled together, nobody ever harassed us.)

After forty-five minutes, the engine fired, and soon the bus was juddering along, passing rickshaws and oxen at a harrowing speed. The road was only one and a half lanes wide, and each time a vehicle approached in the opposite direction, both drivers swerved off the pavement, a maneuver neither felt warranted a reduction of speed.

In another hour, we reached the ferry crossing to Patuakhali town. Four buses were lined up ahead of us. The driver cursed and shut his engine. It would be a thirty-minute wait. Passengers fanned themselves with magazines. Those without seats disembarked and mulled around a cluster of shops. Thousands of flies hovered above bowls of cut papaya. I got out to jot down some notes and was immediately surrounded by a dozen men pressing close to catch a glimpse of my pad. Across the road a high-voltage tower lay on its side, having been downed in the 1991 cyclone. Some boys boarded the bus to peddle candies, chocolates, and chewing gum. Another young boy followed them. He had a handsome

Loading up the bus

face but the bottom half of his body was so mangled that he could get around only on all fours. A money pouch hung from his neck. He wore flip-flops on his hands.

A ferry carried the bus across a muddy river to an unmemorable town of weather-beaten buildings. Except for the buses at the depot and the odd motorcycle, the only vehicles in Patuakhali town were rickshaws, and they filled the narrow streets with the sound of bells. We hailed a rickshaw *wallah* who appeared to be in his fifties. For the five-mile trip to the Grameen Bank's Dibuapur branch, the driver quoted a price of 12 takas—equivalent to thirty cents or three pounds of low-grade rice at local prices. He anticipated a counteroffer and was pleased when we just climbed in.

The Dibuapur branch stood by the roadside, a quarter mile down from a flagging bazaar. By contrast to the wood and tin huts we had just passed, from afar the two-story brick and cement office seemed virtually indestructible, an enduring feature of the landscape, like a grand old banyan tree.

The Dibuapur branch had been open eight years, and up close it showed its age. Outside, the walls needed a fresh coat of paint. Inside, the sinks and fixtures had decayed because years before management had determined that the cost of installing running water in hundreds of branches was prohibitively high. Upstairs, only two of the four sleeping rooms were occupied, giving the place the feel of a half-abandoned army barracks. Most of the staff, recruited during the bank's first major expansion in the mid-1980s, had married and moved into their own houses. Only four of the eleven cots had bedrolls on them—three young recruits and one old bachelor. There was plenty of room for guests.

We were welcomed with exuberance by the branch manager, a high-spirited and meticulous fellow. Everything was in order with our bedding, he explained. Blankets, sheets, pillows, mattresses, and mosquito netting would be delivered later that afternoon from the zonal office in town. We could take our meals with the staff, or in the restaurants in the bazaar, but we had to be careful; some were not so hygienic. Or his wife would be delighted to cook for us. Did I eat rice? Fruit, vegetables, and toiletries could be obtained in town. The staff had candles and flashlights. Electricity was sporadic. If we gave him a list of items, he'd be happy to pick up anything we needed when he did his household shopping. (This was advisable, since he'd be charged less in the bazaar than a foreigner. No offense intended.) The zonal office had a fax machine if we needed to communicate with the head office. Any letters or faxes received in Dhaka, similarly, would be routed to Patuakhali and delivered here. Had he left anything out?

"Where are the villages you work in?" I asked.

The manager made a wide circular motion with his hand. "Everywhere," he said.

8

It's All on Trust

After our initial exchange by the pond, Aleya Begum had invited us to her house, a two-story building made of wood and tin that appeared newer than the other houses in the village. Along the way we were thronged by children. They massed in front of Aleya's house, waved through the windows, and pressed their eyes against the slits in the bamboo walls. Considering the heat, I was astonished by their energy.

"There are too many children," a friend of Aleya's commented grimly. "They die by ones but they increase by twos." She was not exaggerating. It is estimated that half the deaths in Bangladesh are children under the age of five, yet 45 percent of the population are younger than fifteen.

Aleya shut the door because the shrieking had begun to drown us out. "Is this a bazaar?" she yelled through the window. "Doesn't your mother take money from the bank?" she chided one boy. She apologized with a smile. "Grameen Bank members' children are better behaved."

Aleya did not smile often, and when she did it was an abbreviated gesture, lasting only a few seconds. At first, I assumed she was shy, but when I asked questions she answered them directly and looked me straight in the eye, something many Bangladeshi women would not do.

She explained how she had come to join the bank six years earlier. Even before the Dibuapur branch—the bank's 115th office—opened in 1984, the manager had introduced himself to the shopkeepers in the bazaar and begun walking around the countryside.

Before long, rumors of his evil designs had taken on a life of their own. Some said the bank was run by Christian missionaries; some said it was a socialist plot. Others warned that if you borrowed money and failed to repay it, the manager would confiscate your possessions and send you to jail. Mullahs said the bank worked against Islam and warned that anyone who joined would be denied a proper burial. (But according to the mullahs, just about *everything* you did went against religion, Aleya later commented.)

One day, a friend told Aleya that she was thinking of forming a group. Would she join, too? One center had already been formed in their village and none of the horror stories had materialized. Now another was getting started. Aleya's friend had met the manager and liked him. She heard that he often visited members' families, and he never accepted any food or gifts, not even a glass of coconut water. He was young, too, only a few years out of university, with a master's degree. Both women had the same question: So why had he accepted such a job?

That evening Aleya broached the subject with her husband. Ansar Ali Malek worked in a printing shop in town and earned just enough money for the couple and their three daughters to live on. He owned a little land, but he had no savings and was having trouble keeping the house intact. Termites had eaten holes in two of the bamboo walls and Ansar knew that he would have to find money to repair the thatch roof before the monsoon season.

Ansar didn't believe the gossip about the bank. Missionary conversions were a thing of the past, he told his wife; and the idea of a bank going through the trouble of constructing an office in the countryside just to bully a few villagers seemed ridiculous. He'd read newspaper articles about development and figured this was probably something the Americans had cooked up. He was skeptical about one thing: this business with women.

Aleya recalled exactly how her husband reacted when she told him she wanted to join. "He laughed at me. He just said, 'Oh, you think you're going to get money? Even men can't get money from a bank without land certificates. So how are you housewives going to get money?' "

If other wives had taken loans, she said, why couldn't she?

Ansar continued to voice doubts.

"Oh, I'll show him," Aleya said to herself. "I'll go and get the money and show him."

Ansar recalled a different conversation. "I started hearing things about the bank," he told me one morning while Aleya was gathering hay outside. "So I wanted to encourage her to join. But I also worried because, with ordinary banks, taking out money is a big hassle. You need to show how much land you have. You need to show deeds and certificates. There's an unwritten law in Bangladesh: They only lend money to people who have money. I didn't believe they would lend money to a poor person like me. You don't need documents, papers, nothing. It's all on trust."

In the middle of Ansar's explanation, Aleya entered. When her husband finished, she added with only the barest trace of a smile: "And they lend money to housewives."

"And they lend money to housewives, not to men," Ansar concurred. He continued: "So then she asked me, 'What should I do?' and I said, 'Go. If it is good, go.' Then there were a few days of training and after the training she came home with the money."

"Then he was a little scared," Aleya added. "Because he worried, 'How are you going to pay the money back? If you can't pay the money back they'll come and clean out the house and take the cow away. You have to pay the installments no matter what.' "

Ansar reflected that much time had passed since that day. "Now I've been in the Grameen Bank for five years," he said.

"Six years," corrected Aleya.

"Now I rely on the Grameen Bank," he said.

"Are you a member, too?" I asked.

"No. But her going and my going is the same thing."

It took a few weeks for Aleya and her friend to form their group. "When I went to the bank they told me to get five people," she explained. "They said, 'Your spirits must be in agreement; you have to share opinions about things; and you can't be in a group with someone who eats from the same cooking pot as you.' "

Aleya borrowed 2,000 takas the first time. She received 1,900 takas in hand (5 percent was deposited into the Group Fund). She bought a cow and sold milk, earning between 10 and 20 takas each day. Each week she paid her installment of 40 takas and deposited a few takas in her savings. "At first it was difficult, but I had no complications."

Over the next fifty weeks, Aleya set aside 163 takas for her interest payment. (The bank was then charging 16 percent interest calculated on a declining balance.) An additional 41 takas had to be paid into the Emergency Fund (25 percent of the interest). At the end of the year, the cow belonged to her.

"How did you feel then?" I asked.

"Inside, my heart and mind stayed the same," she said. "But I also felt happy."

"Then?"

"Then I said, 'The cow is ours.' "

A month later, Aleya borrowed 3,000 takas and purchased another cow and started all over again. Over the next four years, her loans grew progressively larger: from 3,500 to 4,000 and finally to 5,000 takas.

Appropriately, the couple decided to diversify. It was risky to tie up all your capital in one asset, especially in an asset that could die. Ansar leased a small plot of land for rice cultivation and Aleya raised chickens and grew vegetables for sale. The couple began saving for the wedding of their eldest daughter, Halima. Rather than deposit money into an account at the bank, where it would earn 8.5 percent interest, they purchased stocks of lentils in season, stored them, and resold them later in the year when the price doubled. In a small house with a leaky roof, however, there was a limit to the scope of this business.

9

Stirring the Money

"Has he seen rice?"

The question referred to me and was put to the crowd by Rani Begum, whose voice rose in volume above all the others. We were crowded inside the front room of her house with about a dozen people, while another dozen stood just outside the door. Rani's house faced Aleya's across a mud courtyard. All of the husbands in this *para,* or neighborhood, were related.

It was early afternoon, a time of day when villagers often take a short break from work if they can afford to. Aleya and her daughters were present, along with Rani, her husband, and their children. Rani was large-boned and sinewy, one of the most powerful-looking women I had seen in Bangladesh. She had borne five sons and one daughter and her husband laughed heartily at her jokes.

A woman named Sahera, who lived two houses over from Aleya, stood by the front door cradling her baby boy, covering his head with a corner of her sari as she breastfed him. "Oh, Allah, it's hot," she sighed intermittently. The air hung still. Rivulets of sweat ran down my back. Rani's daughter alternately fanned herself and my translator.

Over the past two weeks, all of the women in this *para* had invited us to their homes. Upon our arrival, they would sit us down and disappear into the kitchen only to reemerge with plates of puffed rice, eggs, biscuits, molasses, coconut water, and fried lentils. As we ate, the questions began. They were many and various, but inevitably the first five were the same: What is your country? Are you married? How many brothers and sisters do you have? Are your mother and father alive? What are your educational qualifications? Sometimes an answer of mine would elicit peals of laughter, as on one occasion when I was asked if people in

America kiss before they marry, and I replied, "They often have children before they marry."

Such banter caught my translator and me off guard. The development texts I had read back home—most written by Westerners—were full of generalizations about how Muslim women in Bangladesh have "internalized their inferiority" to such a degree that many perceive themselves as virtually worthless. Patuakhali is not a terribly conservative district within Bangladesh, and these women, having been members of the Grameen Bank for years, were necessarily bolder than average. Even so, my translator, a graduate student (who had spent little time in villages), found them remarkably self-assured. For my part, I had anticipated difficulties interviewing Bangladeshi women and was pleasantly surprised by the relative ease of communication.

My translator laughed each time another dish of food was forthcoming. I laughed, too, although I could not help but estimate the cost of the food and wonder what sacrifice it entailed for our hosts. And I understood why bank staff were strictly forbidden to accept food or gifts from borrowers.

"Would you like to see rice?" Rani asked, pursuing her line of inquiry.

Another woman interrupted, saying it was a ridiculous question. Of course, Americans know about rice. Didn't they? (I had explained that I came from Canada, but villagers were interested in hearing only about "America.")

Americans eat rice a few times a week, I replied, but usually as a side dish. "Side dish" was translated as a plate of food in which the rice lay near the edge. Bangladeshi villagers eat rice at every meal, three times a day if they're fortunate, and they usually mix their food with their hands in a single bowl. There is no Western equivalent for rice. The closest thing would be water.

Rani took the opportunity to divert the conversation toward some of the ways she knew how to cook rice: You could grind it into flour for breads, make pudding, fry it in ghee, smash it and serve it with grated coconut, or puff it and, if you like, mix it with date molasses. That was a favorite among the children, she explained. "But if they're not good, they don't get any," she added in a menacing tone, which caused a tremor of giggling to run through the hut.

The children were quiet today because Rani's husband was present. Some had darted over after school and a few still had their books. I asked Rani if our visit was keeping them from their homework.

"Unless you give them a swat," she explained, "the kids don't sit to study."

The hut erupted in laughter.

"Sometimes you even need a stick," she added.

This comment produced an enormous uproar. One eight-year-old boy pulled his T-shirt up over his face because he was laughing so hard.

"When they're naughty, I hit them with a stick," Rani continued. "And then after a while, I give them the puffed rice."

"But after a while, you don't have to use the stick," I said. "You just have to show it. Right?"

"No, you have to apply it. They're little devils."

The children paired off, boys with boys and girls with girls, arms around one another. Among children and adults, physical intimacy with the same sex is common in Bangladesh, and men can often be seen holding hands while walking along village paths. Except for the behavior toward young children, these are the only acceptable displays of affection in a Bangladeshi village. While Aleya's sixteen-year-old daughter, Halima, ran her fingers through the hair of Rani's daughter, her mother shared a chair with her friend Zainub. The two women sat shoulder to shoulder, knee to knee, with their hands resting on each other's thighs.

Zainub lived in another *para*. "Before we were in the Grameen Bank," Aleya said, "we didn't have this friendship."

"What do you usually do when you are together?" I asked.

"We talk," Aleya said.

Zainub nodded but she would not speak.

Rani jumped in: "We discuss the work we do. We sit on the veranda like this."

"In the full moon we sit outside," added Sahera, rocking her baby.

"We go for walks in the fields," another woman added.

"What do you have the most fun doing?" I asked Rani.

"You're asking me what I like eating best?" she replied.

My translator laughed and explained that the word she used to translate "fun" was also used to describe something that tastes good. She rephrased the question.

"We don't have any fun," Rani said.

"There are weddings," Aleya said. "We put turmeric on the bride. Then we bathe her and sing and dance and feed everybody sweet rice pudding."

"What about on ordinary days?"

"I work in the household," Rani said. "I cook. I make chili paste. I scale and cut fish into pieces. I dry and husk rice."

"But that's all work," I said.

"That's what it is," she added. "That's it. We don't have fun. At weddings we have fun and at Eid time and at Korbani Eid time. And when a child is born we shave his head. Then we eat sweet rice pudding. Other than that we don't have any fun."

Sahera had been the last woman in this *para* to join the bank. Although the others seemed to be getting along, she had worried about the responsibility of assuming a loan. Finally, her husband urged her to approach some women who were in the process of forming a group. "They checked me out and determined that I was a reliable person," she said. Like Aleya, Sahera used her first loan to purchase a cow.

"Were you worried about repaying the money?" I asked.

Sahera hesitated before speaking. Villagers are often reluctant to say anything negative to a foreign visitor. In this case, I guessed that Sahera was also being cautious. Since it was known that the Grameen Bank received money from abroad, it followed that a foreigner who came to Bangladesh to investigate it was very likely checking up on his money. Indeed, when I first arrived in Dibuapur, I had had to explain many times that I was not associated with the Grameen Bank, that I was merely a guest. Villagers did not wish to say anything that they imagined might harm the bank, so they were inclined to censor bad news. Only after repeated visits and reassurances did they begin to speak more openly to me about their difficulties.

"What is there to be worried about?" Sahera finally said.

Aleya, who was more forthright, cut in: "The bank loves us, but they keep us in jail. If you can't pay, you must ask your group for help. If they won't help, you can ask the center. If they won't help, then you're out. No matter what, the bank has to get its money back."

"Then do you think of your loan as a burden?" I asked Sahera.

"Yes," she replied. "That burden is necessary. When you are holding another person's money, don't you have to worry?"

"Is it worth the anxiety?" I asked, prodding.

"Yes," Sahera said. "Because we improve."

"How do you improve?"

"By stirring the money," Sahera said. "When you stir it, it cooks and makes more. To make her point, she reiterated: "I buy a cow; I sell milk; I lease some land; and the money grows."

"Can everybody do it?" I asked.

"We don't accept completely poor people into groups," she said. "What if they don't repay their loans?"

"Why wouldn't they?"

"When you borrow the money, you have to work it intelligently," she explained.

"Aren't there intelligent poor people?" I countered.

"If you have a little bit of good sense then you can't get absolutely poor."

"What if the situation is beyond your control?"

"Then you have to sort out a way for yourself. You have to develop a system to carry on."

"There are family members and neighbors to help out," added Aleya.

"But isn't that what the Grameen Bank is for?" I asked.

"If the group won't accept someone, she can't join," Sahera said. "Everybody tries to understand and cooperate, but first we make sure she's a reliable person."

"What if people who've never had money have had no chance to prove themselves?" I asked.

"Yes, that can happen." The reply came from Rani's husband, the first words he'd spoken. "Sometimes you accept people like this and watch whether they'll invest the money or consume it. But some people who've been given loans have taken all the money and eaten it up."

"The first time someone borrows money, it's enough to tell," Aleya said.

"If we see that she's reliable, then we authorize more loans," Sahera added.

"There are a lot of people at loose ends," Rani's husband commented, "people who want to get into the Grameen Bank but can't join."

"I'll tell you this," Rani said. "Whether we eat or not, whether our household runs or not, we pay the money back."

"If the bank lent money to men," her husband added, "they wouldn't get it back so conscientiously. Women have the discipline to manage such things."

"That's why the Grameen Bank is made up of women," Rani added.

"Why?" I asked.

"Because they profit by it."

10

Sabina Yasmin

One morning I took a walk with Sabina Yasmin, the oldest bank worker in the Dibuapur branch, to visit her centers. Sabina had two collection meetings, one at nine o'clock, and one at ten-thirty. We had arranged to meet at seven o'clock by the barber shop in the bazaar.

My translator and I arrived ten minutes early and found Sabina waiting for us by the roadside, discussing business with a local shopkeeper. Over her sari, she wore a hooded garment called a *burkah,* with a veil flipped back off her head. She carried a black handbag brandishing the Grameen Bank logo, a red and green arrow.

Sabina was in her late twenties, but she conducted herself with an air of professionalism that made her seem older and made me reluctant to disturb her with trivial questions. When I first asked whether I might accompany her on her collection rounds, she hesitated. I imagined that she was concerned about being seen in the company of a foreign man. In fact, she was trying to remember which centers she would be visiting the following day. Some were more than five miles away and Sabina was not sure I would be up to the trip.

Today it would be a one-hour walk to the first center meeting. During the monsoon season, the same trip took two and a half hours.

Soon we came to a bamboo bridge. "Can you swim?" Sabina asked, hopefully.

During the monsoon season, the water can rise to a level of eight feet, swamping the high road and inundating the countryside. On high land, houses become small islands. On low land, villagers build wooden stands and live, sometimes for weeks, twelve inches above the water. They cook and sleep on the stands and get around on floats constructed from banana trees.

Sabina Yasmin

The monsoon season was only eight weeks off, and with summer approaching, Sabina complained that the days were growing hotter. By 8:00 A.M., the heat was such that any movement of air, even the thinnest zephyr, seemed a blessing. (One might imagine that Bangladeshis would be used to their climate, but just as New Yorkers hate mugginess and Montrealers can't stand the cold, Bangladeshis grumble endlessly about heat and rain.)

A woman dressed in a black *burkah* and carrying a black umbrella darted across the path. I commented to my translator that the woman must be melting inside, and she just smiled and told me that this was far from the worst heat; the worst heat was "mango-ripening heat." (To

Bamboo Bridge, Patuakhali

experience this in its fullness, she added, I would have to take a walk at midday in a district called Rajshahi, in the northeast. As it turned out, I did go to Rajshahi, in the month of June no less, to visit a woman named Manjira, who was to become the most famous member of the Grameen Bank: the woman about whom the staff would come to say, "If you were truly lucky, you had *the luck of Manjira.*")

The season Sabina liked best was winter, when it was cool and dry enough for her to take shortcuts across fields. "I hate mud and I hate storms," she declared. Sabina kept an extra sari at the office to change into when she returned soaking wet; on a few occasions she had slipped off slick paths and had had to swim to safety. "I never once lost my deposits," she added.

She had taken this job eight years before, after completing tenth grade. Like most of the staff, initially Sabina had little idea what she was getting into. "I knew nothing about the fieldwork," she recalled. After a two-day briefing in the bank's training institute, she was dispatched to a branch for two months where she learned how to manage groups and centers and how to keep accounts. She spent long days interviewing villagers, following the "case study" model that Nurjahan had developed in Jobra. She returned to the head office for a week of seminars and was reassigned to the same branch for two more months, this time with shared responsibility for a few centers. She was then transferred to a different branch for two more months to gain experience dealing with problem borrowers. Finally, she was assigned to a third branch for normal duties. After five months, in which her performance was closely monitored, she passed a comprehensive written and oral examination (she passed the first time; many candidates have to repeat it). By the time her probationary year was finished, one third of her class had dropped out.

"When you were first hired, what did you think about the bank?" I asked.

"I had no idea how they were going to accomplish what they said they would," Sabina replied. "Before working for the Grameen Bank, I had the preconception that poor people were not very bright. I didn't think they would pay back the loans."

We passed a band of boys, about seven or eight years old, playing a game that involved a metal hoop two feet in diameter, and a metal rod with a hook at the end. The object was to run alongside the hoop and use the rod to guide it and keep it rolling. Though the path was bumpy, some of the boys managed to keep the hoop going for about thirty yards.

They were dressed in ragged shorts. On leather cords around their necks hung amulets called *tabiz*, believed to ward off illness. By the side of the path a girl watched them play. She supported an infant against her hip and held a toddler by the hand. She appeared to be the same age as the boys.

She reminded me of a girl named Hasina, perhaps a year older, who worked in one of the restaurants I frequented in the bazaar. While her mother cooked in the back, up front Hasina took orders, served food, tallied checks, washed tables, and fried bread on a skillet over a fire. From the tobacco shop across the road she procured for her customers cigarettes and *pan,* the smoky-tasting combination of betel nut, betel leaf, and lime that villagers enjoy throughout the day and especially after meals. (*Pan,* which stains the mouth blood red, is said to alleviate hunger pains.) Hasina also argued with the men over their bills—always something of a judgment call—and on one occasion that I know of, even chased down a deadbeat customer who said that he had "forgotten" to pay. (I suspect she did not believe him.)

Sabina had plenty of time to think about her own children on these walks to center meetings. Both her son and daughter attended elementary school for half the day. Each day Sabina awoke at 5:00 A.M., prepared breakfast, and left for work before her children went to school. She tried to get home to prepare lunch on most days, but often she was detained at the office and had to rely on neighbors. "When there are rainstorms, they stay with my daughter," she added. "And when I have to travel to a workshop, their grandmother stays with them."

Throughout Bangladesh, children can be seen working and taking care of themselves. On busy thoroughfares in Dhaka, buses and trucks lumber alongside ten-year-old boys clumsily pedaling rickshaws. Elsewhere their younger brothers, and occasionally their sisters, can be found walking barefoot along the asphalt, toting baskets loaded with candy, nuts, and cigarettes.

In villages, mothers are often too busy to watch over their children. They try to keep tabs on them by tying bells to their waists. Still, with most huts situated near a pond or stream, drownings are commonplace.

Children under the supervision of older children play with nightmarish toys—things like sheets of tin and wooden boards with rusty nails extending from them. Their parents can be maddeningly careless as well. I have seen babies whose skin is covered with rashes and scabies sitting naked in the dirt, while their mothers worked on mats only six feet away. Among young wives, one common cause of death is fire, which occurs when a woman is cooking and her sari catches the flame.

Buses in Bangladesh often pass men sleeping dangerously close to the roadside. Once I saw a man sleeping with one leg extended twelve inches into the road. The bus driver blasted his horn and swerved around him.

How to explain the lack of prudence? Malnutrition and its corollary, extreme physical and mental fatigue, were the most common explanations I received from locals. Sabina said that many villagers, perceiving no escape from their problems, were apathetic about life.

When I asked her how she thought Bangladesh might be different in five years' time, she replied, "It's impossible to say—but I can tell you this: Five years from now, there will be less poverty and people will be more aware than they are now. The things I have to repeat over and over again—in five years, I'll only have to say them once."

11

The Center Meeting

The center house was a hut with bamboo walls and a tin roof measuring about seven by fifteen feet. Inside, twenty-eight women sat in six rows (two were absent). When Sabina arrived, the women stood up, saluted, and returned to their positions sitting cross-legged or squatting on the mud floor. Some rested on tiny benches two inches off the ground. Several children crowded by the door. "Go away," yelled one member. "There's no sweet rice pudding here."

The center house is the nucleus of Grameen's operation. Bank workers refer to the weekly meeting as the "heartbeat." Each center accommodates between six and eight borrowing groups, or thirty to forty members. More than 60,000 of these huts are scattered throughout Bangladesh today, in 35,000 villages, more than half the nation's total.

In a 1991 speech, Yunus outlined the function of the center house: "People should not [have to] go to the bank," he said. "The bank should go to the people." When a villager is asked to come to an office, it becomes a symbol of terror, he explained. "You are put in a line, you don't know the rules. Somebody says, 'You go there.' Somebody else says, 'You better go there.' Somebody says, 'Where are your papers?' and, 'No, you come next time.' The people at the bottom are terribly scared of this kind of situation. They would rather not deal with you."

The hut also provides borrowers with an opportunity to undertake a collective activity. After a few groups are formed, members must begin accumulating money to build the hut and then agree on a location. (Until it is complete, meetings are usually held in members' houses.) Like any group activity, the process fosters competition. "Look at the other

Approaching the center house, Dibuapur Village

center houses," Aleya told me. "Some don't even have walls. You saw ours. Wasn't it nice? Every year we put up new bamboo walls."

Sabina took her seat at a table and chair in the corner. She inquired about the two absentees. The villagers explained that one woman was tending to her sister-in-law after she'd been bitten by a snake, and another was repairing her house, which had been struck by lightning the night before. Both absentees had sent their installments with someone else.

Sabina signaled the center chief to begin the meeting. The women rose, saluted, recited the Grameen Bank credo—"Discipline, Unity, Courage, and Hard Work"—and did a minute's worth of arm stretches and knee bends, before sitting down. Sabina asked for the passbooks. Each group chairman, in the right-most position of her row, collected the yellow books from her members and passed them to the center chief who handed them to Sabina. Sabina flipped open each one and handed the enclosed money to the center chief who counted it while she initialed the passbooks and recorded the payments in her ledger.

Sabina explained that the members of this center made very few errors; it saved time to assume that their installments were in order. Afterward, if the totals were off she would search for the problem. Most of the time everything added up. Her approach reminded me of a difference Yunus had pointed out between Grameen and other banks. "Other banks assume that you are a potential cheat," he told me. "That's how they tie you up [with collateral]. We assume that you are the best person ever. And there are margins of error in both cases. But if their repayment is 98 percent and so is ours, they're *wrong* in 98 percent of the cases and we're *right* in 98 percent of the cases."

Sabina keyed in totals on her calculator while the center chief stacked the notes in neat piles by denomination: blue hundreds, red fifties, green twenties, pink tens, brown fives, orange-green twos, and orange-purple ones. The paper was old and worn, having gone through many monsoons. You couldn't riffle through these notes; counting took time.

Outside a cow brayed. Dogs and chickens went about their business. Sitar music emanated from a radio. Inside, the back of the hut was dark and the last group barely visible. Sunlight filtered through the bamboo walls, spreading a mirror-ball pattern and producing tiny bursts of color from the women's saris. A narrow shaft of sunshine entered by the door over the children's heads, providing light for Sabina and the center chief to work. The members chatted softly: The night before, a child in the village had died of fever.

An installment was inserted in the wrong passbook and suddenly the center chief shouted at the chairman of group number six: "You should be more careful."

The chairman remained silent, but one of her group members shouted back, "She is careful."

"After seven years you're still making these mistakes," commented Sabina without raising her eyes.

Another woman was 2 takas short. Her group members shouted instructions to a young boy outside who quickly returned with the money. Sabina finished her calculations and put her papers aside. "This is a very bad time for diarrhea," she said. (The days were getting hotter and it was very easy to become dehydrated.) "If you get sick go to the doctor right away. You know how to prepare oral rehydration solution. Make sure to cover your food. Make sure you and your children wash your hands before eating. And even if the tubewell is very far away, never wash your plates and crockery with pond water.

"Plant the seeds we've given you before the monsoon season. Check if your kids are really going to school and talk to them at night."

Inside the center house

The center chief rose to conclude the meeting. The women stood up, saluted, recited the Sixteen Decisions, and departed. Sabina had collected 2,500 takas. She placed the bills in a three-inch-high pyramid (higher denominations are bigger), wrapped two rubber bands around the stack, and dropped it in her handbag with her collection forms.

"This center runs well," she said.

Over the years, the center meetings had evolved to incorporate the salute, the slogans, the exercises, and the Sixteen Decisions—the bank's social development manifesto. In 1980, Grameen began organizing workshops and center schools, and providing members with items such as iodized salt, vegetable seeds, saplings, water-purification crystals, and textbooks. The bank always charged a small fee for these items, even if it was just a token amount, because Yunus was adamant that Grameen not be perceived by members as another giveaway program. Bangladesh had far too many.

The workshops were the bank's principal forum for addressing a wide range of social problems. Today, Grameen conducts almost 3,000 workshops each year, some one-day affairs, some lasting a full week, focusing on health care, nutrition, family planning, child care, and business opportunities. Some workshops involve exchange visits among branches; women look forward to these rare opportunities to travel and meet strangers.

Once every two years Grameen holds its National Workshop, a five-day conference that brings together center chiefs from one hundred branches across the country. The first national workshop, in 1982, produced ten resolutions for members to carry back to their areas and disseminate. The second, in 1984, added six more resolutions, which delegates voted to incorporate into a new document called the Sixteen Decisions, which was to be recited at each center meeting.

The next meeting was a mile away. In an hour, the temperature seemed to have doubled. When we arrived at the second center house, we quickly removed our sandals and ducked inside, where it was cooler. We were early, but several members had already taken their positions in the six-by-five matrix. Sabina reviewed the day's business. One member had recently applied for a new loan. Another had applied for a loan from her Group Fund.

The members were engrossed in their own preparations, counting money, settling private debts, and making change for one another. Bills and passbooks moved back and forth like chips in a poker game. One woman fanned a small child in her lap with her yellow passbook. Another used the end of her sari to muffle a throaty cough.

"Are you sick?" Sabina asked.

The woman nodded.

"Then why have you come?"

"I have to for my group."

Sabina glanced at her wristwatch. A few minutes remained. While others arrived in ones and twos, filling the center house, I imagined a similar scene being played out across the country. Bank meetings are held five days a week, two per morning. So, at each designated time, about 6,000 centers are gathering, each containing thirty to forty borrowers. An hour and a half before, 200,000 villagers had assembled, and now another 200,000 were preparing for a second round.

Imagine the range of problems that might arise in these meetings. Bangladeshi villages are split along clan, class, religious, and, in some cases, caste lines. The anxiety produced by extreme poverty leads inevitably to hostile competition among different factions. Villagers fight

The Sixteen Decisions

1. The four principles of Grameen Bank—Discipline, Unity, Courage, and Hard Work—we shall follow and advance in all walks of our lives.

2. Prosperity we shall bring to our families.

3. We shall not live in dilapidated houses. We shall repair our houses and work toward constructing new houses at the earliest.

4. We shall grow vegetables all the year round. We shall eat plenty of them and sell the surplus.

5. During the plantation seasons, we shall plant as many seedlings as possible.

6. We shall plan to keep our families small. We shall minimize our expenditures. We shall look after our health.

7. We shall educate our children and ensure that they can earn to pay for their education.

8. We shall always keep our children and the environment clean.

9. We shall build and use pit-latrines.

10. We shall drink tubewell water. If it is not available, we shall boil water or use alum.

11. We shall not take any dowry in our sons' weddings, neither shall we give any dowry in our daughters' weddings. We shall keep the center free from the curse of dowry. We shall not practice child marriage.

12. We shall not inflict any injustice on anyone, neither shall we allow anyone to do so.

13. For higher income we shall collectively undertake bigger investments.

14. We shall always be ready to help each other. If anyone is in difficulty, we shall all help him.

15. If we come to know of any breach of discipline in any center, we shall all go there and help restore discipline.

16. We shall introduce physical exercise in all our centers. We shall take part in all social activities collectively.

over control of land and water. It is not uncommon for a family to split apart over a land feud, or for a strong brother to steal the inheritance of a weak one. Centers are by no means insulated from the tensions in their communities. Almost every one of the two dozen centers I visited had at least one major division that ran through it like a geological fault.

Admirers of the Grameen Bank are fond of retelling stories about centers that have united to protest injustices. Indeed, the image of forty village women confronting a wife beater is inspiring. But such moments are the exceptions. More compelling is how well Grameen's system operates under normal conditions: how it compensates for a lack of goodwill, and how its rules act as a tight web around the center—ensuring that villagers are brought together frequently in a setting where they are forced to answer for their actions before all eyes. Despite the great potential for anarchy, most of the time things do not fall apart. *The center holds*—and it holds by means of a powerful social pressure that was described two centuries ago by Adam Smith.

"In the middling and inferior stations of life," wrote Smith in *The Theory of Moral Sentiments,* personal success "almost always depends upon the favour and good opinion of . . . neighbours and equals; and without a tolerably regular conduct these can very seldom be obtained. . . . In such situations, therefore, we may generally expect a considerable degree of virtue; and, fortunately for the good morals of society, these are the situations of by far the greater part of mankind."

"Why are you late?" Sabina asked a straggler. "It's not right to be late."

Three spots remained vacant. One woman had contracted dysentery and gone to the hospital in Patuakhali for treatment; another was repairing her roof after the previous night's storm. The last one arrived.

"Why are you late?" Sabina asked.

"I was sick," the woman replied.

"What sickness?" Sabina said, with a half smile. "You look fine."

A few women laughed. Ignoring them, the latecomer took her place and the center chief rose to begin the meeting. The women got to their feet, saluted, chanted, "Discipline, Unity, Courage, and Hard Work," and the meeting was under way.

While Sabina recorded the payments in her ledger, one woman inquired of my translator if she could ask me a question. The woman stood up nervously and proceeded to explain that she had been a member of the bank for seven years, but even after that time her loans were still

Paying the installment

too small. She had heard that other organizations sometimes helped poor villagers. Could I help her?

"Sit down," Sabina said curtly.

The woman continued. The bank had also raised its interest rate, she said. And once after a flood other banks had forgiven their loans but the Grameen Bank had not. "Why should we have to pay when others don't?" she asked.

"Sit down," Sabina said. "Are you a beggar?"

"Why should we pay when others don't have to?" the woman said again. Then she sat down.

Other than development workers and international aid donors, few foreigners visit rural Bangladesh, so it was natural that the woman should assume that I was an aid worker. When I replied that I was only a guest of the Grameen Bank and that I had no influence over it or any other development agency, the woman was disappointed. My translator didn't think she believed me.

Now something was amiss with group number three. Their combined installments were supposed to come to 440 takas, but the center chief had only 390 takas in hand. The woman in the hospital belonged to this group, which complicated things.

"Who is 50 takas short?" asked Sabina.

"I just put all the money they gave me together," the group chairman said.

"Who is 50 takas short?" asked the center chief.

"They gave me the money. I just put it together. I don't know," the group chairman replied.

"Do you know?" asked Sabina, addressing the others in her group.

The chairman turned to her members. Who is short? Somebody has to be short. Who is it? Nobody knew. Ten minutes passed. The shortfall was not discovered. Next time, the chairman said indignantly, she would check each passbook individually. She had lumped payments together because one member had only a 100-taka bill. Next time, if her group members did not bring the exact amount she wouldn't accept their installments. Why should she have to be their banker?

Sabina had seen this sort of confusion arise countless times. Sometimes a small discrepancy—in this case, most likely an innocent mistake —could destroy a group. The group chairman and another member agreed to make up the difference for the time being and Sabina advised the group to settle the matter as soon as the meeting was over.

She turned to the business of the new loan proposal, which had been submitted by a woman in group six. The members had gone through this procedure many times. First, the woman applying for the loan stood up, along with her group chairman and the center chief. Then Sabina asked the woman, who was barely visible at the back of the hut, to state her name, her group number, and her husband's full name (this is necessary because many village women have the same names).

"How many loans have you taken?" Sabina asked.

"Six."

"What was the amount of your previous loan?"

"Three thousand five hundred."

"What for?"

"Clothes making."

"How much do you request this time?"

"Four thousand."

"What for?"

"To buy a sewing machine."

"Will you repay it?" Sabina's tone was firm.

"Yes."

To her group chairman: "Do you agree to this?"

"Yes."

To the center chief: "Do you?"

"Yes."

"Okay then."

The woman smiled, saluted, and sat down. The center chief signed a form that already bore the signatures of the loan applicant and her group chairman. (Before they join the bank, all members must learn to sign their names.) Sabina told the woman that if there were no complications, she would receive her money within two weeks.

Now Sabina addressed a woman who had received a loan for a rice puffing business earlier that week, reminding her that she had to invest her money within seven days. "I'll come visit your house after next week's meeting to see your business," she explained.

"I know," the woman replied.

Some more business: A member had applied for an interest-free loan of 2,000 takas from her Group Fund to purchase medicine for her husband. She had completed the necessary form and gotten her group members' signatures. Before completing the paper work, Sabina tried to persuade her to borrow only 1,000 takas. They settled on 1,500. "It's their money," Sabina told me later, "but her husband is not that sick. If she takes too much now, there won't be enough left when she really needs it." A few weeks before, all the groups had elected new chairmen and secretaries. "Don't forget," Sabina told the woman, "the *new* chairman and secretary have to come with you to collect the Group Fund loan."

Finally, the center chief informed Sabina that the members had agreed to withdraw 300 takas from the Special Savings to purchase sweets and decorations for an upcoming festival. A sheet was circulated for all twenty-eight women to sign. Sabina reminded the center chief that she would have to obtain signatures from the two absentees.

She wound up: "It's very hot now. Be careful with your food. Diarrhea is bad now. If you get sick, go to the doctor right away. Always use tubewell water for drinking and for washing your plates and crockery,

Sabina Yasmin and Grameen Bank members

even if the well is very far away. Plant the seeds you have before the monsoon comes."

The members got to their feet, recited the Sixteen Decisions, saluted, and departed.

According to one version of Grameen Bank apocrypha, the origin of the salute was an incident involving a manager named Mohammed Mortuza. One day, Mortuza was driving in a car when he spotted a man on the ground by the roadside with a goat by his side and a police officer standing over him. The man recognized Mortuza and began gesturing frantically in what appeared a salute. Mortuza stopped. The policeman explained that the goat had been stolen but the man insisted that he had purchased it with a Grameen loan. Mortuza drove the men and the goat to the police station, where he informed another official that he could document the loan. The matter was dropped. "If he hadn't alerted me with some identification," Mortuza told me, "I couldn't have helped him."

The tale of the villager, the goat, and the policeman mirrored the abuse of authority commonplace in rural Bangladesh, and demonstrated how institutional affiliation could offer the landless an additional measure of security in their lives. Why shouldn't all borrowers be able to identify themselves with a uniform gesture?

The story struck me as too pat to be the whole truth. When I questioned others, I heard similar tales but the details always varied. Some said the story had little to do with Yunus's real motive for introducing the salute, which was that he was embarrassed when villagers bowed their heads before him and touched his feet.

In Bangladeshi villages, women reflexively lower their eyes when they encounter a man who is not part of their extended family. Often they will pull the ends of their saris over their faces and peer hesitantly from their cloth enclosures. The salute obliges a woman to look her banker in the eye. "When people are grateful to others, they bow their heads," Mortuza told me. "We say, 'Salute and say, "Salaam." ' Do it as if you're saying, 'I'm a person to be counted. I'm not going to bow to anyone.' Dignity grows out of a straight back."

12

It's Their Problem

Sabina's handbag was bulging with money. Weeks before she was unsettled when a colleague from a nearby branch was robbed at knifepoint. One might imagine that bank workers would make attractive targets for theft. In fact, attacks are surprisingly rare. Sabina thanked Allah that she had never been robbed, although her good fortune could also be explained by the fact that villages afford almost no privacy. With Grameen members scattered in so many places, bandits are often identified within days. As one villager explained: "Thieves are not able to digest the money they steal from the Grameen Bank."

On our way back to the branch, Sabina seemed deep in thought. The woman who had complained in the center meeting had upset her. Sabina understood the source of her frustration. In 1991, the bank raised its interest rate from 16 percent (the commercial rate) to 20 percent after the government awarded a salary hike to all civil service employees. (Grameen followed the government pay scale.) "It has made their burden heavier," Sabina explained. That same year, following up on a campaign promise, the government forgave all commercial bank loans under 5,000 takas and waived interest on those under 10,000 takas. The move created a backlash against the Grameen Bank, which occasionally restructures loans but never forgives them.

What continued to bother Sabina, however, was the woman's request for assistance. "You're our guest," she said. "Is it right that she should ask you for money?"

"What is the main reason that a borrower fails to prosper?" I asked.

"If she doesn't invest the money," Sabina replied. "If she consumes the money." (Borrowers were more specific: "If she *eats* the money," they would say.)

"And how does the bank maintain such a high repayment rate?" I asked.

"Number one, we take weekly installments, and, number two, we go to the borrowers. Then we check up on how the loan is being used. When we give a house loan, we watch the house go up, and we keep checking until it's finished. Only then do we say, 'Yes, they built a house.' When Janata Bank and Krishi Bank give a loan for a fish pond, they never watch whether anyone throws fingerlings into the pond.

"Number three, we keep our promises. If we say we'll be there at three o'clock, we're there at three o'clock. If we say that loans will be disbursed today, then we disburse them today, and if we say that to-morrow is the collection day, we collect the money tomorrow. With other organizations, people say, 'Oh, these are just hollow words,' but with the Grameen Bank it's, 'What they say they're going to do, they really do.' "

Unlike other banks, Grameen staff were specially trained to manage disputes among villagers, Sabina added. But there was no substitute for experience. She had made plenty of mistakes; now other bank workers came to her for advice. I asked her to give me an example.

"Say a member wants a new loan but she has some quarrel with the center chief," she explained. "The center chief might accuse the member of something and not authorize the loan. She's the center chief and must be respected, what should the bank worker do?

"My suggestion would be this: If the center chief has come alone with this accusation, then he shouldn't listen to it. The bank worker should listen only if the center chief stands up in front of all the members and states reasons for her decision. Say the member is always late for meet-ings or has violated some other rules. And the bank worker should never disclose that the center chief had come to him privately. Once the objections are made public, the bank worker can ask the group chairman to respond to them. Ultimately, all parties will have to compromise to come to an agreement. Then in front of everyone, the member will have to promise that she will not come late or violate other rules, and the members can agree or disagree to sanction her loan. This process would force the member and the center chief to speak directly and air their differences. In this fashion, discipline would be preserved."

When it came to the implementation of the Sixteen Decisions, Sabina was both hopeful and skeptical. The most difficult decision to adhere to was number eleven, where members pledged not to give or receive dowry. Villagers found this an attractive idea when their daughters were getting married, but it was a different story when they were marrying a son. (The same applied to the bank staff; it is not uncommon for a branch manager to receive a television as dowry.) "It has decreased a bit," Sabina explained. "But not much."

Family planning was another area where slow progress was being made. In decision number six, members pledge to keep their families small. A number of independent studies have shown that Grameen borrowers are more likely than comparable nonmembers to use birth control (in one study of 2,000 women, almost 50 percent more likely).

Several explanations were advanced: (1) The bank affords villagers better access to family planning information, (2) women who bring an income into the household exert greater influence on their husbands, and (3) the impetus for children (sons, really) is to provide villagers with old-age security. With a reliable source of credit, a family can earn more and accumulate assets, so parents feel more secure as they approach old age. Muzammel Huq, a senior Grameen manager, explained: "You don't have to spend billions on family planning. It's simple. A woman who is not earning any cash cannot tell her husband that she doesn't want to get pregnant. She cannot say, 'We have to take precautions.' But suppose she is repaying a 3,000-taka loan and is hoping to get a 6,000-taka loan? Now she can tell her husband, 'If I get pregnant my group will not recommend 6,000 takas because in three or four months' time I'll be heavily pregnant.' Now, she has a bargaining position."

(Delegates at the 1994 United Nations International Conference on Population and Development, held in Cairo, arrived at the same conclusion: "Experience shows that population and development programmers are most effective when steps have simultaneously been taken to improve the status of women.")

But personality and emotions also figure into the equation in unpredictable ways, Sabina added. While some husbands may be prepared to stop after three daughters, others demand no less than three sons. And parents with several sons often hope for at least one daughter, so they can enjoy the prestige of marrying her off in an honorable fashion. "Our motivation is working but there are accidents," explained Sabina. "People don't take their pills regularly. Some don't use permanent methods." Still, the drop in the number of women who brought babies with them to the center meetings was the most significant change Sabina had witnessed since joining the bank. "Didn't you notice in the first center?" she said. "Nobody had a baby with them. When I first started forming groups, everyone had a small child.

"But next year, those same members might have another child," she added quickly. "We have to consolidate what has already been accomplished. And we have to lend more money to more people."

Not until I returned to Dhaka did I discover that many individuals in the development community found the bank's rituals coercive. Initially, I found them unsettling, particularly the exercises, which appeared to have been imposed on the borrowers. I was impressed with the salute, despite the fact that it remained an easy target for criticism. "The Germans don't like the salute," Mortuza told me. "They find it too regimented." But the military comparison struck me as reflexive and facile. Men and women cannot shake hands in Bangladesh, and the salute seemed a respectful alternative. Borrowers and staff members greeted one another in a relaxed manner, saying *"Salaam Aleikum"* ("Peace unto you," in Arabic) while touching their right hand to their foreheads. Older members saluted in an offhand manner, the way a veteran baseball player tips his cap after hitting a triple. "The bank workers salute us and we salute them," a villager told me. "It's mutual." The salute also extended to family members and guests of the Grameen Bank. I often found myself encountering village women I'd never met, who smiled and saluted as they passed.

The chanting of slogans has a long tradition in Bengal, a land where the majority of the population have always been illiterate. For a Westerner reared during the cold war, however, slogans celebrating the virtues of "hard work" carry an overtone of Stalinism. Some villagers find them tiresome—"They taught us how to chant slogans and all this other garbage," one woman told me—but others don't seem to mind. "If I go to another bank," a villager explained, "I can't receive a loan unless I have collateral or land. But the Grameen Bank will give me a loan just on my word, and all they ask is that I say these slogans; so I can do that." An older member added: "If we're disciplined, we humans receive dignity, money, everything." (Sometimes, when the slogans are chanted quickly, the result is comical, such as when villagers merge decisions nine and ten and pledge to "drink water from pit latrines.")

Within the bank there were mixed feelings about the exercises. "I don't think they are important," Dipal said. "Only the discipline is important." (In 1994, he told me that management had decided to abandon the exercises.)

Yunus saw the features of the center meetings as a way to turn the tables on tradition. His experiences in the United States in the late 1960s never seemed far from his mind, and they emerged when he expressed mistrust for the government and in his fondness for describing Grameen as a "counterculture." "We're counterflow," he told me. "Banks look up; we look down. Banks ask you to come to them; we go to the borrowers. Banks ask you to give your property; we say forget it. Banks ask borrowers to sign legal documents; we don't have any legal documents, and still we deal with millions of dollars.

"Other programs look for experience and certifications; we say forget it.

"And women are not supposed to get involved in income-generating activities; we say they're the ones. Traditionally, women were asked to speak softly so that men could not hear their voices; we say get together and chant slogans. The traditional modesty is to look down; we make them look eye to eye. And the traditional greeting is a very meek, limp kind; we say give a salute and be proud."

How did Yunus respond to the aid workers and middle-class Bangladeshis who labeled the bank's meetings coercive?

"Let them think what they want to think. What do I care?" he told me. "The people who say these things never help you in anything, so why should I care what they have to say? It's their problem."

13

Can You Walk Far?

Grameen launched its operation with nineteen branches in Tangail and five in Chittagong. Each office was staffed with a manager and guard and five bank workers who carried out the same work that Yunus's students had been doing in Jobra: organizing and training villagers, disbursing and collecting loans, and troubleshooting.

Dipal supervised half the branch offices, another student took charge of the others. Nurjahan took responsibility for female bank workers and borrowers. Daiyan remained the numbers man, overseeing monitoring and budgeting. The office had little in the way of amenities, just a few wooden tables and chairs and metal filing cabinets. The project had been allocated one English-language typewriter.

Yunus rented a room near by. The year before, his wife had decided to return to the United States after giving birth to a daughter. "She thought this wasn't the country in which to raise a child," Yunus explained. At the time, the credit project in Jobra was just getting under way; Yunus was spending more and more time in the village. "She left hoping that sooner or later I would follow," he added. "We were divorced."

Would Yunus have given up his teaching post and moved to Tangail had his wife and daughter remained in Bangladesh? He paused a moment to consider the question. "The way I was moving, I probably would have taken the challenge." Then he added: "I don't know. These are things that one has to run speculative computer programs on."

One afternoon, Daiyan borrowed Yunus's key to check on his lodgings. "It was dusty and full of mosquitoes," Daiyan recalled. "He didn't even have a net. I must have killed one hundred bugs. He never even had time to set up his room. When he left the office, he just went to sleep."

• • •

The project required more than a hundred employees. With a glut of educated youth in the country, any advertised job drew reams of applications. Yunus had no problem finding young men with the required academic qualifications—for a branch manager, a master's degree in any subject, and for a field-worker, twelve years of schooling. However, to open up positions for more women, he had to drop the requirement to ten years of schooling.

An early recruit named Firoza, who was later to become the first woman promoted to branch manager, recalled her job interview. "Professor Yunus, Dipal Barua, and an assistant general manager from the Janata Bank were there," she explained. "At the time, I thought Grameen was a normal bank. First the AGM from the Janata Bank asked about my education level. Then Professor Yunus asked: 'Can you walk far?' "

"I rarely walk a mile," Firoza said. "I lived close to my school."

"But you'll have to walk miles and miles," Yunus said.

"If I get the job, I'll walk."

"You may be sent to other places in Bangladesh," he added.

"If it's part of my job," Firoza replied. "I'll go."

Another old-timer named Saleha recalled how she had been gently plied by Nurjahan, whom she knew from the women's college in Chittagong. "We need Muslim girls to speak with the women in this area to bring them out of purdah," Nurjahan told her. "They think that borrowing money is a sin. We need to explain to them that it's not, but to do that we need women."

Saleha had met Yunus years before, when, as a college sophomore, she had approached him about the possibility of transferring into his department. Yunus encouraged her, but after her friend failed the economics entrance exam, Saleha decided to stay with her in the women's college. When she identified herself, Yunus leaned forward and asked, "Are you *that* Saleha?" She nodded. His first question was why she had decided not to transfer to his department. "Then," she added in a tone of mock annoyance, "he only asked me about my family, my kids, whether I can work in the rain, in the sun, in the mud, whether I can work with poor people."

"Sometimes you'll get wet," Yunus warned.

"God willing, I can," replied Saleha.

"I knew he was a very prominent figure," she commented. "But the way he asked these questions, it didn't seem like a real interview. It lasted fifteen minutes. He just looked at me as if he were a mind reader and said, 'Okay, you can go now.' I was so angry. I thought I had wasted my time."

Saleha was assigned to a branch called Fathyabad in Chittagong—branch number ten—five miles south of Jobra. Firoza was assigned to a branch called Narandia in Tangail—branch number eleven. "There weren't many rules and regulations," Saleha recalled. Periodically, Yunus traveled to Chittagong to oversee the new recruits. "He used to tell us how to approach the women, how to address them, and how to dress so that they wouldn't be inhibited. Then we'd go to their houses, sit with them, ask them what they're eating and how they're earning. They used to say, 'Yes, we're very poor. It's very difficult. Sometimes we only eat once or twice a day.' They would pour their hearts out to us. So we asked them, if we lent them some money could they do better? And their first response was always, 'Who's going to lend us money?' "

Initially, Saleha's husband was cool toward the bank job, not because he disapproved of the work but because he felt there was no future in it. The couple had two young children. Saleha's husband had a job as an electrical engineer, but money was tight, and the Grameen Bank Project did not pay very well. Soon her husband began urging her to look for other work. "If there's no surety, there's no value," he said. But after he saw how much she was enjoying her work, he softened. "If a woman has her education and wants to be a social worker"—he shrugged—"what can I do?"

Saleha recalled: "Every day I saw with my own eyes how hard these people were struggling. One can understand oneself by witnessing this poverty. Sometimes, if we cannot have something, we become irritated. But I would look at these poor people who had nothing, and they were still alive and capable of happiness. And I would compare myself with them—because we are all humans. And it made me forget my own troubles, all my frustrations and unfulfilled hopes. I felt like I was living in the real world."

"I may have enjoyed another job," she added. "But I would not have learned the truth about things."

On her first day of work, Firoza was told to report to her manager under a tree. "What will people say?" she thought.

Within weeks, Firoza found herself in a village trying to encourage a group of women to join the bank; there she met a thirty-eight-year-old widow named Rabeya. Rabeya had a son and daughter, both of whom had stopped supporting her. "When she heard about the Grameen

Bank," Firoza recalled, "she wanted to join, but groups did not like to accept older women." Firoza persuaded a group of women to accept Rabeya. She helped her to learn to write her name. The day Rabeya received her first loan, for 300 takas, she cried and said that she had never seen so much money.

"Did her situation improve?" I asked.

"At one time she couldn't even count on eating once a day," Firoza said. "Then she got to the point where she could eat three times a day. She husked rice and sold it. She improved—not a dramatic improvement—but she could at least buy one good sari. And later her son and daughter joined the bank and began to help her."

Soon Firoza's father noticed that his daughter was growing thinner; most of the time she left for work at dawn and did not return home until it was dark. "Sometimes I didn't even eat any lunch. I was missing family functions. It got to the point where my father and my brothers started pressuring me to quit. And I myself thought, 'I can't do this job anymore, it's killing me.' But the next morning I'd think, 'No, I'll go and see how they're getting on.' Soon, if I missed one day from the field, I felt terrible." Eventually, like Saleha's husband, Firoza's father relented when he saw how attached she was to her job. "A particular kind of joy comes from this work," she explained. "There was a time when the Grameen Bank was my whole world."

14

A Petticoat

Daiyan was walking in a village one morning when he caught sight of a bank member named Nilu standing by a bamboo thicket. Months before, Nilu's husband had beaten his wife and Daiyan had tried speaking to him on her behalf. When his talk failed to have an effect, he urged Nilu's center members to confront the husband, but Nilu feared his reaction.

"Sir," she called to Daiyan. "Yesterday, I was sick, I had a headache. When I told my husband, he went to the bazaar and bought me some medicine." She added that her husband had not hit her for several weeks. Daiyan said that he was very happy. He inquired about her flour-trading business, which she said was going well.

As he walked away, Daiyan thought to himself: "What more can a development worker ask for?"

Yunus was traveling between the branches in Tangail and Chittagong, grappling with problems. In June 1980, a month after the nineteenth branch in Tangail opened, he attended a bank directors' meeting in Dhaka with several issues to raise. Most serious, his own employees were being treated disrespectfully by the official bank employees and their morale was suffering. His people were doing the hard work of motivating and training the villagers, reviewing loan proposals and collecting the money, while their counterparts in the commercial banks who sanctioned the loans, released and accepted the money, were causing problems. There seemed to be a "communication gap," he said. Rather than cooperating with his staff, the official employees were hindering them. Bank workers returning late in the day to deposit money were being turned away at the office door by managers who informed them that transaction hours were over.

"In rural areas, bankers have no work," recalled Zubairul Hoque, a senior Grameen manager who worked in Tangail in the early 1980s. "They open at nine and close at two. When the Grameen Bank opened, their work increased ten times. Their attitude became: 'If you want a pad, I'll have to file a requisition form; it will take fifteen days.' Women would wait for hours in front of the bank to receive loans and then be told to come back in three or four days. It was frustrating for them and humiliating for us."

Yunus urged the bankers to direct their staff to cooperate with his. He suggested a simplified method for interest calculation to lessen their workload, since the number of transactions was so high.

Meanwhile, other problems were cropping up in the field as villagers rushed into groups, accepting members indiscriminately. This signaled trouble. First, no amount of speed on the part of the villagers would hasten loan approval by the commercial bankers. Yunus remembered how disheartened villagers had been in Jobra when the Janata Bank was taking three months to sanction loans. Second, villagers were joining with the attitude that they could turn a quick profit and then quit.

"We didn't give the members a clear idea of how far the Grameen Bank could take them," Zubairul Hoque explained. "They thought, 'Okay, I got 2,000 takas for a cow. I'll repay it. Okay, I have a cow. It's all over.' Many didn't see it as an ongoing process."

Villagers of unequal means were forming groups where poorer members tended to be ignored. Family members were being permitted to join the same group; naturally, they tended to favor one another. Worst of all, in some centers, the poorest villagers—those who had lost their land from river erosion and were forced to live on government-owned embankments—were being overlooked completely. Yunus recalled: "People would say, 'Oh, they're just a floating population, we don't take them.'" What if these people took their loans and fled? "If you create a condition that will make them want to stay," Yunus replied, "they will stay."

Ideally, a group should behave like five firemen holding a tarpaulin to catch someone about to jump from a building ledge: evenly spaced, each pulling with equal and constant force keeping the canvas taut and centered. Yunus revised the group formation procedures in the Bidhimala to ensure this equilibrium. From now on a group would be comprised only of villagers who were "in a similar economic condition" and who enjoyed "mutual trust and confidence." No more than one member from a household could join the same group. (This was why Aleya was told that she couldn't join a group with someone who ate from the same "cooking pot.")

Among his own staff there were other setbacks—seemingly logical decisions that resulted in unforeseen consequences. One was the staffing of branches with local residents. "We thought that if we hired people from the area it would help the program to run smoothly," explained Zubairul Hoque. "But people were under too much pressure because others knew them as friends." Female bank workers in particular were not viewed as professionals near their own villages; they were someone's daughter or sister or wife, and locals tried to take advantage of them. Ideally, Yunus would have preferred to post women staff to branches away from home, but not many were prepared to defy their families like Nurjahan.

Despite the strains, the project continued to grow. Within a year it had 15,000 clients, slightly less than a third women. More than 11,000 had already received loans. Surprisingly, a small percentage of villagers joined groups, attended meetings, and contributed the weekly savings but opted not to borrow money. Firoza offered an explanation: "We asked about their family life. We saw them each week and took notice of everything and it made them feel important. Before, nobody bothered with them. And Professor Yunus used to have direct contact with the villagers; that appealed to them."

Today, sitting in his spartan office, caught up with the demands of an organizational octopus with tentacles in 35,000 villages, Yunus often misses the intimacy of Tangail. His telephone rings continually with requests for advice and speaking engagements, offers to sit on this or that high-level committee. His time is blocked in quarter hours. Managers file in and out of his office from various departments: audit, establishment, monitoring, administration, central accounts, technology, special projects, training. "I'm so distant from the Grameen Bank," he told me. "I'm caught up with the mail, the visitors, the telephone calls. One of my decisions in the early days was to visit each branch at least once. Probably, I stopped at 600 branches.

"When I go to the field, I see that some of the decisions we took were based on wrong assumptions. I can identify new areas of growth. But now I'm not getting the inputs which continuously feed this institution."

In Tangail, he was getting the inputs hourly, and for the first time he was beginning to see the full potential of his idea manifested in a rich diversity of pursuits. During the second year, the number of female borrowers doubled. By the end of 1981, five thousand groups had been formed in more than four hundred villages, and the bank had extended loans to 22,000 villagers for two hundred different types of businesses, ranging from husking rice to making ice-cream sticks, from trading in brass to repairing radios. Members manufactured brooms, umbrellas, and cigarettes; processed mustard oil, sugarcane, and jute; wove mosquito nets, cane mats, and quilts; cultivated bananas, turmeric, and jack fruit; they sold saris and punjabis, crockery, pots, glassware, and wood; opened laundries and tailoring shops, tea stalls and restaurants; leased land; rented out boats; traded lentils and leather, silver and soap.

The project was still small enough for one man to comprehend its scope, and on any given morning, Yunus would set out in the project's jeep to survey branch offices and villages. One day, while he was talking to a group of villagers, a woman ran up to him and exclaimed: "Do you see what happened to me? Do you see what happened to me?"

The woman motioned downward to something under her sari. "It's very embarrassing for a woman to pull her sari up," Yunus said. "I was looking at her feet. I thought she was wearing new shoes or something, but she was just wearing some old slippers. I couldn't figure it out."

"Okay, okay," he said.

"No, no, no," the woman said.

"She knew that I didn't see. She kept pulling her sari up."

"Look," the woman said.

"So then she separates it out into two pieces. Pulls one up. And I saw. For the first time, she had a petticoat. Never in her life had she worn a petticoat."

PART III

The Organization

There is nothing so little comprehended among mankind as what is genius. They give to it all, when it can be but a part. Genius is nothing more than knowing the use of tools; but there must be tools for it to use. . . . Let two men, one with genius, the other with none, look at an overturned wagon:—he who has no genius, will think of the wagon only as he sees it, overturned, and walk on; he who has genius, will paint it to himself before it was overturned,—standing still, and moving on, and heavy loaded, and empty; but both must see the wagon, to think of it at all.

SAMUEL JOHNSON

15

We Don't Want Windows

Yunus was worried about the future of the Grameen Bank Project. He had signed on for two years with the intention of handing it over to the commercial banks once everything was running smoothly. The banks were then to carry it to every district in the country.

As time passed, he saw this was not to be. The commercial bankers were still treating his staff as unwanted guests. Even after tens of millions of takas had been disbursed and recovered, they continued to voice skepticism about the project's "viability." They pointed out that Yunus's branches could only be profitable at higher loan volumes and near-perfect repayment rates. Yunus said the project was well on its way to achieving such economies of scale. The bankers replied, How long can it be sustained? "You have succeeded because you have worked very hard," they told him.

"Now, hard work is a penalty," Yunus replied in an exasperated tone.

Yunus recalled what Gangopadhyay, the deputy governor of the Bangladesh Bank, had written in 1979 in his initial letter to the bank directors: "It will be appreciated that success of the Project depends totally on active support and cooperation of all the participating banks." Prescient words, he thought. His staff left their houses at dawn, and walked or bicycled miles to get to work. Each day, they spent hours with villagers, settling disputes and arguments, and managing countless small crises. Yet they were constantly running into walls—not with the borrowers and not even with the fundamentalists, but with their fellow bankers.

In 1980, the International Fund for Agricultural Development (IFAD), a Rome-based aid organization created by the United Nations, sent a Project Identification Mission to Bangladesh to provide funds at concessionary terms to agricultural initiatives and farm credit programs. After identifying all the worthy projects they could find, the IFAD mission still had a few million dollars left over and they were finding it difficult to justify returning to Rome with money unspent, particularly from Bangladesh. When an official from the Bangladesh Bank mentioned that they had an experimental credit program working with landless villagers in Tangail, the IFAD mission declined; the project had nothing to do with agriculture and didn't really sound like banking, they said. A few days later, still unsuccessful in their search, they called back. They would take a closer look at the Grameen Bank Project.

Yunus contacted the Ford Foundation, which had funded the Rural Economics Program at Chittagong University and had been supportive of his efforts in Tangail. One of Ford's representatives in Bangladesh, a woman named Adrienne Germaine, had been enormously helpful at a time when most development officials viewed anything that smacked of "capitalism" with displeasure. Now, while IFAD took a closer look at Grameen's operation, Ford offered to guarantee 10 percent of its loans.

IFAD had $3.4 million available, which they agreed to lend to the Bangladesh Bank, which in turn agreed to lend it to the Grameen Bank Project at the "soft rate" of 3 percent interest. The Bangladesh Bank was obliged to lend the project matching funds at 6 percent interest. Yunus drafted a plan proposing to extend the project's coverage to two more districts—one in the north of Bangladesh called Rangpur and one in the south called Patuakhali. He planned to expand to 100 branches.

The Bangladesh Bank officials were nervous. "If you move out of Tangail," some warned, "it will collapse." Meanwhile, others were urging Yunus to move to Dhaka as soon as possible to see how Tangail managed in his absence. "What will I do in Dhaka?" he asked. Finally, he decided that it made sense to transfer the office to a central location with better communications. But if he did, he was going to move it somewhere where the project was operating. So he added a fifth district: the rural area closest to Dhaka. At least he wouldn't be too far from "the field."

In the fall of 1981, Yunus bid farewell to Dipal and Daiyan. Soon the three would be scattered across the country—Daiyan in Rangpur and Dipal in Patuakhali. Nurjahan would join Yunus in Dhaka, responsible for special programs and, later, training. Yunus formally resigned from Chittagong University and began scouting for an office in the city.

In Dhaka, Yunus soon saw that he would need help. On top of having to coordinate efforts with the Bangladesh Bank and the seven nationalized banks, he had to satisfy IFAD's and Ford's reporting requirements. Yunus's old friend Muzammel Huq was back in the country after having lived in Europe for most of the decade. Yunus and Muzammel went back almost twenty years. In the early 1960s, at the age of twenty-two, Yunus had been Muzammel's economics instructor at a preuniversity college in Chittagong.

Five years after Yunus moved to Nashville, Tennessee, Muzammel found himself in Ann Arbor, Michigan, studying political science at the University of Michigan, also on a Fulbright Scholarship. The two resumed their friendship. When Bangladesh's War of Independence broke out in March 1971, they joined forces in a U.S.-based network called the Bangladesh Defense League. Their objective: to get the Nixon administration to stop military aid to Pakistan. (Years later, it was revealed that Nixon had supported Pakistan because it was secretly brokering talks between the United States and China.)

Yunus worked on a newsletter while Muzammel spoke on college campuses. That summer the two shared an apartment in Washington, D.C., to focus their efforts on Congress. "I was the cook," Muzammel recalled. "Yunus did a wonderful job washing up. It was the best of times and the worst of times. Hopes up and down. We had no idea how long the war would last."

As ever, Yunus was the strategist. "He used to keep index cards on every senator and congressman," Muzammel recalled. They worked with others, setting up an information center and compiling a mailing list of every known Bengali in the United States. They would meet for lunch in the cafeteria of the Library of Congress. "We worked on each individual congressman," Yunus recalled, "trying to find out his or her background, what issues he voted for, who was his most effective staffer, how to enter his mind, should we try a hard or soft sell . . . "

"I don't know how much impact we had," he added. "But military aid was stopped."

After independence, Yunus returned to Bangladesh. Shortly thereafter, Muzammel abandoned his Ph.D. in Ann Arbor and followed. "We thought we were missing the revolution," he said.

Muzammel's dream was to run "the best high school in Bangladesh." Back home, he was discouraged by the corruption and political infighting of the new regime. "Things were the same as usual—my dream was shattered." When a professor from Oxford University told him of a position researching the role of the military in the Third World, Muzammel jumped at the opportunity. He remained at Oxford as a research fellow for five years and later joined the International Peace Research

The author's translator, Sadia, and veteran branch manager Saleha

Institute in Oslo, Norway. In 1981, he returned to Bangladesh and landed a job as head of a private college, but again he was frustrated. "I saw there was no way I could run a good college in this system."

Muzammel was preparing to leave for Helsinki to teach at the United Nations University when Yunus, who was preparing to open his first branch in Rangpur, said: "Why don't you try it out with me? People think I'm crazy. People are laughing at me."

Muzammel was skeptical about the project. For years, he had concerned himself with great themes in the sweep of modern history: the postwar alignment, the arms race, the cold war. He admired Yunus, but the sort of incremental improvements Grameen promised did not excite him. "As an academic, I didn't think much of it. Tokenisms. But after spending a month with Yunus, I decided to stay." Muzammel still planned to return one day to his father's village and start a small farm or teach. In the meantime, he would see if Yunus's project had any life in it.

Today, Muzammel occupies the corner room diagonally across from Yunus's on the fourth floor of the Grameen Bank head office. For several years, he was the bank's second in command; now he is third. His is the noisiest room in the building, overlooking Mirpur Road with its interminable wail of buses and trucks. The noise doesn't seem to bother Muzammel. If anything, he seems distracted by the occasional stretch of silence. If his phone fails to ring for ten minutes, he will pick it up and request some document, or tea. He has a great deal of nervous energy. His knees shake beneath the desk. He was a chain smoker before he quit. (Until Yunus gave up the habit completely, he used to bum exactly two cigarettes a day from Muzammel—"one at 11:00 A.M. and one at 5:00 P.M.")

Muzammel wears glasses with thick black rims, partially obscuring a face that has the heavy delicacy of a Bombay film star. What is most curious about him is the way he manages to convey genuine interest in you while he fidgets and glances at files and occasionally drifts off into his own thoughts. Probably because he is genuinely interested: It is surprising how much he remembers about people with whom he has exchanged a few words—the name of a wife or sister, the school someone attended, a plan mentioned in passing. By his own reckoning, Muzammel has visited more than seventy countries; by his colleagues', he has a friend in each one.

His outgoing personality was helpful to Yunus, who, despite having "unshakable confidence," Muzammel sees as "basically a shy person." Yunus would not have approached IFAD, he said, if they had not first come to him. Yunus loved a challenge but he was uncomfortable networking. "He doesn't like to go to people," Muzammel said, adding that Yunus rarely crossed over the line between business and socializing.

So, for those who found it difficult to approach Yunus directly Muzammel acted as a bridge. "I don't go around and say 'hi' to people," Yunus told me. "But he does and he remembers people's names and places. Immediately they relax." You could unburden your heart to Muzammel; you could tell him that you didn't like your posting or you had a personality conflict with your manager. The staff felt uneasy bringing up such matters in Yunus's presence, and he understood this. "When people spill their problems to Muzammel," he told me, "they're hoping they'll come to me."

Having spent five years at Oxford University, Muzammel was also a well-connected ally. His old friends were in government—no small advantage when the government is a military dictatorship. And because he had forgone an attractive opportunity abroad, Muzammel reserved the right to speak critically of Yunus and the management of his bank. His honesty was valued. Yunus knew that his students were hesitant to question his judgment and inclined to shield him from bad news. "He knew I would never say anything to flatter him," Muzammel told me. "He doesn't like flattery—but these days I think he's beginning to like it from the Americans. This worries me. Because they are making him into a kind of a prophet, and once you keep on repeating this kind of thing, it has an effect."

When it came to resolving conflicts, the two were almost total opposites. "Yunus is a peacemaker," Muzammel said. "His presence gets people talking. He's honest and personable and he's genuinely kind." Muzammel was less patient. "If Yunus had not been there, I would have beaten up people." Indeed, when Muzammel was lost in thought, it often appeared as if a fire were smoldering within him. It could be an effective look: It made you want to get out of his way.

Muzammel left for Tangail to learn the operation. In the meantime, branches were opening in Rangpur, Tangail, and in the countryside around Dhaka. By the end of 1982, the project had fifty-four offices and 30,000 members. Later that year, an IFAD appraisal mission visited Bangladesh and sent an enthusiastic report back to Rome. They reported an increase in borrowers' incomes and, remarkably, predicted that the project could begin turning a profit in a few years. They wrote that Grameen was improving the social status of poor women who were "otherwise relegated to a very marginal existence."

The mission members also noted that the attitudes of the commercial bankers ranged from "benign tolerance" to "suppressed hostility." Bankers caused undue delays in processing loans, and forced villagers to fill out a complicated form with each withdrawal from the Group Fund—a procedure they found intimidating. The fear had always been that Grameen's clients would run off without repaying their loans; no one had ever worried that the bankers might make it difficult for the villagers to access their own money. "It is somewhat ironical that this question should assume such a dimension," noted the IFAD mission.

By now Yunus was convinced that the future of the Grameen Bank

Project lay in its becoming an independent bank. He was losing good people because the nationalized banks had shown a reluctance, contrary to their agreement, to give permanent status to his employees. And he no longer entertained the hope that ordinary banks, with their "traditional urban orientation" and natural focus on the "economically fortunate," would ever be inclined to, or even capable of, absorbing the landless as clients. The first-class customers would inevitably push out those traveling coach. In fact, Yunus felt that the only reason Grameen members were not pushed around more often was that more affluent villagers had no desire to attend center meetings. "If you make anything easy it will never reach the poor," he told me. "The powerful ones are standing in line before them. If we had a beautiful center house with cushioned chairs, do you think poor women would get the seats?"

Yunus would need help. There was opposition to the Grameen Bank Project at all levels—from politicians, academics, and development experts, from Marxists and Libertarians alike. Their arguments were diverse; taken together, they formed a remarkably incoherent whole: Grameen was antirevolutionary, throwing crumbs to the poor; credit turned villagers into minicapitalists, drove agricultural wages up, and created an environment of intense competition that destroyed the chances of uniting the landless in revolt. In any event, credit alone was worthless. A development organization couldn't do just one thing well; it had to do many things well. Bangladesh needed *integrated* rural development. Besides, how far could the bank go? Grameen's success rested on one man; large-scale replication was impossible because Yunus could not be in hundreds of places at the same time, and a small-scale operation brought no meaningful change. But even if, somehow, it did grow large, villagers would stop repaying their loans. Or they would soon run out of business opportunities because the market could not absorb so many producers and petty traders. Of course, long before then, it would have run out of funds for expansion.

"Grameen is not radical enough for the radicals," commented Nasreen Khundker, an economics professor at Dhaka University, "and it's not conservative enough for the conservatives. It's the middle path."

The establishment was adamantly opposed to the idea of creating another bank in Bangladesh. The bankers said Yunus was overreacting to a few minor staff problems. Besides, they added, no major study had ever verified Yunus's statement that the Grameen Bank Project was more effective than their banks at providing credit in rural areas or that, as he contended, it generated employment opportunities for the poorest segment of the population "at a speed faster than any other known method."

"Why can't the project continue as a 'window'?" the bankers asked.

"In a house you have a lot of windows," Yunus replied. "At a certain point, if you find that a particular window is not useful, you just close it. We don't want windows; we want doors."

16

Independence

In March 1982, Yunus attended a conference on rural development at which he planned to outline the various options available to the Grameen Bank. For months, he had been debating with himself as to whether Grameen should become a private or government-owned bank and whether it should be for- or not-for-profit. The question was not simply which framework lent itself most naturally to Grameen's objectives, but which one he could get the bankers to agree to.

They had flatly rejected a prior proposal to set up an independent Grameen Bank. And now Yunus was without his biggest supporter—Gangopadhyay—who had left the Bangladesh Bank. However, he soon found another prominent figure attracted to his cause, the former finance secretary, a man named A. M. A. Muhith.

Muhith and Yunus had first met in Washington, D.C., in March 1971, when Muhith was posted in the Pakistan embassy as an economic counselor and Yunus was in Washington helping to organize a demonstration in support of Bangladesh. Yunus worked without pause, designing placards, calling news organizations, arranging police permits. "He had great organizing ability," Muhith recalled. "He also had a very amiable smile and a way of endearing himself to people."

Six years later, when Muhith returned to Bangladesh, he was appointed finance secretary, which made him an ex officio member of the Bangladesh Bank's board of directors. He was only vaguely aware of the Grameen Bank Project, but because he had great respect for Gangopadhyay, when the project came up for discussion, he offered his support. Muhith had earlier been approached by the head of the IFAD mission when they were considering financing the Grameen Bank Project. Because all international aid had to be channeled through the government, he had to give final authorization for the loan. When the IFAD representative, an old colleague of Muhith's, asked his opinion on the Grameen Bank Project, Muhith remained "noncommittal."

When Yunus heard this, he invited Muhith to visit one of his branches in Tangail. Muhith accepted. Yunus took him to a few center meetings, and later they visited a branch holding its annual celebration, where the staff members and villagers participated in a series of musical performances and skits. "In the villages, I saw Yunus in a totally new light," Muhith recalled. "I saw that he had the capacity to enter into a dialogue with the people. I spoke to them; he spoke to them. But there was no comparison. The people's response to him was *overwhelming*. He would say something—anything—and it immediately registered."

Afterward, Yunus said to Muhith: "Come along. See what they're doing with the money."

In 1995, sitting in a restaurant in New York City across from the United Nations complex, Muhith, now in his early sixties, a gregarious man with a gentle fringe of white hair around his head, recalled the villagers he met that afternoon in Tangail: "One was an abandoned woman tending a milch cow, another sold firewood to shops, another sold sweetmeats, another raised chickens, another was a simple retailer." Muhith was impressed with the villagers' industry, but one question nagged him: Where was the market for all these goods and services?

"Who buys from you?" he asked the woman who worked as a retailer.

"Anyone," the woman replied. "But often another member."

Muhith paused and spread his hands over our table in a theatrical gesture. "They had become *each other's* customers," he said, speaking slowly. "And then I saw: This was pure Adam Smith in action. It was creating wealth, and at the same time, creating the market for that wealth."

"That was my conversion to Grameen," he added. "Afterward, I never questioned the soundness of its philosophy."

Two days into the conference, on March 24, General Hossain Mohammed Ershad seized power in a bloodless coup and placed Bangladesh under martial law. Shortly thereafter, Muhith, who had retired from government service the year before, found himself named Bangladesh's finance minister.

After events stabilized, Yunus contacted him, and suggested that Grameen be converted to a private bank with 60 percent of the shares controlled by landless villagers and 40 percent controlled by the government.

"At the time the Grameen Bank was not a high priority in my hat," Muhith recalled. "Bangladesh had no foreign exchange and we were facing all sorts of adverse economic situations, including a recession. Still, it was one of the few things I wanted to do."

Muhith found his opening several months later, after events had stabilized. In a private session with President Ershad, who would go on to rule the country unilaterally for more than eight years, he offered the following counsel: "We're providing benefits to the civil servants; you've satisfied the army; privatizing was for the industrialists; you've released two banks to the private sector and given income tax relief. These are all measures for the well-to-do. We have to do something for the *poor.*"

"Yes," Ershad said. "It's a good point."

Then Muhith mentioned his plan to convert the Grameen Bank Project into an independent bank and Ershad gave his approval. "I had the support of only one person in government—Ershad," Muhith said. "But, at the time, the government *was* Ershad."

Muhith still worried about the resistance from the bankers. In order to reduce "friction," he flipped Yunus's figures, giving 60 percent control to the government and 40 percent to the villagers who had amassed, by mid-1983, almost 10 million takas in savings. He found a chairman who would work well with Yunus and who would be able to keep the other board members in line should they grow uncooperative. "To me, ownership was not a big concern," Muhith explained. "If the government wanted to shut it down, it could have at any time, with or without ownership."

But to Yunus more government ownership represented a symbolic defeat. It wasn't merely a matter of control; he felt it was important that Grameen be perceived by the landless as *their* institution. If was like a ship prepared to carry its passengers as far as they wanted to go, he would say. "You cannot ask the owners to disembark from the ship."

Muhith promised to divest the government shares after some time, but Yunus worried that, in a country with such volatile politics and capricious ministers, what was to stop the next finance minister from sinking the ship?

When I asked Yunus what he would do differently if he had to do it all over, he replied: "I would try to avoid the government completely. If I had to do it again, I'd say 'nothing.' I'd say, 'You don't get anything and we design our own thing.' " But it's hard to imagine that such an approach would have yielded results at the time.

"Yunus had to walk a tough line with Ershad," Muhith told me. "Don't annoy him; don't get too pally." He added: "In eight years, for Yunus to work along with him and not be tarnished is a great accomplishment—particularly with an organization that became so popular that if you set up a branch in your own village it would be considered patronage."

Even though the country was under military rule, the decision had to go through Parliament. Bangladeshi law had no provision for a bank authorized to work only in rural areas, owned collectively by the government and tens of thousands of villagers. Yunus feared that the legal formalities would drag on for months. Muzammel knew Kamal Hossain, the man who had written Bangladesh's constitution. "He was a friend of mine from Oxford. He volunteered to help us. He used to give us eight hours a day. He didn't charge us a penny."

The Grameen Bank Ordinance was passed in September 1983. On a sunny October day, a celebration was attended by 2,000 villagers in Tangail. "It was a very special day," Zubairul Hoque remarked. Muhith, Yunus, and Muzammel listened as the proclamation was read aloud by a borrower. Soon, a new amendment was added to the *Bidhimala:* Each member had to purchase a 100-taka, nonpreferred share in the Grameen Bank.

Earlier in 1983, Yunus had asked his contacts at the Ford Foundation if they knew of "another crazy banker" who could help him develop his systems. After a search of India produced no suitable candidate, Ford's New York office suggested two bankers in Chicago—Ron Grzywinski and Mary Houghton—who had founded a community development bank that worked on Chicago's South Side called the South Shore Bank.

Ron and Mary traveled to Bangladesh and visited Tangail with Yunus. They could not believe the enthusiasm he generated and the way the villagers responded to him. "It felt like traveling in Caesar's entourage," Ron commented. They were "amazed" by Grameen's work, but nevertheless entered into heated debates with Yunus about proper banking practices. Obviously, Yunus did not have to be reminded of the banker's credo: "Know your borrower." But he did have to improve his accounting procedures and focus on such specifics as dual control, audits, loan-loss reserves, and delinquency reporting. In ten days, the three established a friendship that would culminate years later in the first Grameen replication program in the United States.

Muzammel returned to Tangail to supervise the transfer of records from the commercial banks. With seventy-seven branches and more than

45,000 borrowers, there was plenty of room for "leakage." Some of the commercial bankers had sought to compensate themselves for having been inconvenienced. Muzammel had no interest in legal wrangling over small sums; Yunus wanted him back in Dhaka as soon as possible. To recover stolen money quickly, he resorted to what he called his "big stick"—an old college friend who was then the military commander in Tangail.

Daiyan helped manage the nuances of "separation" branch to branch. "It was a lot of work," he recalled one Friday afternoon while he relaxed in his apartment with his wife. "You ask Muzammel," he said. "One day, I forgot to tell my wife that I had to go to another area. For two days I was gone. My wife was weeping. She said to Muzammel, 'Daiyan left two days ago. I have not heard from him.' "

Muzammel started to search. He went from one branch to another. "Hey, have you seen Daiyan?"

"Oh, yes, he was here yesterday."

"Where did he go?"

"He took a bicycle and went to that branch . . . "

"At two-thirty in the morning, he found me working on a big accounting problem. My clothes were dirty. I was dead tired."

"Daiyan," Muzammel shouted, "you've been gone for two days. You didn't tell your family. You didn't tell me. What are you doing?"

"Has it been two days?" Daiyan exclaimed.

He smiled at his wife as he recalled the story. Over the past decade and a half, the two had supported each other's careers. His wife had accepted his long hours and inconvenient postings around the country, and, in turn, he had supported her decision to study public administration at Harvard University, when she was offered a fellowship to do so —even though it meant her being out of the country for a year.

Daiyan resumed: "So Muzammel picked me up from that branch and handed me over to my wife. And within two or three hours, I left again."

17

A New Culture

The scene is commonplace in Bangladesh: Hundreds of students advance up the center of the road like an occupying army, wearing red scarves tied around their heads, shouting political slogans. Their faces are defiant. Many clutch sticks.

Passersby rush out of the boys' path; shopkeepers hastily pull down their metal gates. The wrong word shouted from the street, and knives (and sometimes guns) are brandished.

The boys are members of a student faction of a political party. Most of them have little chance of finding work after they graduate. "Politics" offers them an outlet for their frustrations and some hope: If their party comes to power, a few may receive civil service positions; at the very least, they will be able to cash in on favors from the officials they helped put into office. Of course, if their party does *not* win power, they must "campaign" harder next time.

Yunus was looking to staff his bank with students. He was looking for individuals who were prepared to work under demanding and often harsh conditions. He was not interested in Bangladesh's best and brightest. He didn't want experience. He wanted young men and women uncorrupted by other organizations who would fit into Grameen's "corporate culture"—a culture that he promised would be unlike anything that existed in Bangladesh.

He was off to a good start. Grameen had not evolved in an environment of closed-door meetings, government officials contacting government officials, or memos in triplicate. Now he wanted to preserve the vitality of the original experiment as it grew. He operated on the premise that any organization which tapped the energy and idealism of young people could not help but succeed. What was necessary was to remove the barriers which, in other institutions—such as the nationalized banks—virtually guaranteed poor performance. Institutions in South Asia are notoriously rigid; Grameen was to be an innovator. It was to have at its core an ethos of simplicity, a clarity of objective, and total lack of pretension. Ideas would travel unimpeded through the organization. And it was to be fueled by the raw enthusiasm that comes when people witness their ideas come to life.

Yunus often reflected on his experience as a student in Nashville, when, for the first time in his life, he was encouraged to challenge his teachers. In an environment that rewarded him for using his own judgment, how quickly his thinking developed. "I took three years of statistics in Bangladesh and I never understood it," he told me. "But in the United States, the first course showed me that it was a beautiful structure. I wondered. 'How come I never saw this before?' "

Word was circulated: If you had a good idea to pass on or a grievance to vent, you were free to write to Yunus directly, a practice officials in the Bangladesh Bank would have found startling. As a matter of course, every branch manager had to complete free-form narrative reports, and sent them each month to the "MD" (short for managing director). Yunus would read these reports throughout the day. He would take a stack home and read them over lunch. In the evenings, he would read them as he sat in front of the television, making comments to his wife: "These people are really intelligent. These are very good people." (Yunus remarried in 1980. His second wife, Dr. Afrozi Begum, teaches physics at Jahangirnager University, in Dhaka.)

"I didn't have experience running an organization," he explained. "Maybe that was a strength—I don't know. If I had had experience in other organizations, I probably would have tried to imitate them and I would have screwed up the whole thing. So I had to improvise and that I take as a good rather than a bad thing."

Yunus used the narrative reports to fine-tune Grameen's systems. Through them he was able to respond to problems at field level as they came up, acting on the recommendations of branch managers, bank workers, and, often, the villagers themselves. "If you can show Yunus he is wrong," Muzammel told me, "he will immediately admit it and change. He has no pride about those things." If you were too shy to write directly to the MD, you could also send a note to Muzammel or Dipal or Nurjahan. You were encouraged to be blunt. Indeed, I was always surprised by how forthcoming Grameen's managers were when I questioned them about problem areas. More often than not I would hear something like: "It's not happening" or "This is an area where we have not had much success" or "We have found that some of our assumptions were totally wrong."

Muzammel recalled a note written by a female bank worker addressed to Yunus: "These days, it seems to me that head office does things without even thinking." The head office had blundered in some way—he forgot the details—perhaps a ledger had been distributed containing hundreds more pages than required. Something simple, an unnecessary waste. In Grameen-speak, it was a "mishappening," an experience to be absorbed. The issue of blame was incidental. (Management was uncompromising only when it came to staff abuses involving sex, violence, or theft. If the charges were confirmed, the employee was immediately dismissed.)

Today, when management drafts a new rule or procedure, the field staff are always consulted. "We circulate the first draft," explained Yunus. "Then we have a second draft. And we may circulate a third. Finally, when we circulate it officially, they own it."

"We used to say often, 'You can try out any new idea—and please do —because that's where our future lies. If you fail in that new idea you don't have to go and cry over it. Just keep it quiet. We don't want to hear about it. But if you're successful, let us know. We'll join in the excitement.

" 'Some of your efforts will go wrong. That's the cost of innovating. It is accepted that you'll make mistakes. But never repeat the same mistake.' "

Occasionally, however, the bank would repeat mistakes—sometimes with near-disastrous consequences.

No longer under the control of the Bangladesh Bank, Grameen was free to establish its own hiring standards. "We used to hire people with accounting and economics backgrounds," Muzammel recalled. "But then we found that people who studied literature or microbiology often showed skills in accounting. We saw that once you had some general education, the most important thing was whether you were interested in something or not."

Above all, a staff member had to know when to keep silent. Grameen's collateral was largely based on its borrowers' sense of personal accountability, so it was essential that villagers come up with their own business ideas. If an idea came from their bank worker, a borrower would not enjoy the same sense of accomplishment; and if the business failed, the villager would blame the staff member who advised her.

Muzammel once asked me why I thought the Grameen Bank had

succeeded where so many development organizations had failed. I spoke about the program's elegant design. He laughed and said it was precisely the opposite: "It's because we never had a design. It didn't begin as a project. It began as an approach to a very simple problem of exploitation. Yunus never imagined that it would become a bank. He saw forty people and he knew what their problem was—and it was a very simple problem."

Muzammel told recruits: "Instead of trying to solve other people's problems, first find out whether they have an idea how to solve their own problems. You can say, 'I heard that there was someone in that village who took money for this purpose but she did not do very well' or 'Someone has done extremely well doing this—you might want to talk to her.' But that is the farthest you should go. Start with the premise that they know the solution and give them the information. Then the five of them will discuss it as a group. This is about people managing themselves, solving their own problems, creating their own jobs."

The lecture wasn't always effective. "We still have this middle-class mentality that we have to tell the poor what to do, that we are above them and they should be grateful to us."

Nurjahan saw the training not so much as a way to impart skills but to shape attitudes—just as the case studies in Jobra had shaped hers. "The training program transports you to the people so you can experience what they experience. You have to mix with the borrowers. You have to develop a personal feeling for them."

Many students who applied for Grameen Bank positions often walked into interviews and did a quick about-face when they discovered what the job entailed. Educated villagers do not like to associate with the landless. "Although they come from poor families themselves," explained Muzammel, "they don't consider themselves *this* kind of poor." (In center meetings, bank workers are supposed to sit on mats at the same level as members, but most prefer a table and chair.)

Nurjahan first weeded out those whose academic qualifications were below par. Then she looked at the candidate's family background. "Did this boy come from a struggling family where he helped his parents, where he tried to do something to pay for his own education?"

"I like to see how he feels about poverty," she explained. "If he is emotional about it. Every worker and manager has to work as a motivator. So I give them a topic like 'family planning' or 'education' and say, 'Imagine this is a meeting in a village. Try to motivate me about family planning.' If he cannot speak well, he will find it impossible to carry out this work."

Muzammel had his own favorite questions: "Can you swim? For the men, Can you cook? Would you like to go to a village and find out? For the women, Would you be willing to ride a bicycle? Would your family allow you to work away from home?

"Most say they would work in a village, but they don't realize that within forty-eight hours they will be dispatched to a branch somewhere in Bangladesh. A lot of people don't even go. Some go and come back and quit. Some disappear from the branch. A third drop out—mostly within the first eight weeks."

18

A Natural and Better Fighter

Each morning, as the sun rolls over the Indian state of Assam and the first light crosses into Bangladesh, across the country thousands of public address systems are cranked up to maximum levels, and, at once, through the morning mist, the metallic wail of the *azan,* the Muslim call to prayer, rises throughout the land.

The *azan* sets the rhythm of life in Bangladesh. Five times a day, work comes to a halt, shoes are removed, hands and feet are washed, and millions turn toward Mecca. In villages, a call to prayer is often issued to mark special celebrations, such as the birth or the naming of a son.

However, one occasion for which the *azan* does not sound is the birth of a daughter.

News of the birth of a baby girl is often received by a family like news of a debt incurred. For months before his child is born, a father may pray five times a day for a son. A son brings prosperity and security. He is an asset. He can work the land or try his hand as a trader, a shopkeeper, or a carpenter. He can travel to Dhaka to look for work, and if he finds it, send money home. When he matures, he will bring a wife into the household, and if he is a dutiful son, he will care for his parents as they grow old, protecting their land and ensuring for them honorable burials when they die.

A daughter earns nothing. She may care for the children, cook, tend animals, carry jugs of water hundreds of yards each day, and do countless jobs in and around the homestead, but her work is assigned little value. Not only is she underprized for her work, she is viewed as a liability, sometimes as a *catastrophe.* Ultimately, she will cost her parents a great deal.

The cause is dowry. From the day his daughter is born, a father is obsessed with one event: her marriage. Even the poorest villagers in

Women in *burkahs*

Bangladesh must provide substantial dowries of furniture, clothing, and gold jewelry. A wealthier villager may offer a television, a refrigerator, or a motorcycle to lure a promising bachelor.

Dowry can cripple a poor family. But parents who do not provide ample sums know they are severely limited in their choice of sons-in-law. A poor father may marry his daughter to a man who already has one or more wives—an unattractive idea but generally a less-expensive option. Or he may resort to a moneylender. To not marry a daughter is an unthinkable disgrace.

Once married, a woman—or girl—leaves her home for what she calls the "outsiders' house." Here she assumes the responsibility of caring for her husband and his family. ("If the husband gives the woman rights, then the woman has rights," Aleya told me.) Since she may still be a teenager at the time, her mother-in-law becomes a dominant figure in her life—a friend if she's fortunate or, if not, a rather hard taskmaster.

Bangladesh is one of the few countries in which women live shorter lives than men. Although the mortality rate for baby girls throughout the world is lower than that for boys, in Bangladesh girls lose their natural advantage after the first six months of life; thereafter, their risk of death is greater than for males. The main reasons are that sons are typically better nourished—they eat first at meals and receive larger portions than daughters—and they are more likely to be given medicine by their parents or taken to a doctor when ill.

In the developing world, poverty is measured in terms of daily caloric consumption. In Bangladesh, approximately 80 percent of the population falls below the poverty line of 2,122 calories per person per day, and about half fall below the extreme poverty line of 1,805 calories. (The daily caloric intake in the United States is approximately 3,700 calories, the world's highest.) Lost in these statistics, is an appreciation of the fact that one of the most dispiriting and debilitating sides of poverty is the fear of imminent disaster.

Anxiety is the rule of life in Bangladesh. No people are more vulnerable to the whims of nature, to the erratic movements of rivers, to wind and rain. But villagers are also vulnerable to the whims of their neighbors: As harvesttime approaches, small farmers erect lifeguard-chairs beside their fields and keep watch through the night. Some live with the fear of extortion by wealthy landlords. Everybody fears catastrophes that can strike at random: A rickshaw driver emerges from a roadside tea stall to discover his livelihood crushed by an errant truck. A shop is burned down by a member of a rival clan. A cow dies. A father of six contracts typhoid. A crop fails and a family must sell off their land to eat.

Though nobody in rural Bangladesh has insurance for these calamities, some can shoulder the losses while others cannot. In the end, Yunus felt, *no one* is more insecure than a landless woman. A woman is not only subject to the authority of the state and her religion, but also to her family and husband. Because her employment opportunities are restricted by purdah, she is often dependent on her husband for her well-being. And when the world beats up on him, all too often he beats up on her.

Wife abuse is prevalent in Bangladesh, especially during the monsoon, when millions of houses become small islands for days or weeks at a time. Some abused wives flee from their husbands and return to their father's or a brother's house. But the behavior carries a stigma, and to avoid bringing shame on their families, many women remain with their abusers. They pay a heavy price for their dignity. It has been estimated that half the murders in Bangladesh involve women killed by their husbands. Though Bangladesh is not a religious state, the authorities are often reluctant to prosecute men for crimes against their wives, particularly if it means fighting the decision of an informal village court, which may follow Islamic law (or its own narrow interpretation of Islamic law). Some wives, seeing no escape, choose suicide; the most common method is eating rat poison.

As in all lands, Bangladeshi women face a world of problems unknown to men. Muzammel explained: "Everyone thinks a poor young woman who is divorced or widowed is up for grabs. She sees every male as a threat to her dignity. So a poor young woman has one situation, a poor old woman has another. A poor good-looking woman has one kind of situation, a poor not-so-good-looking woman has another." Even within Grameen, he added, a member's looks can affect the way she is treated by the staff: "There are some centers that our branch managers are more likely to visit than others." (Sex scandals involving bank workers and women borrowers are quite rare.)

Finally, although women in Bangladesh tend to die before men, those who defy the odds usually find themselves alone in old age. Only 20 percent of village women older than sixty-five have living spouses; for men, who almost always remarry, the corresponding figure is 90 percent. A great many of the beggars in villages are old women with no husband or children able, or willing, to care for them.

From the beginning, women borrowers were an important part of Yunus's vision. Over the years, he would often relate the story of his initial encounter with Sufiya Khatun, the woman in Jobra who wove bamboo stools. Between 1978 and 1983, the percentage of women borrowers climbed from 25 to 40 percent. The Bangladesh Bank had not been excited by this development. "We notice a very high percentage of your borrowers are women," one official had written in a "menacing" memo to Yunus. "We cannot see the reason for it. Please send your explanations."

"I'll be happy to explain the reasons for the high percentage of women borrowers," Yunus replied. "Before that, I would like to know if the central bank ever sent any letter to any other bank asking for explanations why they have a high percentage of male borrowers. In the case the central bank did not do so, I don't see any reason why it should make an exception in our case." He received no reply.

Now, with the nationalized banks off his back, Yunus felt there was no reason why Grameen couldn't reach many more women. IFAD was all in favor of it. And the logic was inescapable: Grameen was a bank for the poor, and there was no getting around the fact that the poorest people in Bangladesh were landless women.

But Yunus also wondered if Grameen could do more than mitigate the worst effects of poverty by targeting women. For example, could it be instrumental in changing men's attitudes toward them? Or in changing women's attitudes toward themselves? These questions were of interest to the development theorists who staffed Western aid organizations. They had been focusing for years on improving the social positions of women in the Third World. One of the most common buzzwords in development circles was "conscientization," a term coined by Paulo Friere in his 1970 book *Pedagogy of the Oppressed.* The way to "conscientize" poor people, wrote Friere, a Brazilian, was to foster the "emergence of *consciousness* and *critical intervention* in reality."

What this translated to in rural Bangladesh were workshops, village support groups, and lots of discussions. Yunus had not read Friere, and he told me that whenever he heard the word *conscientization* all it brought to mind was: "Blah, blah, blah." As he said this, he held up his left hand and mimicked a yapping mouth. It made me laugh. Yunus often made satiric, rather dismissive comments about development theorists. When I asked why he adopted this anti-intellectual stance, he replied: "It comes from the Bangladeshi academic environment. It's bookish; it's withdrawn; it has nothing to do with life. The social consciousness is not there. And it disorients the students so that they are no longer products of the soil."

"In Bangladesh," he added, "you see intellectuals talking about the *world.* They say all kinds of things about the *world,* but they won't talk about the *neighborhood.* Because if they talked about the neighborhood, they would have to *do* something."

Perhaps if he had not lived in a country with battalions of development theorists, Yunus might have found more merit in the idea of "conscientization," which overlapped with his own thinking. Since 1980, Grameen had been holding workshops to promote social awareness. But Yunus held that these actions were secondary. Fostering the "emergence of consciousness" among women in Bangladesh proved extremely difficult in practice, and Yunus had little patience for ideas that were not "life-oriented."

Which meant that any intervention was a waste of time unless it immediately addressed the villagers' fundamental problem of survival. Once that was done, however, other things were certainly possible. But in the short term, Yunus seemed always to act according to the adage: Use what is dominant in a culture to change it quickly. And what is dominant in the culture of rural Bangladesh is that an individual's worth is often construed in economic terms.

So he posed a question: If a woman brought a second income into a poor household, could the very same forces that caused her oppression be turned to her advantage?

There was another side to the question. Not only did women experience poverty more acutely than men, they behaved differently because of it. As the number of female borrowers increased, the staff observed that money which entered the household through the mother seemed to have a more profound impact on the family as a whole. "When a woman brings in income, the immediate beneficiaries are her children," Yunus said. A mother was interested in buying better food or cooking utensils, or patching the roof. She paid more attention to the children's clothing and to their bedding.

Yunus had come to see a poor woman, in contrast to a poor man, as a "natural and better fighter." As usual, Muzammel had an explanation: "The father leaves home early in the morning and comes home in the evening. He doesn't have to face the children. But the mother has to manage constantly. If the father is working away from home and he's not able to send money, she has to borrow, she has to beg, she has to tell all kinds of lies: 'The money will be coming any day. I've got the letter. So give me some rice today. I'll pay you back.' Or worse if the child is sick and she's unable to take her to a doctor. And if the child dies, she even has to go begging for the burial.

"So given the chance, she will fight so that she doesn't have to do these things. It all has to do with her dignity and the dignity of her children."

Men were peacocks, he added. Given money, their priority would be "a watch, a good shirt, a radio." "If you wanted development in terms of quality of life—education, housing, sanitation," Muzammel said, "these were coming through women on a much more solid foundation."

It would require patience and tact to reach large numbers of women. Before, the majority of male borrowers helped to diffuse religious opposition to the bank. As their proportion declined, Grameen would become more vulnerable. Firoza recalled how religious men used to threaten women who joined groups: "They would say, 'Allah will pull your heart out' or 'Your grave will shrink and close in on you.' "

Yunus sought no confrontations with fundamentalists. (The Islamic injunction against interest was, in real terms, a fantasy. Everyone knew that well-to-do villagers who made a grand show of piety often doubled as moneylenders.) The environment that best suited Grameen was indifference. Yunus preferred his critics saying in effect, "Who cares if a crazy bank wants to help a few women?"

The rise in landlessness had already made it impossible for the majority of families in Bangladesh to rigidly observe purdah. Over time, villagers had developed highly elastic notions of "inside" and "outside" to accommodate their religious beliefs and survival needs. In practice, this meant that work conducted physically "outside" the homestead by women could nevertheless be deemed "inside" work if it was unavoidable, and if enough other women were doing the same thing. This conceptual loophole allowed millions of women to remain "within purdah" in the eyes of their relatives and neighbors, while still doing what was necessary to support their families. What constituted "inside" and "outside" work varied throughout Bangladesh according to local custom, but often it depended simply on how eloquently a woman could justify her behavior.

Bank workers took advantage of the changing attitudes. "If you take a loan, you'll be helping your husband," Firoza would say. "If you're earning even 2 takas extra, you can save for your children's education. Wouldn't it be better to have your children say prayers for you when you die than to have them blame you for not preparing them for life?

"When the mullahs used to say, 'Don't join groups. Don't chant slogans,' I taught the women to reply, 'If you lend me the same 2,000 takas that Grameen Bank lent me, I'll listen to you.' Mostly, the mullahs didn't like people to get money in their own hands because they learned about moneylending and interest, and they began to understand how moneylenders had been taking advantage of them."

"The villagers appreciated our advice," she added. "We would tell them, 'When your daughter is born, plant a teak or a mango tree. As she grows, the tree will grow. Then when she is to be married and you need money, what can you do? Sell the tree and use that money to marry your daughter.' They were very impressed. They would say. 'Even our parents didn't tell us such things.' "

In Chittagong, Saleha would tell the women who came to the office wearing veils, "How can I lend you money if I can't see you?" Her method was just to keep pressing. "If you keep knocking at someone's door, she'll eventually open it."

One difficulty was trying to ensure that a wife made use of the money herself, or at least a good portion of it. "Even today, women will pass it on to their husbands—but not as much as initially," Yunus explained.

"We had to struggle very hard to make sure she didn't become a conduit for her husband."

He felt that the struggle was worth the effort: Children benefited from growing up in a household where their mother earned an income and participated in economic decisions. While it was impossible to gauge the impact on the children, you only had to visit one village to witness the change in their mothers.

"When you see women who have just joined the bank, they go around the outskirts and avoid people," explained Maheen Sultan, formerly one of the bank's top women field managers. "But once they've been borrowing money for a long time and they're sure of themselves, they walk through the center of the village greeting people. Before they were apologizing for being there, later they belonged. It's their village, it's their territory.

"At the branch the difference between a new borrower and a four- or five-year borrower is very evident. At the beginning, they don't know where to sit, what to do, who to talk to. Later they just come in, they know everybody, they go about their business, signing or asking for the money or arguing back sometimes. In the center meetings, new borrowers hardly look up and they don't speak up. Older ones are chatting away. If the bank worker doesn't agree, they'll argue, they'll go to the manager. They know what needs to be done.

"And in the home as well—because the husband also feels he's a member of the Grameen Bank—the woman speaks up more often. The husband agrees more often or at least doesn't contradict her. You can see that their relationship also changes. He's proud of what his wife has been able to do."

But sometimes conflicts emerge, added Muzammel. "A woman's position undergoes a dramatic change. And this change may not be liked by her husband or by her father-in-law or even by her mother-in-law. If the son's wife is earning an income they think they'll not be able to exercise undue influence on her."

"I haven't come across men who resented their wives' progress," Maheen commented. "But it may be that such men keep away or perhaps the marriage breaks up, or perhaps they take their wives away from the center."

In 1984, for the first time in the bank's history, the number of female borrowers surpassed the number of males. By year's end, the figures were 68,000 to 53,000. Yunus was impressed by how effectively his staff had been able to reach women borrowers. "Now that we're at 94 percent women, we don't talk about it much," he told me in 1994. "But it was a tremendous push. We would applaud a staff member who said, 'I have five new groups—all of them women.' And we said that any branch manager who could ensure that half of his groups were women would get a promotion."

Among the staff, however, there remained pockets of resistance to the new policy. Grameen's employees differed from the mainstream high school– and university-educated Bangladeshis in that they were slightly more flexible in their attitudes toward women. They were not iconoclasts, and although they appreciated the problems of landless women, they had not planned to spend the majority of their time dealing with them. Yunus recalled, "They would say, 'Ahh, women, they don't know anything. Give the money to men. A woman only asks for 500 takas, so how many women do we need to make 10,000 takas? A man asks for 5,000 takas right away. So it becomes cost-effective.' "

"It's cost-effective only if you look at the surface," he would reply. "But gradually this woman will move on. She's a steady person. And your 500 takas will have much more impact on her family."

19

If a Big Dam Breaks

A bony woman dressed in a threadbare sari emerged from the hut. "I heard you would come today," she said in a high-pitched voice. She stood slightly stooped, smiling hesitantly. She called to a child, who immediately disappeared into another hut and returned carrying a chair. The woman invited us into her house and placed the borrowed chair next to the stool she owned, indicating for us to sit. Disappearing into the back room, she returned moments later with a tray containing two glasses of sweet lemon water, two bowls of puffed rice, and two pieces of hardened molasses.

She apologized for not having more to offer us. "I'm a bit tense because my cow is not giving milk," she said. "I'm having a bit of trouble managing. The feeling of hardship runs through my body."

The day before, Rani had told me about this woman, one of the poorest villagers in Dibuapur to join the Grameen Bank. Her name was also Aleya, and she lived about two hundred yards from the other Aleya. This woman had fought tooth-and-nail two years before to be accepted into her center and now she was experiencing difficulties. Although I had taken many walks through the village, I had never seen her. Rani explained that it was because she didn't have time to sit and chat. She spent almost all of her time working in the houses of other villagers.

Rani's daughter had led us to this woman's house by way of a path that snaked around a pond and cut through heavy foliage. When we emerged from the overgrowth, the sky returned, and there appeared before us a mud court ringed by houses, similar to the one where the other women lived but far more squalid. Here the houses were small and broken down, the wood and bamboo rotten, the thatch roofing patched with pieces of cardboard and blue plastic sheets. A half-collapsed cow shed was poised unsteadily against Aleya's house. Strewn about were broken branches, pieces of torn mats, bamboo, and rusty tin. On several occasions, I had watched Rani neatly smooth the ground in front of her house. In this *para,* it seemed, there was little time for such niceties.

Rani had suggested that we visit Aleya at noon, when she might have some time on her hands. When we arrived, the sun was high and white-hot. A half dozen children materialized and grew still as we approached. They were less energetic than the children in the other *para.* They were a dusty lot, dressed in shorts several sizes too small that were held up by leather strips encircling their bellies.

Aleya appeared to be about the same age as her counterpart, although her face was thinner, more angular, and more deeply lined. As we ate her food, she explained how she joined the bank two years before after a bank worker told her that the maximum center size had been raised from six to eight groups, opening up ten more spots in the center. Aleya approached a few women about forming a group, but some center members warned against taking her. A Grameen Bank borrower had to know how to work with money, they said. You couldn't trust someone so poor. What if she consumed the money?

Aleya fought and fought. Didn't she bear the entire weight of a house-hold? Didn't she have good sense? She appealed to her cousin, Hajera, who had just been elected the center chief, and promised that she would not cause problems for the center. She vowed to repay every *poisha* [penny] even if she had to go without food, even if she had to sell the straw off her roof.

Finally, Hajera agreed to help. "She vouched for me," Aleya said, "but there were some meddlers. They said, 'She's got no land. She's got five kids. Her husband doesn't work.' Because of this, one woman was put off and didn't join. But another woman joined instead. Hajera told the others, 'If Aleya can't pay her loan, it will be my responsibility.' "

When Aleya spoke, her body inclined forward, her voice grew louder, and she would manipulate her hands as if kneading dough; and then, quite suddenly, she would come to a halt and drop them in her lap, at which point the tide of her body seemed to recede.

In the far corner of the room sat a gaunt, toothless, elderly man. Aleya hadn't bothered to introduce him and now nobody even acknowledged his presence. Was he her father-in-law? If so, it would be unusual for her to serve us food without also serving him some.

Aleya read my mind. "My husband has been slaving and toiling from an early age. His body has become stooped and broken down."

The man was not old, I now saw, perhaps only in his forties, but he was lost to the present, and when his wife spoke to him, he merely nodded and returned to his reverie.

"This is why I can't educate my eldest son," Aleya said. "Shall I educate him or shall I feed my family?"

Her husband's decline in the past five years had come as a mixed blessing, I was to learn. In previous years, he had beaten her repeatedly. He had also opposed her wish to join the Grameen Bank when she had the opportunity six years before. Over time, as his body weakened, so did his objections; finally, Aleya joined the bank without even bothering to ask his permission. By then all their neighbors knew that he was not supporting his family and so had forfeited a husband's full moral prerogatives over his wife.

But not all: I was greatly surprised when, in reply to a question about whether she intended to have any more children, Aleya motioned toward her husband, who was oblivious to the gesture, and said, "You should ask him."

The year before Aleya had given birth to her sixth child, a boy, who now rested in the arms of his seven-year-old sister, who rocked him and played with his toes. Only two of Aleya's children attended school. Up to fifth grade, classes were free, but because it was shameful to send a child to school in tattered clothes, the girls stayed home. Aleya had wanted her eldest son to complete high school, but he had been forced to take a job as apprentice to a house builder. The family desperately needed another income. Aleya's husband worked only intermittently, and the sums she earned working for other villagers were minimal. Occasionally her brothers helped out. "My father-in-law and mother-in-law are also my burden," she said.

In my notes, I have numerous references to "Aleya #1" and "Aleya #2" and, subsequently, to "Aleya (rich)" and "Aleya (poor)." My purpose was simply to keep track of who said what. I made the notations for convenience, with little appreciation at the time of the importance of such distinctions to the Grameen Bank.

In global terms, all landless villagers in Bangladesh are extremely poor. From a high altitude—a bird's-eye view by contrast to the "worm's-eye view" that Grameen favors—the variations among villagers disappear. Up in the clouds hover the economists' traditional concerns: gross domestic product (GDP), infrastructure, unemployment, inflation, interest rates, and so on.

Aleya (rich), who fits near the top of the poorest third of the population, and Aleya (poor), who belongs, perhaps, to the bottom eighth, are, to the high flyers, indistinguishable. To policymakers, they are interchangeable. On the ground, however, the differences in their daily experiences are enormous. Which is why the most vital work of the Grameen Bank—which has helped millions of villagers to move from one level of poverty to a less oppressive level—is invisible at the national level. No economic indicators exist to measure so many small changes.

When Aleya received her first loan of 3,000 takas, she purchased a cow. Each week, she earned 90 to 120 takas selling milk. This covered her installment of 60 takas and her mandatory savings; the remainder she spent on food. "I paid the installments and rice fell in my stomach," she explained. At the end of the year, she sold the cow for 2,500 takas. Unfortunately, years before, Aleya's husband had borrowed a small sum of money. Interest had accumulated and now Aleya was forced to use the proceeds of her sale to settle the debt.

The following year she borrowed 3,500 takas and purchased another cow. The cow stopped lactating midway through the year, leaving Aleya owing 1,700 takas. She had only one option: to cut down on the family's eating and put everyone—even her seven-year-old daughter—to work. According to bank rules, the cow could not be sold until the loan was repaid.

When I asked Aleya why she didn't turn to her group or center for assistance, she said that it was too soon. She didn't want to lose their confidence. She wanted to prove herself before applying for a Group Fund loan. The other members were watching to see how she handled her problems.

Aleya worked in the houses of wealthier villagers, repairing mud floors and washing dishes and crockery and clothes. Nothing remained from her gains from the prior year. "With my body's labor I'm paying the installments," she said. Now and then, she rented out her cow to a farmer for plowing. But on a daily basis, she had to ask herself, "Will I eat or will I pay?" Usually her family ate two meals a day, occasionally only one. Once in a while her husband summoned the strength to fish. "The prices in the bazaar keep going up," Aleya said. "Our eating is now very little."

She gathered her son from her daughter's arms and tucked his head beneath her sari to breastfeed him. I stepped outside for a few minutes while my translator asked Aleya whether she used birth control. (Her husband had gone to sleep in another room.) She admitted to secretly taking pills. My translator later told me that Aleya seemed to regret having given birth to six children. "I only heard about family planning after I joined the Grameen Bank," Aleya told her, "and I didn't really understand. I found out about the methods from the government family-planning workers."

Suddenly, a woman appeared at Aleya's front steps. She seemed to have come by stealth from the wooded area behind the house, and now she stood motionless holding out a plastic bag. She glanced briefly at me, then dropped her eyes. Aleya removed her son's mouth from her breast and handed him to her daughter. She rearranged her sari and disappeared inside her house, returning moments later with a fragment of a coconut shell containing a small portion of rice. She handed the shell to the woman, who poured the contents into her bag.

"How many houses do you go to?" Aleya asked.

"As many as I can in a day," the woman replied without raising her eyes. She departed quickly.

After she left, Aleya asked, "Do you have beggars like her in America?"

I said yes. She did not seem surprised.

"Begging is not a matter of shame," she said. "It's the way Allah provides for her."

"Allah does not say to beg," my translator said.

"Yes, that's true," said Aleya. "Allah says to work hard. Do you know why she begs? It's easier. If I go to your house one day, then you'll feed me. If I go to her house one day, then she'll feed me. But who is going to feed me every day? For five days you can pull me along. For ten days you can pull me along. But can you do it forever? That's why I became a member of the Grameen Bank."

"Would you accept her in the center?" I asked.

"It would be difficult for her to manage the installments," Aleya said. "Maybe she wouldn't be able to utilize the money. Anyhow, we have a full center."

"What would you do if the center hadn't taken you?" I asked.

"I don't have to think about that," Aleya said. Her tone seemed to say, "Don't give me any additional worries." "I'd get along somehow. I would live according to the will of Allah."

Two months, eight installments plus interest, remained on her current loan. "If, for the next few months, I can make my installments, then I'll be okay," Aleya said. "My cow may not be giving me milk now, but later on when I sell her I'll receive a great deal of money.

"God willing, I'll be able to carry on. If I kill myself with worry, then I might as well get up and leave the Grameen Bank. With Allah's blessing and the blessings of old people, I try not to think about it that much."

Aleya knew she would probably never catch up if she fell behind on her payments. Then she would endanger not only her chances of receiving more loans but her group members' chances as well. That, she would never allow. "If a little dam breaks you can stop it," she said. "But if a big dam breaks, you cannot."

Her eldest son worked every day, the younger children worked to earn their meals, and Aleya was pressing her husband to do small jobs to earn some money, but his labor was no longer valued by other villagers.

"One taka here, two takas there," she said. "I'm struggling very hard to make the installments."

20

This Is Her Factory

The day Ansar, the husband of Aleya (rich), fastened four sheets of corrugated tin to the roof of his house, he thought: I won't have to worry about my family getting wet for many years. Yet when a thunderstorm struck the very next night, Aleya and Ansar and their children were unable to sleep. It wasn't from the excitement of living in a new house; it was from the noise, the great white noise of rain on tin, like a shower of pellets. It would take some getting used to.

A few days later, after the mud steps were smoothed and the finishing touches were being applied to the veranda, Ansar said to Aleya, "It's all yours now." It was the truth: The house was registered in her name. What's more, before the mortgage was authorized, according to bank rules, Ansar had had to make a trip to the land registry office to transfer the plot of land under the house, which he had inherited from his father, into her name as well. Then he was obliged to furnish a copy of the document to the bank for safekeeping. It was the first evidence of ownership that Aleya had ever possessed.

Land, by far the most important asset in Bangladesh, is typically kept out of women's hands. Under Muslim law a sister is entitled to inherit half a brother's share; in reality, women often sign their land inheritance over to their brothers, sometimes for a token amount, sometimes for nothing. This practice is considered both honorable and prudent. When a woman marries and moves into her husband's household, it is seen as a sign of disloyalty to her kin if she takes land out of her father's household. It is also risky for a woman to burn her bridge back home. She is always in danger of being abandoned by her husband or thrown out. Young brides are frequently "returned" for one reason or another —typically due to insufficient dowry.

But ownership of a house changes this. "In one stroke you create a tremendous security environment for the woman," explained Muzammel. "In the case of a divorce, *he* will have to walk out."

Aleya and Ansar appeared to have a respectful, if not observably warm, relationship, and it did not seem to me that she had much to fear. But one morning after Ansar had gone to work, we were discussing her house loan, and Aleya said: "My husband can never tell me to leave. He can never tell me to get out. I can say anything to him."

Many husbands object to the land transfer; however, if a man wishes to live in a more comfortable house, he has no option but to conform to the bank's guidelines. The rules state that only members with flawless repayment records after at least two loans are eligible for mortgages. And all borrowers must agree to purchase from the bank four reinforced concrete pillars and a cement latrine, and build their house according to Grameen's design specifications. The bank wants the houses it finances to be sturdy. (And they are: During the 1991 cyclone, many villagers along the coastline south of Chittagong survived the tidal wave that drowned thousands because they climbed onto the roofs of houses and tied themselves and their children down. First choice were schools and the cement houses of local elites; second were the Grameen Bank houses that dotted the countryside.)

Aleya's house is a two-story structure supported by four reinforced-concrete pillars and a wooden frame, and topped by a pitched roof of corrugated tin. The four support pillars are sunk into a three-foot-deep mud and clay plateau. The walls, made of wood, flat tin, and interwoven bamboo, contain a generous number of windows, which can be quickly shuttered during a sudden downpour. The front door is three steps above the ground. When it is muddy outside, sandals and shoes are always removed before entering. During the monsoon, a jug of water and a rag cloth remain by the door for washing the feet.

The family sleeps upstairs, sharing the room with sacks of rice and lentils. Downstairs is a kitchen and two rooms: a multipurpose work-room, and, in front, a family room where Ansar (and, less often, Aleya) relax and entertain guests. Off in the back stands a concrete sanitary latrine, one of the few in the village.

The house was financed with a 10,000-taka, ten-year mortgage from Grameen. The interest rate on the mortgage is 8 percent (up from 5 percent in 1991). In addition to her general loan installments, Aleya pays off her house at the rate of 40 takas a week. Within limits, bank members can choose to pay off their mortgages faster or slower.

• • •

Like many of the bank's best ideas, the housing program evolved from the field. Yunus found the opportunity to follow through on the idea when the Bangladesh Bank announced a donor-supported program to finance rural housing units costing between 35,000 and 65,000 takas. Yunus challenged a group of engineers to come up with a design for a durable, inexpensive house, and they returned with a blueprint for a structure made of wood, cement, tin, and bamboo that villagers could build easily and would cost 10,000 to 12,000 takas (about $250 to $300).

From the start, the housing program was expected to lose money, even though Grameen received subsidized funds. Charging 5, and later 8, percent interest, the bank did not have enough of a "spread" to cover administrative costs. As a result, some managers felt that, with this loan, the bank was moving away from its stated objective of achieving financial viability. A house generated no income, they argued. What villagers needed was more credit to expand their businesses so they would become better customers and borrow even more money. In due time, they could build their own houses.

"People thought it was a consumption loan," Muzammel recalled. "They said, 'They won't be able to pay it back.' But after starting it, we began to see that people were enthusiastic. Their children's health improved. Then we realized that for the poor this is not a consumption loan. For the poor this is an investment loan. A house for a poor woman is her workplace. This is her factory."

With roomier, drier houses, villagers began stocking rice, lentils, betel nut, and other staples in quantity, taking advantage of seasonal price fluctuations to buy low and sell high. (A house, it seemed, also doubled as a warehouse.) With more land around the perimeter—part of the loan often went to purchase a larger housing plot—members grew more vegetables and trees, and raised poultry. They recycled materials from their old houses to construct cow sheds or outdoor kitchens or to build strong boxes for chickens. These changes led to improved nutrition, less smoke inside the house (from cooking), more comfortable bedding, and better light and more room for the children to study. However, by far the most important and far-reaching consequence of the housing program was simply that drier and warmer houses cut down on illness—the single greatest factor preventing a family's rise out of poverty. So a mortgage could also double as health insurance.

From 1984 to 1986, Grameen built a few thousand housing units and monitored the results. In 1987 and 1988, after flooding had caused widespread damage across the country, the bank hastily scaled up the program. In 1989, Grameen received the Geneva-based Aga Khan Award for Architecture for its housing program, which, by then, had financed 60,000 units. Over the next six years, the bank financed a quarter of a million more houses.

21

A Conversation

One Friday morning, his day off, Ansar invited me to his home for tea and a chat. He had several questions, he said, mostly about the United States and Canada and international affairs. I had pages of questions for him, I said.

As we sat together in the front room of his house, his daughters occasionally passed him on their way outside. Ansar would extend his arm in what seemed an unconscious gesture and offer a light touch. Like his wife, he spoke softly and slowly. He rarely smiled.

Ansar worked as a press compositor in Patuakhali town. He had always been interested in printing presses and newspapers; after completing the eighth grade, he joined a local print shop as an apprentice. A year later, he was offered a full-time position and the following year he was married. "It's very inconvenient to be married if you're unemployed," he commented.

Ansar had a copy of his favorite newspaper, *The Inquilab,* open on his lap. He turned the pages gently. "We get news about Bangladesh from Dhaka on the radio," he explained, "but for me the overseas news is most interesting."

Poverty creates the need for services rarely found in wealthy countries: In cities, newspapers are pasted onto billboards for public reading. Along sidewalks, rows of typists accept dictation from people who cannot read or write. "I am a poor man," commented Ansar, "so I'm not able to buy this newspaper for 4 takas." His boss usually gave him the paper after he was done with it.

"What is the literacy rate in Canada?" he asked.

I replied that it was close to 100 percent. Ansar nodded and commented that Bangladesh's literacy rate was quite low, about 25 percent. He was the first and only villager who asked me a question about "Canada" rather than "America." It didn't last long, however. Within a few minutes his focus had turned to the United States and the subject of democracy. "Democracy is a very beautiful concept," he said. "Lenin's way—do people want that anymore? Religion is restricted; work is restricted; all possibilities are limited. You're accountable to the government. But in a democratic state, if you've earned it, you keep it. You receive the benefits of your hard work."

Ansar's view of the United States came from newspaper and radio accounts and television. At his boss's friend's house in Patuakhali town, he watched CNN and had seen untranslated episodes of, among other shows, *MacGyver, Dallas, L.A. Law,* and, oddly enough, *Northern Exposure.* He also spoke frequently with a local villager who had spent a year in Washington, D.C.

He was critical of politics in his own country. "During the Ershad government," he commented sarcastically, "for eight years the nation was not *obliged* to go to the ballot box." He contrasted the transfer of power in Bangladesh with what he knew of American elections: "In America, there is no thuggery. The incumbent welcomes the new president. In other countries, far from welcoming them, they try to kill them."

Indeed, since the assassination of Sheik Mujibar Rahman, Bangladesh's first prime minister, in 1975, the country had experienced a succession of military coups. Shortly after Mujib was killed, General Zia-ur Rahman, who had led the Bangladeshi freedom fighters in the war against Pakistan, took over as chief martial law administrator, and later assumed the presidency. In 1979, Zia's party, the Bangladesh National Party (BNP) won two thirds of the vote in a national election. Two years later, Zia was assassinated in an attempted coup. In 1981, another election was held, in which the BNP again won two thirds of the vote. But the following year, General Hossain Mohammed Ershad seized power and placed the country under martial law. Ershad never delivered on his promise of elections and, finally, in 1990, after stories of his corruption were widely publicized, he was toppled by a popular uprising led by students around the country, and put in jail. In 1991, Bangladeshis went to the polls and once again elected the BNP, this time led by General Zia's widow, Khaleda Zia.

In America people can speak their minds freely, Ansar said. "Here, if you try to speak the truth you're in dangerous waters." Local political officials, supported by wealthy landlords, were totally corrupt, he added. And they did not tolerate public criticism.

"Is there corruption in the Grameen Bank?" I asked.

"In the Grameen Bank, there's no corruption and no bribery. That's the beauty of it. If you want to borrow money from another bank, if you want, say, a 5,000-taka loan, you'll spend at least 1,000 takas on the bribe. You'll be exhausted from running around. Then you need to show all kinds of documents and deeds and then you even have to buy them *tea.* In the Grameen Bank, you go to the bank and they place the money in your hand."

"Are there poor people in the United States?" he asked.

"Four *crores,*" I replied, using the Bangla word for 10 million. (Ansar expressed the population of Bangladesh as "12 *crores.*")

What did it mean to be poor in America? he asked. Did people starve? Did they have houses? In response, I found myself describing ghettos and drug abuse, homelessness and crime. I glanced outside and noticed two teenage boys chatting. It was Friday morning. There was no school. One sat on a mud step whittling, the other drew a picture in the dirt with a stick. It was the Bangladeshi equivalent of a Norman Rockwell scene.

I told Ansar about the worst incarnations of violence in urban America, about street gangs and metal detectors in public schools. (My translator explained the purpose of a metal detector.) He nodded. None of it seemed to shock or disappoint him. He had been a youth during Bangladesh's War of Independence, which saw some of the most heinous atrocities committed since World War II. "The Pakistani army walked through villages," Ansar had earlier told me. "They raped women and threw babies onto open fires. In the whole district, not a single house was left standing."

But Ansar's neighbor had told him about Washington, D.C. and now he commented: "If you go to Washington, you would not know that there are poor people." True, I replied, you could live in parts of Washington without seeing poverty. But it was there if you looked.

How odd to be speaking about American poverty with a Bangladeshi villager. Was it possible to compare the two? I recalled Yunus's comments on the subject. Poverty, he believed, was similar in character everywhere. "The frustration—not seeing any opening, being cooped up in a kind of walled world—it's the same feeling whether you're in Bangladesh or in a ghetto in New York or Chicago."

"The expressions and descriptions may be different," he added. "In the United States, the degree of frustration may be one hundred times more because you *see* everything but you cannot *do* everything. Here, I don't see much, so I justify my poverty by God, by my fate. Or, 'Yes, that's the way it has been.' Or, 'I must have done something wrong in my previous life, so I'm being punished.' Or, 'Everybody is in the same position, so I don't feel too bad.' "

Writing about poor Americans almost thirty-five years ago in *The Other America,* Michael Harrington arrived at pretty much the same conclusion as Yunus. Poverty, he argued, could not be defined simply in terms of material deprivation; it had to be viewed in relation to what a society could realistically provide for the majority of its citizens. "To have one bowl of rice in a society where all other people have half a bowl may well be a sign of achievement and intelligence; it may spur a person to act and to fulfill his human potential," he wrote. "To have five bowls of rice in a society where the majority have a decent, balanced diet is a tragedy." He went on: "Poverty should be defined psychologically in terms of those whose place in the society is such that they are internal exiles who, almost inevitably, develop attitudes of defeat and pessimism and who are therefore excluded from taking advantage of new opportunities."

Without question, poverty in Bangladesh is more physically debilitating than its American counterpart; and the intense competition for scarce resources often leads to cutthroat behavior among villagers, exemplified in the extortionate practices of moneylenders, in stories of brothers who swindle brothers out of their inheritance, and husbands who brutalize their wives because of insufficient dowry. However, anthropologists have argued that, despite the material deprivation and the frequent explosions of violence in villages, the multilayered, social character of village life mitigates the most demoralizing aspects of poverty in a way industrialized societies do not. Decades of want in Bangladesh have not produced widespread alienation such as you find throughout Harrington's "other America" and in many parts of the United States today. Bangladeshis live harder and shorter lives than the poorest Americans. Whether their lives are more "brutish" is another question.

The journalist who has written most authoritatively on the subject of villagers is Richard Critchfield. As a journalist-cum-anthropologist who has "covered" village life for four decades, Critchfield, an American, has no contemporary equal. In *Villages,* a compilation of twelve years of personal reportage, he summarized the "character of village life" in a chapter aptly titled "Look to Suffering, Look to Joy," tracing a seminal debate between anthropologists Robert Redfield and Oscar Lewis that began in the 1950s and is still unresolved.

In 1926, Redfield studied a Mexican village called Tepoztlán and published what Critchfield calls a "warm and sympathetic interpretation." of village life. In 1943, Lewis returned to the same village and found it "awful": full of violence, disease, " 'fear, envy and mistrust.' " Lewis attacked Redfield for romanticizing village life; Redfield accused Lewis of taking "his own values" to the village. Critchfield quotes Redfield explaining: " 'The hidden question behind my book is, "What do these people enjoy?" The hidden question behind Dr. Lewis's book is "What do these people suffer from?" ' "

Throughout their lives the two men would remain true to their initial findings. "Redfield kept emphasizing *enjoyment* and Lewis *suffering,*" commented Critchfield. It was Lewis's book that enjoyed more commercial success, a fact Critchfield feels "distorts our perception of the Mexican poor and, to some degree, all poor people." In the end, Critchfield indicates that he views Redfield as the greater anthropologist, and he leans toward his more-optimistic worldview when he concludes: "Each man's portrayal of villagers and the poor, taken by itself, seems incomplete. . . . Their work should be read together. The villagers may be no more stable and happy than we are; they are certainly no less so, which is what matters to them and (eventually) to us."

What of the comparison between Bangladesh and the United States? Critchfield believes that poor villagers are no less happy than "us," by which he means his readers: ordinary Americans. Of course, Bangladesh is exceptionally poor, even by Third World standards. Yunus and Harrington, standing on opposite ends of the earth, seem to agree that, to gauge the "suffering" inflicted by poverty, one must understand how an individual perceives his or her self-worth and opportunities for advancement—although one does not necessarily need to know his or her *income.*

And what do the numbers say? The per-capita income in the United States is a hundred times greater than in Bangladesh. Yet toward the end of the twentieth century, in the world's poorest nation, you will find a great many poor people—like Ansar and Aleya—walking around in what appears to be higher spirits than many of their counterparts in the world's richest nation.

I asked Ansar what kind of books he read.

"I like books on religion," he replied. "I don't spend my time reading trashy novels. With religious books you get a special feeling. You can learn about the life of the great prophet and other illustrious people."

A devout Muslim, Ansar prayed five times a day. During the month of Ramadan, he consumed no food or water from dawn to dusk, and abstained from smoking. (During the month of the fast, out of deference to local mores, the bank suspended the chanting of slogans.) Ansar's views on purdah were, by his own admission, "conservative," although he acknowledged that they had been tempered over the past decade to accommodate a working wife. "Purdah is disappearing," he added. "It was much stronger during the Pakistan time. There's no Islamic law in Bangladesh. It's only called an Islamic state because 85 percent of the people are Muslims. In Saudi Arabia, if you steal they cut off your hand. If you're a *dakoit,* they kill you. They'll stone a prostitute. You can't even have a chat with a woman outside. But this goes on all the time in Bangladesh."

"What about the problems the Grameen Bank has encountered with mullahs?" I asked.

"Religious men say, 'Ahh, the women go and sit amongst men.' But these people are confined within their narrow limited sphere, which today ordinary Bangladeshis don't abide by."

Things had changed markedly over the past ten years, he added. "Women didn't used to go to schools and colleges so much. It was not looked upon favorably." Ansar turned to my translator. "You can understand what he says. But if I kept you locked in the home, then you wouldn't be able to study in the university and you wouldn't be able to speak English with him. You need education to develop a country. Education can coexist with purdah. It's in Islam. We are demanding improvement and progress."

"You may not be wearing a *burkah,*" he added, "but you're still in purdah. Maybe you don't cover your hair, but you can follow another kind of purdah."

He turned to me. "You don't have purdah in America. It's not an Islamic country. There's always purdah in an Islamic country. It's written in the Koran. But nowadays, it's more up to your discretion. I know how women dress in America. I've seen it on television."

"Why should a woman have to wear a *burkah?*" I said. "Why can't a man just close his eyes?"

Ansar's brother had dropped by to listen to our conversation. He was standing by the door, enjoying the exchange. "Did you hear that?" he exclaimed to his brother, laughing. "He made a good point."

Ansar nodded seriously and returned to his thought. "I've seen in America that they wear small clothes—I don't know what you call them. I know this kind of dress and that kind of dress are a vast difference. But doesn't this look beautiful?"

"It is beautiful," I said.

"Our situation is different."

"A *burkah* seems very hot," I said.

"Women in Bangladesh have to dress the way they do," he said. "That's their hardship."

22

Peace of Mind

Back at the branch office, my translator and I ate dinner with the male bank workers, sitting cross-legged on the dormitory floor around bowls of rice, vegetables, curried chicken, and fish. The staff in this branch had been sharing sleeping quarters for more than a year. At night, they usually talked, wrote letters, or played the harmonium and sang together. This night, after dinner, we decided to take a walk to the bazaar for tea and sweets. Once a week, the bank workers splurged on 7-Ups or Cokes, which cost 7 takas a bottle (about one tenth their daily wage). Tonight, they insisted on treating us.

The road leading to the bazaar was lined on both sides with arching trees that gave the impression of passing through a tunnel. On cloudy nights we navigated by flashlight and the lanterns that swayed beneath rickshaw carriages; tonight the moon was full and bright.

A barefoot man came toward us balancing a great basket on his head. Under the weight, he moved in quick, fitful steps, with that hip turn characteristic of Olympic racewalkers. I turned to watch as he passed. He was so thin, I could imagine his spine snapping like a twig.

Near the bazaar, the road cut across a stream. The shops extended over the water on either side, supported by hundreds of vertical bamboo shafts. The shops were constructed of broken wood, thatch, and rusty sheets of tin. Most stocked dry goods, cigarettes, soap, and sundry items. Also in the bazaar were a barber, a laundry, two pharmacies, two tailors, and two clothing shops: one for *lungis,* skirtlike wraps worn by village men; and one for saris, the long cotton cloths women wind around themselves from shoulder to foot.

Two restaurants served rice, dal, bread, and tasty curries. (One was "good" and one "bad," the branch manager explained, although I never discovered which was which.) There were three tea stalls that served

Bank workers relaxing on the roof of their branch, Patuakhali

sweet tea with cardamom and condensed milk—one taka per cup—and
sold puffed rice and molasses by the roadside. The sweets were delicious,
but with each passing bus a fresh layer of dirt settled on top of them.

Daylight does not permit illusion. Which is why bazaars in Bangladesh
are most inviting at night, when the shops are illuminated only by kerosene lamps or single lightbulbs. Amid the dark hush of nature, approaching a tea stall with a glow and the distant sounds of voices always
gave me a small thrill. At such times I would think how remarkable it is
that with almost nothing human beings can create laughter; and, at such
times, it struck me as a particularly great loss for all that, in Bangladesh,
none of this nighttime laughter, none of the arguments or gossip, ever
included a woman's voice.

(Except for my translator's voice. Indeed, while the bank workers,
who were in their mid-twenties, enjoyed hearing from me about life in
"America," they seemed more interested in hearing from my translator
about life in Dhaka. Our working arrangement gave them a rare opportunity to speak casually with a woman their age, a woman more worldly

than they, who had a master's degree and whose family permitted her to travel in the company of a foreign man. Such exceptional circumstances occasionally led to exceptional disclosures. Some unmarried bank workers even admitted to having female "friends" back home.)

A heavy plank lay over the mud at the entrance to the tea stall. It had rained heavily each night for the past week and the roadsides were sloppy and thick. In late April, the Bay of Bengal is ferocious. During storms, the wind blows with such force that coconut trees take the form of catapults and limbo dancers. The night of my first storm, the screaming wind jolted me awake. The bank workers jumped out of bed and ran to fasten the shutters. After they were secured, the wind sounded even more harrowing. I expected it to shatter the glass panes. The explosions of thunder were unbelievable. The sky was a discotheque.

It seemed impossible that these little shops in the bazaar could withstand such storms, yet they did. And each morning they reopened, and smoke rose anew from their cooking fires. The morning after my first storm, I asked a bank worker how much more powerful a cyclone was.

"At least one hundred times," he said.

The tea stall was filled with the pungent smell of damp wood and smoke. Two gnarled men sitting at another table stared at us in a hangdog manner. We ordered soft drinks and biscuits and one of the bank workers paid 2 takas for a Gold Leaf cigarette, which he planned to smoke on the way back to the branch. Two of the four bank workers I had come with were in their mid-twenties and had recently married; the other two were waiting for their marriages to be arranged.

"Will you allow your wife to work?" I asked Shahidul Alum, a bachelor, and the most forthcoming of the group.

"My friends say, 'If a woman works, she will rise above the man and there will be disharmony in the marriage,' " he replied. "But I say, 'If she's a good girl, even if she has more experience and more money, she won't get out of control.' "

"Friends back home think that it's better to keep women screened away," added Nurul Amin. "I've tried to explain to them that women should work—not necessarily have a career—but that they should generate income."

"In my family, my father was the only income earner," Shahidul Alum went on. "And we never had enough money. But if we had all done something—mother and brothers and sisters—then we would have prospered. After seeing the economic improvements these women in the Grameen Bank have brought to their families, I promised myself that when I bear the weight of a household, I will encourage all the members of my family to work, so that socially and economically we can advance." He added: "I'm not sure I would be saying this if I had not had this kind of experience."

The bank workers spoke with enthusiasm about developing their country and helping poor families get ahead. They saw the value in banking with women, not because they cared to overturn tradition but because women were so obviously underemployed. It seemed that only a minority of bank workers saw the social logic in providing employment opportunities to women, while just about everyone I spoke with saw the economic logic in bringing another income into a household.

But staff members whose spouses worked had to overcome logistical problems. In Grameen, there is no telling where you will be stationed; many branches are located in backwater areas with few, if any, employment opportunities. Working couples often have to live apart for both to hold onto their jobs; some go months without seeing each other. If they are lucky and find jobs in the same area, it doesn't last long. Every two or three years, bank workers receive new postings. "At any moment I may be transferred with no consideration given to my family situation," explained a bank worker. Frustrated by repeated postings in outlying areas, some bank workers told me that they would leave the bank if they could find other work.

Although bank workers put up with the Grameen Bank's working conditions primarily because jobs are scarce in Bangladesh, most of the staff seem to approach their work as more than just a job. They complain about the pay, the transfers, the separation from their families, and the constant fieldwork—as an indication of the nature of the job, bank workers received allowances for sandals and umbrellas—but their discontent often vanishes when they speak about the borrowers.

Aside from witnessing firsthand the impact on the lives of poor villagers, one attractive feature of the job is that it offers young people the opportunity to manage others. When I asked one of the bank workers what he would miss most if he were to quit, he replied: "Every day I speak with sixty or seventy people. I would miss that."

Elsewhere in Bangladesh, junior employees are entrusted with clerical duties and the responsibility of serving tea to their seniors. Bank workers, by contrast, see themselves as advisers. On the bulletin boards inside many branches is a framed quotation from Yunus: "We are all teachers and we must not behave otherwise. Ours is a creative work and we must always bear that in mind."

Something else makes working for the Grameen Bank a refreshing experience, Shahidul Alum explained. "Every other organization in Bangladesh is full of corruption. Here, you can be an honest person and it's possible to remain so."

Everybody nodded. Nurul Amin recalled the process that had led to his being hired. "They wasted no time," he said. "I didn't need influence. I didn't have to pay a bribe or do anyone a favor."

Muzammel once told me that the easiest way for a job applicant to disqualify himself would be to have a well-connected friend or relative place a call to the head office on his behalf. "Anyone who approached the job that way would not be right for us."

On a visit to Jobra, I ran into a cousin of Dipal's who had recently applied for a job with the bank. Dipal had sent him the same form letter that every applicant receives, instructing him to report for an exam on such-and-such a date. He offered no advice; he didn't even wish him luck. Later, I was told that his cousin didn't get the job.

In Dhaka, one of the staff's favorite anecdotes has to do with the time, immediately after the office on Mirpur Road opened, when Yunus refused to pay the obligatory bribe to expedite phone installation, and for weeks the Grameen Bank, with 400,000 clients, had one telephone.

Maheen Sultan recalled: "Professor Yunus went around everywhere, to any meeting, and to whoever wanted to know why he couldn't be reached over the telephone, he said, 'Well, our telephones haven't been installed because the telephone authority is asking for us to pay this bribe and obviously this would be totally dishonest.'

"He went around saying this until it happened in a meeting where somebody from the telephone authority was present. And he was so embarrassed that he went back and ordered immediate installation of the Grameen Bank's phones."

Such stories were widely circulated. Yunus wanted the staff to feel that their institution was unique; and he used the bank's international acclaim to boost the pride of the staff, saying effectively, "The whole world is watching you. You're building the future of this country. People are coming here from Africa, from Asia, from America, to learn from you." It was a powerful motivation. Susan Davis, who represented the Ford Foundation in Bangladesh in the late 1980s, commented: "Those Grameen people walk with a certain pride—with an extra puff of the chest."

But how could an organization that managed so much money in such a poor country remain pure? In Dhaka, among intellectuals and businessmen, the cynicism runs thick. "Nowadays, it's almost as if the

The walk to the bazaar from the Dibuapur branch

honest people are the stupid ones," Maheen Sultan told me. "The honest people are the ones who'll be left out at the time of retirement with only their pensions. They'll be the people who haven't been able to send their children to the right schools."

Shahidul Alum offered an explanation: "The thing is mainly peace of mind. People who are corrupt are not always happier. For every five they receive in bribes, they have to pay out three. They have to pay bribes for holidays, for raises, for everything. For a file to be moved from this table to that table, you have to pay a bribe. And then it takes three months."

"Also, there is little opportunity to be corrupt in the Grameen Bank," he added. "There are too many eyes."

23

It Was Like a Fish Market

Within a year of Grameen's independence, Yunus was faced with the situation he had always hoped to avoid: a failing branch. The branch, Shajanpur, located in Tangail, had been struggling for two years. The loan recovery rate had fallen steadily for more than a year; then, in 1984, members in dozens of centers suddenly stopped attending meetings, and repayment plummeted, hitting 50 percent, then 25, and finally reaching a low of 14 percent. Soon, word that Shajanpur's members were not repaying their loans reached other branches and default began spreading through Tangail.

"People began to think that Yunus was crazy," a senior manager recalled. "The Grameen Bank couldn't last. Villagers had seen development organizations come and go. They thought, 'So why should we repay?' "

Muzammel added: "The bankers had projected that after we became a bank, we would collapse. They said we would not be able to close our books. They said that when the Grameen Bank became big it would burst like a balloon."

Shajanpur was one of the original nineteen branches in Tangail. When it opened in 1980, demand for loans was tremendous. Bank workers registered groups as fast as possible and Shajanpur filled up in a year. That same year, Bangladesh was hit with severe flooding, and many of the borrowers suffered losses. Now, as management looked for an explanation as to what had gone wrong, the field staff blamed the flood. Many borrowers had never fully recovered, they said. Problems had accumulated invisibly with time. In 1982, defaults cropped up; they snowballed in 1983; and by 1984, the situation was out of control.

The cleanest solution, some felt, was to close Shajanpur and get to work repairing the problems elsewhere in Tangail. But when Yunus ordered the branch closed, Shajanpur's staff refused to comply. "Why should the villagers be penalized for our mistakes?" they said.

It wasn't a matter of the bank workers protecting their jobs—they would have been transferred to other branches. It was a matter of principle. In the past, Yunus had told the staff many times: "If something goes wrong it is not because of the shortcomings of the borrowers, but because of the lack of skill and understanding of the staff."

And: "For every problem, there are several solutions; one of them is the best."

Now, they countered: Was closing Shajanpur the best solution to this problem?

There wasn't much time for experimentation. Shajanpur had to be contained. From Dhaka, a number of "spies" were dispatched to diagnose the disease and report back. Their initial investigation revealed a problem management had suspected: Shajanpur lacked a "healthy" composition of borrowers. There were too many married couples, both of whom were members, and too many "faulty selections"—members who exceeded the bank's eligibility criterion. These villagers tended to be less loyal to the bank and they often treated poorer members disrespectfully.

But the spies also reported two serious problems the head office had not anticipated: "loan adjustment" and staff corruption. Borrowers had indeed been hurt by the 1980 flood, but that was only one contributing factor in the crisis and, as it turned out, not the most important one. "Loan adjustment," a practice by which the bank settled old debts with new ones, was more serious. Here, if a borrower had an overdue balance of 1,000 takas on a prior loan, the staff might offer him or her a new 3,000-taka loan and then "adjust" that loan by immediately subtracting the overdue 1,000 takas. This meant that the villager had to pay installments and interest based on a 3,000-taka loan (60 takas per week) but had only 1,850 takas to invest (3,000 takas minus 1,000 takas overdue minus 150 takas for the Group Fund).

Simply put, this was bad banking. By not restructuring old debts, the bankers were not giving borrowers a fair chance to get back on their feet.

What caught management completely off guard, however, was the revelation that several staff members were stealing money from their members and failing to deposit or properly record their payments. If bank workers in Tangail had closed their eyes to their borrowers, it seemed that the head office, in its zeal to expand to new districts, had grown complacent and lost touch with its oldest staff members—a small portion of whom, management now discovered, were involved in what is today euphemistically described as "left-hand practices." (One Grameen manager told me: "In almost every case where the bank has a problem, if you look closely you will find the problem is the staff member. And when a man gets in trouble it is usually for one of two reasons: *money* or *sex*.")

Yunus never had the illusion that his staff were incorruptible; nevertheless, he was surprised and hurt. "This was the bank's first major crisis," commented Dipal. "It woke Professor Yunus up. It woke everyone up."

It wasn't the first time the bank had encountered such problems. When Grameen had separated from the nationalized banks, the official bank employees had taken advantage of the confusion and appropriated money belonging to villagers. As far back as the Three Share Farm, when the farmers of Jobra had shortchanged him at harvest time, Yunus had been aware of the need for unrelenting supervision. Reflecting on this, he wrote: "[The] Grameen system is built on trust. But it monitors everything, checks everything continuously and ferociously, as if its life depended on it." The bank could maintain excellence "only if its monitoring system can reach out to all the remote and dark corners of the system and keep them clean."

In the fury of expansion, the dark corners were neglected and certain bank workers found it impossible to resist the temptation of pocketing some of the money that daily passed through their hands.

"Expansion was the crucial issue," Muzammel explained. "It was bound to happen and when it happened we had no experience handling the situation." "A close inspection of the books at the time," commented another senior staffer, "would have revealed an institution that was very shaky."

What was the situation?

M. Abul Hossain, a top-notch staffer, now connected to the International Training Unit, recalled what he discovered as a freshman branch manager in Tangail: "It was like a fish market. There was no discipline in the centers. Bank workers had been playing with the interest rate. They weren't letting members get loans from the Group Fund. There were long delays in sanctioning loans because some bank workers were not depositing villagers' interest payments. They were lying to them, saying their loans had not yet been authorized.

"Bank workers were keeping the information from branch managers so there was no quick way to discover problems. I had to go directly to the center chiefs to find out what was going on. I sat down and had discussions with the members and found lots of inconsistencies. My bank workers tried to cover them up by saying, 'Oh, they're illiterate. They don't know.' "

Breaks in communication had occurred everywhere. Abul Hossain reported what he saw to the Tangail zonal manager, Mohammed Mortuza (the same man who told me the story about the salute).

Mortuza is an exuberant individual with a great deal of the showman in him. He has a colorful manner of speech and a talent for making a hard point simple. He is the sort of individual to whom you would expect children to naturally gravitate. Like so many other senior managers, he had been Yunus's student at Chittagong University. Before he joined Grameen in 1981, he worked for the Bangladesh Bank, where he ran into the same corruption and gridlock that frustrated Yunus. "I found the system very polluted," he recalled. "Grameen promised less security, but I thought it would be a challenge."

Mortuza began by dealing with the most serious cases of corruption. He fired the worst offenders and demoted several others. It was more critical to act quickly to restore members' trust. Much damage had been done, not only by the employees' malfeasance but by management's initial attempt to restore discipline when members were unable to make good on their "adjusted" loans.

"We thought we could solve things by being tough," Mortuza recalled. Faced with large-scale default, bank workers panicked. They bullied villagers; some even threatened to lock them up in branch offices. It was a knee-jerk reaction and it backfired. Villagers grew embittered. They spread rumors: The Grameen Bank won't be around much longer. Why attend the meetings? Why repay the money? Others, more fearful, took loans from moneylenders to pay their installments, putting themselves in jeopardy of losing everything they possessed. "People had lost faith in us," Mortuza said. "I knew if we wanted to survive as an institution, we had to help these people survive."

Mortuza directed bank workers to visit the members at home, informing them that their payments were on hold, and urging them to attend center meetings—not to pay their installments but to discuss their problems and the possibility of receiving additional loans. "It is not enough to go to the meetings and collect the money," he reminded his staff. "You have to talk with people: How is your situation? How is your sanitation? How are your children's teeth? Banking is not like ice; it is warm and changing. And it's not a one-shot game. It takes twenty or thirty meetings."

Mortuza spent his days visiting branches and centers. Abul Hossain recalled: "Mortuza had a car, a baby taxi, a motorcycle, and a bicycle, and he used them all to do his job."

In the flooding of 1980, borrowers' houses had been damaged. They had lost animals and food stocks. Four years later, they still had not replaced them. Mortuza introduced new loans to help villagers recover their productive assets. He knew that he could not forgive loans—that would establish a dangerous precedent—but he could restructure them, spreading the burden over years, so that borrowers could manage both their new and old obligations, and still get ahead.

Villagers who attended center meetings for three months and deposited one taka each week in their personal savings became eligible for capital recovery loans, regardless of past performance. Mortuza wanted to make sure that the message villagers received was unmistakable: The Grameen Bank responds to your problems not by curtailing credit but by providing even *more* of it.

How had the staff members become involved in "left-handed practices"? When I asked Abul Hossain, he replied, "They were corrupted because they had the opportunity." Most of the bank's employees were, themselves, quite poor; some were only a little better off than the villagers they served. And many worried that the officials who said the Grameen Bank would "burst like a balloon" were right. If they were soon going to be out of work, they might as well make it worth their while now.

Mortuza and Yunus saw the Tangail problems as an inevitable consequence of bold experimentation. "We wanted to go fast," Mortuza said. "At first, everything looked okay, but internally the system was fouled."

"We relaxed," added Yunus. "Our accounting systems failed."

As Mortuza worked to rebuild Shajanpur, new groups were formed. Concerned that the attitudes of old members would carry over into new groups, Mortuza ordered separate meetings to keep the "pure" members from the "corrupted" ones until the bad habits were corrected. Most of Shajanpur's members were men. After they quit the bank, many had fled to Dhaka to find work. "People rented rickshaws; some sold their blood," Mortuza recalled. "They said they had been treated like animals. They wanted back in." The villagers were surprised when the bank refunded some of them money from overpayment of interest years before. "Many came back with lump sums to repay their previous loans, but we didn't take the money."

Rebuilding the branch would take many years. By 1987, most of Shajanpur's members had returned to good standing, explained Mortuza. "In three years," he added, "Tangail was completely changed. When Yunus came to visit the branch, 1,700 members turned out for the ceremony." Despite the bank's corrective measures, however, the mistakes that were made in the early 1980s in Shajanpur could still be felt a decade later.

24

Little Checks and Big Checks

Despite the problems in Tangail, Yunus felt confident. Free of the commercial banks, Grameen could sanction its own loans, solve its own problems, and grow at its own pace. Two criticisms were now directed at the bank. One said that it was moving too slowly, that it would take hundreds of years before it could make a dent in poverty, and the other said that if the bank expanded too fast it would soon break apart.

The bank's biggest constraint was the six months it took to train bank workers. Since 90 percent of their training took place in the field, expansion was limited by the number of branches that could be used as training sites. As the bank added branches, however, it could absorb more recruits. And once these new recruits were ready for service, the bank could open more branches and these branches would allow for an even larger number of recruits the following year, and so on. Grameen would grow exponentially.

Based on estimates of the proportion of branches available for training and the number of recruits each branch could hold, management calculated the number of branches Grameen could be operating by 1988. "The conservative estimate was three hundred and the optimistic was six hundred," recalled Muzammel. "So Yunus said, 'Maybe five hundred is a good number. We have groups of five, so let's say five hundred.' "

Immediately, the number crunchers went to work calculating the financial requirements to establish five hundred branches capable of serving 10,000 villages and reaching 500,000 borrowers. They estimated credit requirements separately for male and female borrowers—at the time the split was roughly fifty-fifty—and made allowances for an increase in loans to women in line with the bank's new policy. The figure they came up with was $38 million.

Muzammel recalled IFAD's reaction: "They almost fell off their chairs. 'Five hundred branches!' "

"Everybody said it was crazy," Yunus added. "We said that's what we want. If you can't afford to give us all this money, give us the amount that you can afford. But don't say it can't be done. If it can't be done, along the way, we'll find out ourselves, but at the moment we believe that it can be done. And it *should* be done."

The mission IFAD dispatched to assess the proposal found the bank's forecasts unrealistic, even in light of its prior performance. Such rapid expansion, they felt, could only lead to a deterioration of quality because the close personal contact between the staff and the borrowers that accounted for Grameen's success would be lost in a network of five hundred branches.

Yunus argued that the ratio of bank workers to members would not change with expansion since each staff member would still be responsible for the same number of centers. His plan called for a new management layer to be wedged between the zonal office and the branch: the "Area Office." The new hierarchy would be: head office, zonal office, area office, branch office, center, group, member.

A full zone would supervise approximately ten areas; an area, ten branches, a branch, sixty centers; a center, six groups; and a group, five borrowers. If the head office could supervise, say, ten zones, in theory, Grameen could accommodate 1.8 million members. If a center could hold eight groups rather than six, then, without adding a single staff member, the bank's capacity jumped to 2.4 million borrowers. (Yunus envisioned Grameen growing much larger until a day in March 1991, when he was faced with a crisis that threatened to destroy the bank.)

Yunus's experiences in Washington had given him insight into the workings of governments and donor agencies. He understood that aid officials had to move large sums of money in order to advance their careers, and he knew how to tailor his sales pitch to meet their needs. "Donors find it easier to give big money than small money. If you ask for $10,000 or $15,000 or $20,000, donors don't care. If you ask for a million dollars, then it's 'Let's have lunch.' "

After a decade of development washouts in Bangladesh, he also knew that aid agencies were eager to attach themselves to successful projects. By the end of 1984, Grameen had lent half a billion takas and its borrowers had accumulated close to 40 million takas in savings. The problems in Tangail notwithstanding, Grameen remained the most efficient lender in rural Bangladesh. Elsewhere, loan performance was something of a comedy. Despite their security requirements—the wall of collateral that poor people encountered—commercial banks in rural areas had repayment rates as low as 30 percent; for industrial development banks the figure dropped down to 10 percent. Sometimes the names of defaulters were published in newspapers to embarrass them into paying. But the lists were too long and the company too good. Besides, with so much aid money keeping the government bureaucracy afloat, top managers at the nationalized banks had little cause for alarm. Nobody was threatening to foreclose on *them*.

The Ford Foundation had given the bank $125,000 for institutional development and staff training. And it provided an additional $770,000 as a recoverable grant to guarantee against loan defaults and foreign exchange losses. This grant was similar in function to Grameen's Group Fund; it protected the bank's loan capital from eroding, ensuring long-term viability. Now, Yunus explained that more than a third of the $38 million Grameen requested was to be placed in a "revolving loan fund" that, by agreement, would never be depleted. Unlike conventional aid, this money was not to be used up and replenished by another donor; it was to be recycled and reinvested. There was nothing particularly new about this idea, except that this is how businesses traditionally operate, not development organizations or social-welfare programs. "This is not a giveaway," Yunus said, "it's a revolving fund. We'll take the money out and we'll put it back. We'll make it bigger and bigger as we go along."

To donor officials, the idea was enticing: Long after they had left their current posts for greener pastures, the money they sanctioned would continue to revolve.

Years later, after Grameen had become famous, Yunus found himself receiving hundreds of unsolicited checks—for $25, $50, or $100—from individuals around the world. Usually, the sender had read or heard about the bank and been moved by Grameen's no-frills, no-charity, poor-people-are-entitled-to-a-fair-deal approach. A typical example is a Canadian woman named Muriel Guest who heard a radio interview with Yunus shortly after the 1991 cyclone and wrote: "[I] thought that the bank somehow would know more directly than most what to do with a small donation to those affected by the storms."

"We didn't know what to do," Yunus recalled. "So we made a decision after seeing that this was a nonending process of receiving little checks.

"Our policy is we take that money and put it in one of our branches, open an account in the name of the person who sent it and write, 'We have opened an account in your name. The moment this money is deposited it has started to work for poor people. It goes out as loans, it's paid back. Your money continues to serve the interest of poor people again and again in a recycled way.' "

"In many cases," he added, "we get more checks from the same person, saying, 'I'm sending more money to put in my account.' It's not a charity. Somebody is just putting some money in a bank account. But putting money in a bank account in Grameen Bank strangely helps people to do their own thing without feeling that somebody is helping them with charity and making them feel obligated. So here you can deposit money. On demand you can get it back. But while it is here resting, it is working very hard to help poor people uplift their own positions."

IFAD agreed to provide Grameen with $23.6 million and suggested that Yunus approach the Asian Development Bank for the difference. "So, one day, a guy came from the ADB," Muzammel recalled. "He put one leg up on a chair and said, 'We want to finance you.' Yunus said, 'Have we asked you to finance us?' He didn't like his attitude. That meeting decided it."

Yunus was put in contact with USAID (U.S. Agency for International Development) and the World Bank, which had earlier given him the "cold shoulder." But now he felt he could be more selective. "I don't think we can handle such big organizations," he told Muzammel. "All their regulations. I don't think we'd be able to cope."

Yunus had heard that the Norwegians and Swedes were looking for "grassroots" development projects that targeted women. IFAD made the initial contacts with the Norwegian Agency for International Development (NORAD) and the Swedish International Development Authority (SIDA). After a brief period of negotiations, each agency agreed to commit $7 million, bringing the total to just under $38 million, most of which would be channeled to Grameen through the Bangladesh Bank as a twenty-year, 2 percent loan, with a ten-year grace period.

PART IV

The System

He who is satisfied with pure experience and acts in accordance with it, has sufficient truth.

GOETHE

25

Laying the Foundation

Yunus had designed a logo for the bank, a red and green arrow: "The red signifies speed and the green is the future. Life and peace—that's the target." Now, throughout Tangail, Chittagong, Rangpur, Patuakhali, and Dhaka, branch offices were springing up along roadsides, with large red and green arrows rising high above dusty bazaars and wide-open rice fields.

In late 1984, Yunus was informed that he had won the Ramon Magsaysay Award, the Manila-based honor, informally known as the Asian Nobel Prize. He had won in the category of Community Leadership, established "to recognize leadership of a local, national or international community, especially toward action that helps the man on the land more fully realize his opportunities for a better life."

Note the twist: Grameen was helping people *without* land, and now mostly women. Yunus conveyed his surprise at having been selected: "I still cannot make out how the trustees of this prestigious foundation could notice a small effort such as ours, which has reached only some 100,000 in a population of more than 90 million. I can only admire the foundation for taking a big risk in choosing me, and in demonstrating its confidence in our work when we need it most."

Back in Dhaka, the head office was brimming with excitement. Recruitment was proceeding faster than ever. At the end of 1983, the bank had 824 staff members; by the end of 1985, it had close to 3,000. Up to 1984, the bank had lent 500 million takas; in 1985 alone, disbursements were 428 million. The bank's membership had grown to 172,000 villagers, of which 112,000 were women.

By the end of 1985, Grameen was operating 226 branches. Each newly constructed branch was an identical two-story, brick and concrete structure. On the ground floor was the office, sparsely furnished with

Branch office, Dulahazara

wooden desks and chairs and green metal filing cabinets and a guard's
sleeping quarters. On the second floor were two four-bed dormitories,
one double room with a balcony and one single room. (The dormitories
were only for men; female bank workers had to find their own accommodations.) Branches had installations for lights and ceiling fans, but
in many cases a decade would pass before electricity ran through the
wires.

A stairway led to the roof, where bank workers hung their hand-
washed and rain-drenched clothes to dry in the afternoon sun, or, when
the nights grew unbearably hot, laid out their bedrolls and slept under
the stars. In the early evenings, they often relaxed on the roof, enjoying the view of the surrounding countryside—a checkerboard of saf-
fron, honey, and lime. From up there, they could observe men plowing
and children playing, and espy the occasional woman walking quickly
through the fields, careful to keep her head concealed within her sari.

The bankers' lives followed a set pattern: from Saturday to Wednesday
they attended two center meetings each morning. In the afternoon, they
visited borrowers or completed office work. "Meetingless Thursday" was

a light day, reserved for miscellaneous accounting. On Friday, the Muslim sabbath, the office was closed.

Meals were prepared in a small brick building to the side of the office, usually by a local woman to whom the staff paid a monthly salary. A hand-operated tubewell supplied bathing and drinking water. The branch was surrounded by a barbed-wire fence, like many buildings in rural Bangladesh. In one corner lay stacks of concrete pillars for houses and cylindrical sections for latrines, which the bank sold at cost to members who received house loans.

Over the years, Grameen had refined its system for branch openings. Before an office was established, the branch manager prepared a report on the demographic and geographic features of the area, providing details on local agriculture, communications and transport, the political power structure, the extent and nature of poverty, and the strength of local mullahs. (Grameen never situated a branch near a mosque.)

Next, the manager called a meeting, open to landowners and landless alike, where he officially introduced the bank and explained its policies and procedures. Here, wealthier villagers were told that the bank made loans only to people with less than half an acre of land, or whose total family assets did not exceed the value of one acre of "medium quality" land in the area. Under no circumstances, explained the manager, would the bank make an exception to this rule. "When laying the foundation for a branch," a manager told me, "the worst thing you can do is let yourself be influenced by local elites."

Many elites suspect, correctly, that the bank will put the landless in stronger bargaining positions, force up wage rates, and hurt their moneylending activities, and they often threaten poorer villagers not to join. In the short run, they are often able to mount effective opposition, but over time their efforts inevitably fail. There is not much they can do against a well-financed institution operating with full government support. Grameen is simply too popular: Its target market, the landless, is half the population.

This is why self-interested elites typically cloak their opposition to the bank in Islam. At best, this strategy slows things down; most villagers are aware of the true motivations behind it. Indeed, the hypocrisy of elites is often glaring: Powerful villagers and mullahs usually exhibit tolerance toward the destitute women who move from house to house begging for rice, because one of the five "pillars" of Islam is charity. However, when these same women borrow money from the Grameen Bank and begin moving from house to house as peddlers, they are castigated as "shameless" women.

"Grameen Bank doesn't please the rich people," a borrower told me. "Why should they like it?" The landless were easily exploited, she said. "Where the labor rate is supposed to be 50 takas, rich people can get away with paying only 20. Now we can take a loan from Grameen Bank and start our own business. And another thing: The person who has a little bit of land can afford to farm that land. He doesn't have to sell it off."

"If I'm secure in my faith what can people say to me?" she added. "People join Grameen Bank due to the imperatives of their stomachs. Does Grameen Bank say don't keep fasts? Don't say your prayers? No. It doesn't say anything like that. People only have one thing to criticize about the bank: 'Purdah has been corrupted.' They say that if you join Grameen Bank you don't have any self-respect left. That's garbage."

After the meeting, the branch manager and a senior assistant begin walking around the villages closest to the bank, introducing themselves to residents, answering questions and allaying suspicions. Their movements are carefully planned. A branch is supposed to expand roughly in concentric circles until it reaches about thirty villages in a five- or ten-mile radius. In this fashion, a bank worker never has to pass through a village that does not already have Grameen representation.

26

I'm Not a Woman Anymore

Saleha threw her hands into the air. She was describing the changes she had seen during her twelve years with the bank. Now, when I asked whether she had encountered difficulties as a woman in Chittagong—one of the most conservative areas of Bangladesh—she almost knocked over a stack of files on her desk, recalling the time she had to establish a new branch by herself.

"Do you know what it was like?" she exclaimed. "I arrived in this bazaar and I knew no one. There was no hotel. I thought, 'Where will I stay? Where will I eat? How should I travel from one place to another? I'm a woman.' I had to create a whole office. I felt helpless. I wanted advice. I wanted to quit."

After several hours, Saleha discovered a shop in the bazaar owned by a Buddhist. Buddhists do not follow purdah. "I need a place to stay the night," she told the man.

He was incredulous. "You, a Muslim woman, alone?"

"I'm not a woman anymore," declared Saleha. "I'm a *manager.*"

According to design, three of the six bankers in each branch were to be women. But Grameen ran into a problem: more men applied for the job, and, once hired, women often quit—usually due to family pressure. "We tried to station women close to their families, but family members interfered," explained Nurjahan. "So we moved them a bit farther away, but then their husbands and fathers objected. Husbands expect their wives to be at home when they return to the house."

"Men are fearful," she added. "They don't want us changed too much —or spoiled."

The majority of the bank's clients were now women, yet Grameen was recruiting mostly men as bank workers. Over time, it had become more acceptable for men to manage women's centers. Although purdah held that women were not supposed to be seen by men outside their "extended families," the notion of "extended family" was defined broadly, encompassing cousins, friends, neighbors, godparents, and, as the Grameen Bank discovered, even bank workers.

A question remained: Who was a more effective staff member—a man or a woman? Certainly, women had a much easier time getting close to other women and broaching sensitive topics such as spousal abuse and family planning. "A woman can identify a central problem more quickly," Saleha explained. "Men can oversee more centers, but women are more effective."

Most of the bank's managers tended to disagree, arguing that the social limitations women faced made them less effective, or at least less *cost-effective*. Sensitive topics, like family planning or wife abuse, could be raised in workshops conducted by women. But men could move around easier. Why not leave the banking to them?

Branch managers, who were mostly men, tended to view any constraint to freewheeling growth as an encumbrance. "Every manager wants to have male workers," Yunus told me in a frustrated tone. "They say, 'Women cannot walk to distant places. They take maternity leave. They have to go home early. They're weak. They're not good at numbers. They make all kinds of mistakes, etcetera.'

"At the same time, you see women workers who stay until ten o'clock and eleven o'clock at night."

One problem was supervision. In a country where men and women have little opportunity to meet socially, interaction at the office is somewhat strained. "People are always worried about what others will think," explained Maheen Sultan, who, in 1993, was one of only two female area managers in the bank (an area manager supervises approximately ten branches). "Managers are very careful about how they treat female bank assistants so no rumors start up. And then they go to the opposite extreme; they don't give them enough supervision."

Another problem was antagonism from local mullahs. Saleha recalled: "I used to work days and nights, and I would talk to everyone—male or female. The mullahs started making trouble, saying that I went from village to village without purdah. What kind of a woman does this job? A fallen woman."

Saleha handled these problems herself, although she said that at times she could have used some assistance from the bank. She quickly added that even if management did pay more attention to this issue, most women in Bangladesh would still be reluctant to take jobs in the

Grameen Bank. "Women are interested in working in things like schools. You start at 9:00 A.M. and you come home at 4:00 P.M. Who wouldn't want such an easy job?"

Even her daughter, Rozie, had little desire to join Grameen after she graduated from university. "It was my hope that at least Rozie could work for the bank," Saleha said. "When she didn't get into medical school, I thought, 'Okay, she can work for the Grameen Bank.' But she said she wouldn't want to spend her days talking with the members."

Recruiting women for managerial posts was particularly difficult, explained Nurjahan. "Women who have completed master's degrees have no intention of holding positions that require fieldwork," she told me. The bank could hire women for junior posts and then promote them faster than men, but this was another contentious issue. "Men do not like having to work under the authority of women," added Nurjahan. "If they could cease their hostility, a lot of these problems could be overcome."

Today, women make up almost 95 percent of the bank's membership but less than 10 percent of its staff. Grameen has many critics in Dhaka's extensive aid community, where hundreds of development organizations jostle for funds from the same pool of donors. Yunus is not terribly bothered by most of the disparaging remarks aimed at his bank: Grameen makes villagers "jump through hoops"; Grameen makes "poverty bearable"; Grameen is a "one-man show"; Grameen is only "redistributing wealth" while "saturating the market with petty traders"; Grameen is not "providing a meaningful increase in productivity." But the one criticism to which he is sensitive is the accusation that Grameen is a "brotherhood."

The criticism is often coupled with skepticism about the bank's explanation for its focus on women. The official version is that women experience poverty more acutely than men and tend to spend more of their income on their children. The skeptics suggest that Grameen targets women mainly because they are easier to keep in line. Men are more difficult to track down and more likely to fight with their bankers. Most of the defaulters in Shajanpur were men. But if women were easier to control, that did not change the fact that they were also poorer. Still, critics asked: If Grameen was interested in bringing about social advances for women, shouldn't it try harder to hire more of them?

It is a sign of his frustration with the issue that Yunus, who likes to engage most problems head on, prefers to skip over this one. When I brought it up, he replied: "There's tremendous pressure for women to quit their jobs. It's very difficult to take them on. We still try but we have not succeeded. This is one area where we have failed miserably. We didn't do it." He spoke quickly. He wanted to move on to the next question.

The likely source of Yunus's frustration are Grameen's donors, who have complained about the low numbers of female bank workers. "It's a blind spot," explained Joan Hubbard, who represented a consortium of donors assembled in the late 1980s. "It's one of those issues that's an untouchable."

Here Yunus finds himself in the uncomfortable stance of having to straddle two very different worlds. While Grameen's Western donors press the bank to adopt affirmative action policies to boost the proportion of women staff—such as promoting them faster, building separate dormitories, or promising women special perks like motorbikes—Yunus has to worry about how the rest of the staff will respond to these actions. To begin with, many staff members do not like the idea of women spending their days walking through the countryside. Should Grameen also initiate programs designed to change their attitudes? Some said yes, and they said the place to begin was with their own wives.

"If the staff really believed in these things, they would practice them at home," explained Maheen Sultan. "The men don't treat their wives as equals. Most of them wouldn't like their wives to be working. Those who have wives working for the bank are supportive of another salary coming in, but very often they're not supportive in sharing the housework and child care. If they work in the same branch the husband would be willing to do his wife's office work so she could spend more time with the child, but he wouldn't be willing to do more of the housework so she could do her office work."

At the heart of the issue was the question of Grameen's mission: Was it a development organization concerned primarily with the advancement of women? Or was it a bank for the poor whose goal was to provide financial services as efficiently and inexpensively as possible? The bank's social and economic goals were not always complementary; in this case a tradeoff was unavoidable: Grameen would have had to slow its growth in order to hire more women staff members.

Most managers also felt that a branch could become profitable in less time if staffed with men. However, male villagers were also capable of investing larger loans than women, and years before, despite this, Grameen had opted to concentrate on village women. If a village woman was a "natural and better fighter," was a woman bank worker also a better fighter?

In recent years, the bank has instituted a quota for women recruits. "But when they hear about the fieldwork, many still back off," Nurjahan explained. She continued to push for motorbikes and other incentives for women, but Yunus was reluctant to adopt such measures. In the meantime, he was exploring the idea of creating "all female areas"—ten branches reporting to an area office, all staffed by women. "If you can do that, women have a chance," he explained. "If you can't, women have no chance."

27

The Logic of Grameen

Because half the population fit into Grameen's target market, managers were supposed to be selective when establishing a new branch. Ideally, the first members admitted should come from the poorest families; next, slightly better off villagers; and last, those at the upper limit of the bank's eligibility criterion. In reality, many branch managers diverge from this ideal because they find it easier to work with the less poor. The same applies to villagers: both Aleya (rich) and Aleya (poor) told me, in identical words: "We don't take the absolutely landless. They *eat* the money." Poorer women are free to form their own groups, but they generally have little influence over other villagers. And they are often reluctant to speak up for themselves. To overcome this, bank workers must actively seek out the poorest villagers and help them into groups.

Many do. Idealism remains an important lubricant in the mechanism of the bank. A few older managers even described themselves to me as "freedom fighters." Having fought against Pakistani soldiers in 1971, they now feel that by slowly building national capacity, they are weaning Bangladesh from its reliance on foreign aid. A number of managers I met had forgone soft jobs in towns, only to be stationed in remote areas away from their families. But even with their best efforts, there is resistance at all levels to taking on the most difficult cases: the bottom poor.

There is no easy solution to this problem, and, indeed, some bank managers feel that it cannot be solved, only controlled. Ultimately, it stems from the bank's fundamental contradiction: trying to achieve financial viability while serving the "poorest of the poor."

"We keep on reminding ourselves, but we don't succeed all the time," Yunus told me. "There are a lot of people within our areas who would have been the first priority of the Grameen Bank but still they're not members."

Branch managers are evaluated on a series of subjective and objective criteria, of which, in theory, financial performance is only one consideration. In practice, just as university admissions offices tend to give more weight to SAT scores than free-form essays, Grameen managers tend to place more emphasis on hard data than qualitative measures. Loan performance is paramount. If a branch manager tries to penetrate the very bottom poor, he will naturally have a tougher time covering his costs. This manager can explain the reasons for his low disbursements in a narrative report, but his area manager, who supervises ten branches, and who is also evaluated on financial performance, may not be interested in the story behind the numbers.

This imperfect evaluation system can lead to inconsistencies and policy contradictions, especially in the hands of less idealistic, more expedient managers. "Encouragement is given officially to take in the poorest," a branch manager told me. "But, informally, some managers give hints that it's better to avoid the very poorest people. They won't say it directly but they'll let you know."

"The people we're talking about have no permanent residence," he added. "They're floaters. One day they're here, one day they're there. Where would we find them?" I recalled what Yunus used to tell his staff in Tangail when they said the same thing: "If you create a condition that will make them want to stay, they will stay."

Today, the pressure on the bank to demonstrate financial viability is stronger than ever and the question of how well the bank is reaching the lowest segment of its target market continues to be debated within the head office. Without a doubt, loans go to the poorest half of the population and, within that subdivision, Grameen certainly reaches a great many extremely poor villagers. But among the staff, some now question whether they are capable of reaching the "poorest of the poor" in large numbers, or whether reaching the poorest "economically active" villagers —say, above the bottom 10 percent—is the most that Grameen, or any bank, can realistically strive for. "Now that we are stabilizing our growth, we'll be making a special drive to reach these people," Muzammel told me in 1992. "We may put in columns on reports: How many widows do you have as borrowers? How many women who have been deserted? Now we think we are in a comfortable position to see whether what is considered 'nonviable poor' can be brought in, in large numbers."

Two years later the debate was still raging. Meanwhile, rumors were circulating in the head office about villagers in Tangail who fell above the eligibility threshold being admitted to the bank. This was strictly prohibited in the *Bidhimala*. Nurjahan had already dispatched spies to the zone. "The situation is unclear right now," she told me in a matter-of-fact tone. "But one thing is *very clear:* If the staff have accepted people above the limit, they will be punished."

Elsewhere, she was experimenting with special loans-in-kind programs targeted at the hard-core poor. "We have to take it upon ourselves to recruit these hard-to-reach people since the members are reluctant to take them. We are trying to bring in those who have absolutely no hope in life."

While the head office investigated Tangail, Yunus had forbidden new groups to be formed in the zone. "We get very concerned when we hear this," he told me. "We want to see the people at the bottom come in, but the tendency for the staff is to look up. I keep arguing, if that's the logic, then you'll be looking for the richest guy in the village. Because the logical conclusion is that you end up as a commercial bank."

28

Begum Rokeya

The forty-mile trip from Dibuapur to Barguna is a half-day's journey. The ferry crossing takes only an hour; the delay is due to the road, which is constructed of loose bricks that shift over time (particularly during floods) leaving fissures large enough to swallow bus wheels. In some stretches, the road is layered with a macadam of makeshift rocks—Bangladesh has almost no stone—and the ride improves. Travelers can thank the rock makers along the roadside. They sit cross-legged atop small foothills of red bricks holding their hammers double-fisted—young girls and old women—smashing bricks into pieces one at a time—chink, chink, chink—from sunup to sundown.

Begum Rokeya lived in a village called Mono Shatoli, three miles from Barguna, a bustling riverside market town with a reputation for contaminated water and dangerous men. The men were actually boys in the youth wings of Bangladesh's political parties who periodically held rallies and played out their frustrations against one another. The water was more hazardous than the boys, however; in Barguna, there was typhoid and cholera.

Begum Rokeya's name had come up several times in conversations with local villagers when I mentioned my interest in the Grameen Bank. Although she had been a member for only three years, she had gained a reputation as something of a Grameen expert. "Talk to Begum Rokeya," villagers advised. "See Begum Rokeya."

Most Muslim women in Bangladesh append the word *Begum* (akin to "missus") after their name. To show respect, bank workers would address Aleya as "Aleya Begum" and Rani as "Rani Begum." But Rokeya made a point of placing the "Begum" before her name. The distinction, I learned, was significant; it implied higher status. The prime minister of

Following the stream to Begum Rokeya's house

Bangladesh is "Begum Khaleda Zia" and never the reverse. But there was another reason for Rokeya's choice, which she later explained: One of Bangladesh's greatest feminist writers was named Begum Rokeya.

Finding Rokeya would not be difficult, villagers explained. Following directions, my translator and I crossed a bridge, passed a row of tea stalls and dry-goods shops, crossed another bridge to a path shaded by date palms and tamarind trees, and followed a muddy stream for about two miles. When the path began to curve right and the stream narrowed, it meant we were close to Rokeya's village—at which point, villagers had instructed us just to ask anyone where Begum Rokeya lived.

Before we had a chance to ask, from behind a row of hedges, a woman called us over. Did she know the house of Begum Rokeya? we asked. Yes, yes, she replied. But first, we must come visit *her* house. I was eager to meet Rokeya. However, from prior experience, I knew that it was next to impossible to decline such an invitation. So rather than put up a struggle, we followed Minara to her house, a stumpy, dilapidated structure. We sat on her bed while she left us to prepare tea and food. Her two-year-old daughter lay asleep on a quilt, with a mosquito net forming a small tent above her.

While Minara was in her kitchen, her husband, Muhammad Abu Hanif, returned home. He carried a transistor radio that he was trying to fix. He called to his wife to bring him some tea, and continued tinkering with the radio. A few minutes before, when I had asked Minara if she was a member of the bank, she had replied: "My husband won't allow it and I cannot disobey him."

"Is your wife a member of the Grameen Bank?" I asked Hanif, after explaining the purpose of my visit to Bangladesh.

"No, I told her not to join," he said, lifting his eyes from his work. "I fix radios and I can't even make ends meet. How will *she* be able to?"

Minara returned with a tray containing tea, eggs, biscuits, and glasses of water sweetened with pink, rose-flavored syrup. She stood by the doorway while the rest of us sat and ate.

"In the future I would like to get a loan myself," Hanif added, after some thought. He said he didn't like the idea of his wife having to join a group with other women. "I'm prepared to go without eating. But I don't want to have to listen to other people."

"If I borrowed money," his wife said, "we could rent out a microphone and loudspeakers [commonly used for weddings and other celebrations] and start a service charging people's batteries."

"If she took a loan, I would constantly have to worry," Hanif said. "She couldn't manage it. Look at her. What's her work? Cooking. Feeding. That's all she does."

"I could manage," Minara said. "I could help him along in life. There's a woman who only sells two seers [about four pounds] of rice a day. Paying the installments is nothing for her."

"I'd take a loan if I could manage it by myself," Hanif said. "I've never objected to women working. But I have to pay house rent every month and I don't want another thing to worry about."

He held up the radio. "Whenever I fix somebody's radio, they always recommend me to others."

"He does very good work," Minara said.

"Let our daughter grow up a bit," Hanif said. "Let things stabilize, then we can try a new tack."

I didn't understand what he was referring to until my translator explained that by "new tack" he probably meant trying to secure their future with a son.

"What if you have another daughter?" I asked.

"That's another question," Hanif said.

Begum Rokeya had gained her reputation by working harder than anyone else at everything she did. Before a Grameen Bank branch opened near Mono Shatoli, she joined a center near her father's village six miles away. One morning each week, she left her house at 6:00 A.M. for the three-hour walk to her meeting. Now she lived fifteen yards from the center house she had established after a branch opened nearby.

Rokeya juggled several businesses. She raised chickens, goats, and ducks. She had two cows. She traded rice and pulses. She made molasses. She planted coconut, date, banana, and guava trees. And she grew her own vegetables, some for sale. Her husband, Muhammad Alum Munshi, owned a tea stall along the path to Barguna, and Rokeya put some of her loan capital into his business so he could stock a larger assortment of biscuits, breads, and snacks. Recently, the couple had begun leasing land for rice cultivation.

Rokeya was grinding chili peppers into a paste for curry when I arrived. Her twelve-year-old daughter, Amena, sat beside her chopping green beans. A younger daughter, Taslima, nine years old, was outside taking a bath. The girls had just returned from school and Rokeya was rushing to prepare lunch. She apologized for her lack of hospitality and then disappeared into the kitchen, returning with a bowl of puffed rice mixed with fried lentils and mustard oil. "Before, when people used to come to my house like you've come," she explained, "I would have tea and many snacks before them. But now when people come, I'm overcome with shame. My heart wants to give you more. But I can't. I have to think first about money."

Rokeya squatted on the mud floor, leaning forward, mashing the red chilies with a stone mortar and pestle. Noticing my interest in her work, she commented: "You see my daughter. When I was even younger, my mother-in-law made me grind chilies. I don't make her do it. She's a young child. Won't her hands burn? Later on she'll have enough of it."

At thirty, Rokeya had a healthy glow in her face but her body seemed tiny beneath her sari. Only when she stood up to reach for something on a shelf did I realize that she was pregnant. Later, she told me that she was in her eighth month.

We sat in the main room of the house. One door led to a front room with a porch, another to her kitchen. A ladder led upstairs, where the family slept. Against one wall stood a wooden chicken box with a padlock. The previous year thieves had stolen half a dozen chickens while Rokeya was visiting her father. In another corner, bees swarmed around a hive. Rokeya did not seem to mind their buzzing. The money she would earn selling the honey would help pay for her daughters' schooling.

After the birth of a son six years before—their third child—Rokeya and Alum had decided against having more children. A government family-planning officer had offered 125 takas and a free sari if Rokeya would undergo a tubal ligation. She and Alum considered the offer but at the last minute opted for a contraceptive injection—just in case.

When their son, Ali Haider, was four years old, he fell into a pond and drowned. Afterward, it took Rokeya more than a year to get pregnant again. Now everybody was praying for another son. "The government says to have only two kids," Rokeya said. "But my husband has his heart set on a son. And my daughters have their hearts set on another brother."

When a Grameen Bank branch opened near her village, Rokeya asked Alum to tell the manager that she wanted to establish a center. She received permission to transfer from the other branch and soon began holding meetings and training sessions in her house. For six months, her home served as the center house. "My house was so crowded," she recalled. "People said, 'How can you take it?' But I put up with it. I supplied all the tables and chairs, betel leaf, tea, snacks, all from my own expense. Some people came in the morning for training and stayed until evening.

"Now my hope is that in the future I'll continue to improve my situation. And I hope, God willing, that we get no bad name for this center. To this end, we've selected people very carefully. With unethical people, can you do an honorable thing? This is a matter of thirty people. You have to be very strict."

"Do you take in the absolutely landless?" I inquired.

"Those are the people that Grameen Bank has targeted to help," Rokeya said. "But some people who are absolutely landless can't manage their loans. We have two of them in our center, and in a new group they have two more, so that's four—if the new group is confirmed." Rokeya pointed outside to a woman walking along the path by the center house. "Her husband just paddles a boat. They don't have any land. Nobody wanted to take her in, but I had faith in her. She and her husband won't be bad debtors. I've known them since we were children. They're well behaved and their children are also well behaved. God willing, they'll manage. Even if they don't have land, they're not thieves. Besides, they

Taslima and Rokeya

don't live far away. If they lived far away we wouldn't take them. Otherwise, on what trust should we accept them? Somebody who's got nothing and we don't even know their characters? On what faith?"

Taslima returned from her bath after having washed her school clothes and changed into a T-shirt and harem pants. At nine, she was still young enough to play in these clothes. Amena, just three years older, dressed more conservatively, in a knee-length tunic over baggy trousers, with a scarf draped over her shoulders.

Rokeya served rice, potatoes, bean curry, and milk. She squatted by the fire, resting on her heels, watching Taslima and Amena eat; she would not take any food until everyone else had eaten. When Taslima finished, she cleaned her plate by curling a finger and sliding it over her bowl, alternating directions like a window washer, until she had scooped up every grain of rice. She poured water over her eating hand, her right hand, to wash it, and let the water fall into her bowl, where she mixed it with the remaining film of curry and drank it.

The past two years had been a struggle, Rokeya said. Alum had gotten into debt with a local moneylender and had used part of her loan capital to cover his payments. "We've been running the tea shop on borrowed money," she said, referring to the loans Alum had taken from money-lenders. "If you run something on that kind of money it can never prosper. That's why we've been behind. But this year, I've repaid that debt. Now, with God's grace, I'll stay in the Grameen Bank and I won't borrow money from anywhere else."

The theft of her chickens last year had shaken her up. "I had gone to visit my father's house and my husband sent a letter," she said. "When my father read the letter aloud, tears fell from my eyes. He said not to feel too upset, but a woman feels a lot of attachment to her chickens. We work hard to raise them." All the effort she had put into establishing her center earlier in the year had also sapped her energy. But none of these problems accounted fully for the waves of despair that had been hitting her recently. It was Ali Haider, she said. "Ever since he died, my body has been drying up and my mind has been eaten away with worry. And it has seemed that there has been even more scarcity in the house-hold. Ever since that woman in my group died in childbirth, I've had a fear in my heart. And I ask everybody to pray for me that Allah will keep me well."

Rokeya excused herself to eat and I joined Taslima and Amena in the front room. Amena asked me my name. When I replied, she said, "Like David Copperfield?"

The front door and windows were wide open and sunlight flooded in. Much of the life of the house took place in this room. At one end was a guest bed where, in the early evenings, Alum sat and chatted with friends over tea and betel nut. At the other end was a wooden table with three chairs where Alum worked on his tea shop accounts in the evenings and the children studied by the flame of a kerosene burner. Rokeya occasion-ally entertained her in-laws here, although it is customary for women to sit in the inner room.

The girls had their schoolbooks open on the table and were preparing to do homework. Above their heads, on wooden shelves suspended from the ceiling by ropes, were piles of old lesson books, their pages flaking from the humidity. On the shelf sat a rusty geometry set containing a protractor and compass, a jar of glue, a few pencils, and one fountain pen, which the girls shared.

My presence was clearly a distraction. Taslima had a mischievous grin on her face. When I asked what was up, she explained that a few minutes before a couple of neighbors had poked their heads in the door asking about me, and she'd told them that I was a writer who had come to interview her mother because she had been selected as the smartest woman in the Grameen Bank.

Amena broke out in laughter, pulling her scarf over her mouth. Taslima giggled. She was the more carefree sister. She could still make up stories and run in the fields and play the games of village children, at least for a few more years. In a half hour, in fact, she was going to meet some friends to play in a field next to her uncle's house. She explained the game: "There are two teams and two areas. Everybody holds hands and one member of the other team will try to hold her breath as long as she can in the enemy's area and touch someone and go back before she lets out her breath, but they try to capture her first."

Taslima looked just like her mother, but she had her father's playful personality. Amena was the reverse: she had Alum's heavier features, but she was quiet and forthright like Rokeya. When the two were together, it was Taslima who did most of the talking. Her favorite subject in school was English. She was a star pupil. With Amena's prodding, she recited a nursery rhyme she had memorized a few years before:

> There was an old woman, she lived in a shoe
> She had eleven children—she didn't know what to do.
> She gave them some soup without any bread
> And beat them all soundly and sent them to bed.
>
> There was a young woman, she lived in a shoe
> She had only two children, so she always knew what to do.
> She gave them some fish and dal with their bread,
> She played with them nicely and sent them to bed.

Rokeya finished her lunch and joined us. She usually rested for a half hour at this time of day. Today she said she could chat for a while. She sat on the edge of the guest bed beside Amena. She was smaller than her daughter and her feet barely reached the ground.

Rokeya had gotten married when she was twelve years old, the same age as Amena. "At the time, I had no understanding of what it meant to be husband and wife," Rokeya said. "I was completely shy and simple. I wouldn't understand things if they were said even the least bit indirectly. My husband had to explain everything to me."

After leaving the security of her father's house, Rokeya was terribly anxious in her new family. Would she live up to their expectations? Would they approve of the way she cooked and kept house? Had the dowry been sufficient? Would they like her appearance?

The answer to the last question, unfortunately, was no—and shortly after Alum brought his new bride into the family, his parents demanded that he divorce her.

Amena stared down at her math textbook, open on her lap, while her mother spoke. She had a test coming up in a few days. Taslima sat on the stoop combing her hair.

"My mother-in-law gave me a very hard time," Rokeya continued. "And why did she do that? Because I was dark. She wanted a fair-skinned bride."

Alum's parents kept pressuring him to "return" Rokeya. Every time they heard of a man looking to marry off a fair-skinned daughter, they intensified their efforts. Why stay married to a dark girl when you can have a fair wife? they asked. Neighbors made comments about Rokeya's appearance to Alum's parents. "Your family has a little land," they said. "Why has Alum married such a dark girl?" It was generally agreed: The family could have fared much better in their choice of daughter-in-law.

But Alum wouldn't budge. "My husband would tell them," Rokeya explained, " 'She may be black outside. But inside her heart is not black.' " Alum was greatly impressed by Rokeya's industry and common sense. The way she always offered him things before he asked for them made him think that she could read his mind. And he never once saw her behave in a disrespectful manner to anyone.

"She used to fast and say her prayers five times daily," Alum told me one afternoon in his tea shop. "She never lied. If there was a problem in the household, she solved it herself. It was difficult to go against my parents' wishes, but she was a loving wife and she had faith in me."

Alum also believed that Rokeya was *lokki,* a concept derived from the Hindu goddess, Lakshmi, who is associated with prosperity, goodness, and happiness. A woman who is *lokki* is thrifty and hard-working and knows how to manage her household wisely. She brings prosperity and good fortune to her family, and her husband is deemed fortunate. His wife's industry shines favorably on him.

This was important because Alum was only a fair businessman himself, and he seemed aware of the fact. "I would be nothing without

Begum Rokeya," he told me on more than one occasion. He was a small, wiry, affable man with bright eyes and a quick wit, who loved to sit in his tea stall and weave improbable tales for his customers. But he was not a fighter, and when the family's land was distributed among the five brothers, he ended up with less than his fair share. He said he was not bitter about this. His brothers were more ambitious so he let them have their way. But privately, Rokeya admitted that their lives would have been a great deal easier if Alum had received his full inheritance.

Taslima jumped up from the stoop, tossed her comb on the table, and scooped up her English reader. She dropped down on the edge of a chair and glanced around the room. She wore red-and-white plastic sandals that she occasionally clicked together like Dorothy. I asked her what she wanted to do when she grew up.

"A job," she replied.

"What kind?" I asked.

"Office work."

"I want to be a teacher," Amena said. "Maybe a high school teacher."

"Do you study hard?"

"Not too much," Taslima replied.

"After we come home from school, we study a few hours," added Amena. "Then at night from six to ten or seven to eleven. And sometimes in the morning from seven to eight."

When Amena had begun reading years earlier, Rokeya used to sit with her and try to follow along as Amena passed over the letters in her exercise book, sounding out each one. Rokeya had been pulled out of school in the third grade so that a younger brother could attend classes instead. Only fragments of her early learning remained. She recognized a few words and could make others out laboriously. When she joined the bank it had taken her two days to learn how to sign her name. (Although she could not read the writings of her namesake, Begum Rokeya, she knew her story well. Begum Rokeya was born in 1880 in northern Bangladesh. Her parents did not permit her to attend school, but at night, with the help of her brother, she taught herself to read, and in later years became an acclaimed writer and social activist, fighting against the subordination of women in Bengali society.)

"As much as I wanted to study, my father could not afford it," Rokeya told me. "Now so many people say to me, 'You're a poor woman. Are you going to make your daughters study?' And they try to discourage me from sending Amena to school.

" 'You have trouble just eating and dressing yourselves,' they say.

'Your husband keeps on wearing the same clothes over and over. They're old and torn.'

"For the girls' school fees he just had to pay 112 takas. But even if he had to borrow the money, he would pay for school.

"Still, he asks me sometimes, 'Shall I educate my daughter or shall I send her away?' "

"Send her away" meant marriage. Amena was a pretty girl, slightly fairer than her mother, though still dark-skinned by Bengali standards. With her education level, her parents had a reasonably good chance of finding a well-schooled son-in-law. But education can be a double-edged sword. Most men do not like to marry women who are better educated than they are. Which means the longer Amena stays in school, the fewer men will want to marry her. Of course, the longer she stays in school, the better her prospects of landing a job as a schoolteacher. But that's a long shot.

Rokeya prayed that her daughter would be blessed with all three: a good education, a good husband, and a good job. She was in no hurry. It was Alum who felt more of an immediate pull. Young brides are often less expensive to marry off, and there is always a father's fear that his unmarried daughter will bring shame upon herself. The longer he waits the more opportunity for this to happen. Then no one would marry her.

And, of course, each year the school fees and the price of books, supplies, and school uniforms increase. "No matter how much I suffer now," Rokeya said firmly, "if she's happy, then I'll be happy. If I can educate my daughter and her fate is good, then she'll get a good husband. And if I can't, she'll stay spiritless inside the house."

"Some people only pray to Allah," she said. "But don't you need to try yourself? If I don't educate my daughter, can I hope to find her an educated husband? No. Never."

29

The Death of Ali Haider

I visited Rokeya a few days later while the girls were in school. It was mid-morning and Rokeya had been up since the dawn call to prayer. She had cooked breakfast for her family, swept the house, collected new cane screens to repair the center house, fed her chickens and ducks, made sticks of dung and straw for cooking fuel, washed her pots and pans, ground chilis and turmeric, and let her two cows out to graze.

Now, as she shelled peas, she began to reminisce about Ali Haider: how he would never let his sisters use his personal glass or plate; how he would never wash his hands in a bowl of water after someone else had touched it; how handsome he looked the day he left to visit his grandfather's house, the last time she saw him alive.

"He had just stopped wetting the bed," Rokeya said. "The hard work was over."

"The way he died left me in a terrible state," she explained. "Nobody else turned out like my son. Even my daughters turned out black. My father used to say, 'The boy is so fair and good-looking, only four years old but already quite tall.' The day he went to visit my father's house, he waved and said, 'Mother, I'm going with my uncle, I'll come back in the morning.'

"When he arrived there he asked my mother, 'Grandmother, can you make puffed rice?' So they boiled the rice and put it in the sun to dry and then they husked it. And while my mother was husking the rice, he was sitting on the porch and playing. In our villages, little children play by making holes in the ground and putting date pits in them.

"In the meantime, he had to go to the bathroom. Amena took him to the side of the pond where there's a fence. When she went to get the washing jug, she made him stand beside the haystack next to the pond, and she told him, 'You stand here.' She couldn't find the jug so she went back to get him, but he was already gone.

"Around my father's house there are three paths: a southern way that leads by the pond, a northern path, and another way in between. My son fell along the middle path, in the place where they had cut the ground for a new fence. But Amena thought, 'Oh, I left him standing here. He must have gone this way.' Allah made her take the wrong path.

"At that time my son's health was good. He was round. He'd just eaten three helpings of rice with milk. So he had his belly full of rice.

"All this weight took him below the water.

"My father had tied a fishing net to a bamboo stick and called out, 'Ali Haider, would you like to come fishing with me? Go put on your sandals, Ali Haider, do you want to come with me?' Soon he realized, Was Ali Haider there? No. And then my father dropped his net on that spot. He knew that Ali Haider had fallen into the fishing pond."

Rokeya paused to wipe her eyes with a corner of her sari. "After two daughters I got a son. He was everybody's darling. He was four years and two months old when he died. But I had been scared to put him in the water so that he could break his fear of the water. I hadn't let him go in the pond. I used to fill jugs and wash him. He even used to come and sleep with his father if it rained.

"My father screamed and ran. Everybody was eating. They left their food and ran out and then Amena said, 'He was standing here.'

"My father and his brother ran around looking for him. One ran this way and one ran that way. My uncle found him. Then my brother went for a doctor. They tried so hard to save the drowned boy, but nothing helped.

"At the time, I was here repairing the porch. The mud was still wet. It was the first day of Ramadan and I was fasting. I felt terrible. I didn't know why. I told Taslima, 'Go and get some water and bathe my head. Go and fill a bucket. Why is my body doing this?'

"She bathed my head from the bucket and then I smoothed the mud and took a bath. I said my prayers and lay down to rest.

"But my body seemed to be breaking apart. My aunt came and asked, 'Why have you become so weak? Has the house-repairing work exhausted you?'

"I said, 'Aunt, I don't know why but my arms and feet seem to be breaking up.' At that time, he was already dead. I didn't understand that it was for this reason I was suffering.

"Later, I cooked for the break of the fast. A person who's fasting doesn't have much strength. Meanwhile, I sent word to my husband that I was feeling ill.

" 'Could you bring a coconut for me?' I said.

"He sent one over with a neighbor. I drank the coconut water and said my prayers again. Then the news reached my husband. My father had sent a messenger and told him, 'Say that his father-in-law is very ill.'

"So that's what he told him. My husband came running and found me. He said, 'You and I better have some rice quickly.'

" 'What's wrong, what's going on?' I said.

" 'You serve rice quickly,' he said to me. 'Father and Taslima can eat later.'

"I said, 'Tell me what is going on. What has happened?'

"He said, 'I need to go to your father's house. I have work.'

" 'What work do you have?' I said.

"He said, 'I have work.'

"I served him rice and I took some, but I couldn't swallow it. I had this feeling that somebody had died. But it hadn't come to me that it was my own son.

"Then I told my husband that I couldn't eat. 'Somebody has died,' I said.

"He said, 'If you can't eat, then just leave it.'

"I didn't change my clothes. I didn't even put the *burkah* on. I put it in a bag and set off walking. And my husband, who walks so well, that day I was walking faster than he.

"When we came to my father's village I saw that there were a lot of people gathered at the ghat. Everybody said, 'Your father is ill. He vomited once or twice. The doctor came but now he's better. You don't have to hurry. Calm yourself and go.' But that didn't reassure me.

"Then I arrived at the house and I looked through the crack in the door and I saw that there was a dead body covered with a sheet. And as soon as I put my foot on the doorstep, I saw that it was small.

"If my father had died, why would it be small?

"Then I saw my father sitting there. The room was filled with people. As soon as I set foot inside, I said, 'Who is it that's so small?' and I pulled the sheet.

"I saw that it was my golden moon, lying there as if he were sleeping. His face had grown bigger and he'd become even fairer. What my heart felt, I can't tell you. My heart told me, 'Bang your head against this pillar and die.'

"I went to hit my head but somebody put their hand in the way.

"All through the night, I sat on the boy's bed and looked at him. With God's grace, there was no blemish at all. There was no disfigurement.

"All night I looked over his body, his hands and his feet. That he was from my womb nobody would have believed. If somebody had told me that God had made him with some imperfection, even then perhaps I might have gotten some consolation. I spent all night like this.

"Oh, Allah." Rokeya sighed. "Then we brought him home and bathed him. His father was in such a state that he got up at night and ran to his bed and then ran to the edge of the pond and screamed, 'Ali Haider.'

"Ever since that boy died, the house has been tense and strained. And we haven't been able to struggle out of it. But I say to Allah, 'If we can just get through this year, then we'll get by.' "

30

Don't I Think of These Things?

*W*hen I dropped by the following afternoon, Rokeya was sitting with her sister-in-law, Parveen, who had recently joined a group in her center. Parveen was preparing for an afternoon training session and she was worried because two of her members kept forgetting the rules when the manager quizzed them. At this rate, they would have to undergo another week of training before the bank would confirm the group. As center chief, Rokeya was responsible for the group's training. But she was tired. This year, she had already gone through the routine five times.

In the center house, Parveen sat alongside four women in a straight line. She occupied the rightmost position, the designated spot for the group chairman. The five women wore five brightly colored saris: green, yellow, pink, purple, and orange. The branch manager wore gray trousers and a light blue, short-sleeve button shirt. He sat cross-legged six feet from the women, with a notepad on his lap. Outside, a few children tried to peek through holes in the bamboo walls. Darts of sunlight flew across the hut. The manager saluted as Rokeya entered. "From now on if anyone comes even one minute late, they'll stand outside," he was saying. "This is not how meetings are supposed to run. I'll empty the center. I don't care. What a state you're in!"

He had been drilling the same points for a week.

"Parveen Begum: If you leave the bank, what happens to your personal savings?"

"We get it back."

"Sufiya Begum: Who will keep the accounts of the group fund?"

"The group chairman."

"Monwara Begum: How much is required in the Group Fund to buy shares?"

Parveen (left) and her group members

A pause, some whispering.

"*Only* Monwara Begum," the manager interrupted.

"Five hundred takas."

"If you buy a share, that means you own part of the bank. Do you get it back if you leave? Hasina Begum?"

"Yes."

"How?"

Silence.

The manager waited a few seconds, then, with a sigh, said: "You have to sell your share back to the group. Monwara Begum: What are the three types of savings?"

"Personal, special . . ."

"And?" the manager said.

Silence.

"The children's welfare fund. Khobirunessa Begum: What are some vegetables you can grow in winter?"

"Beans, cauliflower, carrots, red spinach."

"Also peas, marrow, tomatoes," the manager added.

Rokeya stood off to the side, occasionally prompting the women. She pointed out the two group members she had mentioned before, the ones who were destitute. "These people break their backs just to feed their stomachs," she whispered. "Their mothers and fathers weren't able to teach them even the most basic things. That's why they're having difficulty learning."

"Parveen Begum," the manager said, "what is decision number six?"

"We shall keep our families small."

"Hasina Begum: number three?"

"We shall not live in broken houses. We shall build better houses."

"Monwara Begum: number ten?"

"We shall drink tubewell water. If we don't have a tubewell, we shall boil the water."

"Good," the manager said. He smiled.

I asked Rokeya if the teachings of the Sixteen Decisions had been new to her when she first heard them. "We knew that water from the stream was bad," she said. "We knew that germs have a good environment in the ponds. That you have to drink tubewell water, keep clean and tidy, plant vegetables throughout the year—most of us were already aware of these things."

"For some it is hard work to learn them," she added, "but for most of us the Grameen Bank has only reminded us of what we already know."

"What about the discipline of the meeting?" I asked. "Is that something new?"

"In any work, in anything you do, don't you need discipline?" Rokeya said.

It was getting late and the manager had a two-mile walk back to the branch and several hours of paperwork to finish up after the session. He closed his notebook. "Remember," he said, wrapping up, "you have to pave the way for your children's lives. Tomorrow, I'll come again in the afternoon and we'll do the accounting."

Afterward, Rokeya felt that she had disappointed the manager. As center chief, she was never completely sure how to behave. Should she have been tougher on the women? Was the manager upset with her? It was so difficult to find time these days to help group members study. "A lot of times people say to me, 'Why didn't you scold them? Why didn't you tell them off?' But is that my role? I want the center to flourish so that we can make a name for ourselves. But what I had to do I've done already. If they don't listen to my advice then what's the point of turning them sour? They feel bad enough coming late. Don't you remember how they looked? And if I scold them, too, what would be the point? All people have a sense of dignity."

Back at her house, Rokeya reassured Parveen. Parveen had been hesitant to accept the two extremely poor villagers in her group when they came forward and said to her, "Listen, would you be able to get us into the Grameen Bank?" She had turned to Rokeya for advice. "Those people are good," Rokeya said. "They'll do business with the money." At her former branch, Rokeya had seen other women in similarly desperate circumstances come a long way, even after just two loans. These people were used to hard work, she explained, and they were loyal to anyone who gave them a chance.

Reassuring Parveen seemed to raise Rokeya's spirits. By contrast to that of the women she was championing, her situation did not seem so dire. Her family ate three meals a day; the women Parveen was worried about ate only twice a day, and during some times of the year, only once. They were "absolutely landless"; Rokeya and Alum were only "functionally landless"; their small plot of land was well under the bank's eligibility criterion.

The distinction was important. Even a little land—one or two tenths of an acre—provides a slim margin of food security and gives a family the recognition of being "permanent residents" in an area, a necessary designation for villagers who wish to join the bank. Members are reluctant to accept people in a group who they feel are not anchored. This was what troubled Parveen.

"They'll work the money properly," Rokeya said. "One of them has this cockerel business," she added, turning to me. "They have only one child. They live on someone else's land; they've been existing like this." She seemed impressed.

Rokeya wasn't telling Parveen anything new, but she appeared to be getting through to her. "The people who have courage," Parveen finally agreed, "they'll be able to pay the installments better."

"Inshallah," Rokeya said.

"Inshallah," Parveen said.

Like most villagers in Bangladesh, Rokeya would say *"Inshallah"*—God willing—almost reflexively whenever she referred to any future event or dared to be hopeful. It is remarkable how often the reflex manifests itself during the course of a day even among Dhaka's secular elite. The electricity will return, the phone call will go through, and *Dynasty* will be televised at its regularly scheduled time—*Inshallah*. On a short flight I took from the north of Bangladesh to Dhaka, the pilot announced: "Thank you for flying Biman Airways flight 492 from Saidpur to Dhaka. We will be flying at an altitude of 11,000 feet. *Inshallah,* our flight time will be forty-five minutes."

"Who controls the future?" I asked.

"Of course it's all Allah," Parveen said. "Do you know what's going to happen to you?"

"It's not as if Allah is going to do everything," Rokeya countered. "It's not as if it's *all* Allah. You've got to do something, too.

"Some of the problems people face are the consequences of their own actions," she added. "Say one place is good and one place is bad. If I can see that and I still go to the bad place, then I brought that on myself. Did Allah tell me to take the bad path and not the good one? Is that Allah or is that me? Some people, when they suffer, call themselves unfortunate and blame Allah. And then they say, 'Why are so many people so poor?' "

"When you can't tell and something happens to you, that's Allah. And when you bring it on yourself, that's you," Parveen said.

"If you want your life to go well, you have to learn how to choose well," Rokeya said. "You have to look where you're going."

"Does Allah always give alternatives?" I asked, prodding.

"Yes," Rokeya said. "You know I'm poor. God has made me poor. But I can raise ducks and chickens. I can work with date palms to make molasses. I have a cow. I can give the cow grass and feed and then if I sell the milk, I can buy a *seer* [about two pounds] of rice. Then I can sell my ducks' and chickens' eggs and make some money. Don't I think of these things?"

"The Grameen Bank has provided us with pumpkin seeds," she added. "My husband has to sit in the tea shop all day, so he can't do much work at home. But still, you have to put something in your stomach. You have to pay for the two daughters who study. You have to keep paying installments. So I planted the pumpkins myself. Now, if some pumpkins grow, then I won't have to pay 8 or 10 takas to buy them. *Inshallah*."

31

The Wisdom in Smallness

Dipal had gotten married before assuming the post of zonal manager in Patuakhali, but his wife had decided to remain in Dhaka to finish her studies. "I didn't want to disturb her education," he recalled. At night, he wrote poems and sent them to his wife. "For two and a half years we were apart," he said.

He was spending most of his days traveling throughout the zone, overseeing branch openings and tailoring Grameen's systems to Patuakhali. In Rangpur, Daiyan was similarly experimenting with new programs and modifications to procedures.

Though Bangladesh is geographically small, each district differs markedly—so much so, that Bangladeshis believe that temperaments also vary sharply from district to district, or about every thirty to forty miles. In my travels, I have been told that Chittagonians are "too political," Sylhetis are "into themselves," people from Noakhali are "still barbarians," those from Barisal are "excellent cooks," and women from Bogra are "very forward" and "too smart for their own good." Residents of Comilla are "progressive," people from Mymensingh are "tough," and those from Kushtia, the birthplace of Rabindranath Tagore, speak the "purest and most beautiful Bangla." Bangladeshis generally feel "neutral" toward their countrymen from Khulna and Jessore, and they respect people from Rangpur and Rajshahi. Villagers from Patuakhali tend to "like luxuries" but are "uneducated and lazy."

Folklore aside, the disparities are real and Dipal and Daiyan had to respond to them in their respective zones. Patuakhali, on the Bay of Bengal, has a high level of salinity in its soil, which prevents villagers in certain areas from planting more than a single rice crop each year. Elsewhere in Bangladesh, two and three rice crops are the norm.

Rangpur sits on the western bank of the Jamuna River, which carries water from the Himalayas and then overflows into Bangladesh. As a rule, Bangladesh has either too much or too little water. Eighty percent of the rain falls between May and September while only 6 percent falls between November and March. In Rangpur, this disparity is even more pronounced. During the winter and early spring, after the monsoon and before the Himalayan snowmelt, Rangpur gets as dry as Arizona. Occasional patches of green paddy and yellow wheat stand out like fresh paint on weathered wood. There is a good deal of water in Rangpur, but it lies forty or fifty feet below the ground, and only well-to-do landowners can afford to bring it to the surface and harvest a winter crop.

Both Rangpur and Patuakhali have poor communications and transport. Road travel in Patuakhali is interrupted by frequent water crossings. Rangpur is cut off from the rest of the country by the vast Jamuna River. (A bridge spanning the river is expected to be completed in the late 1990s.) In both areas, commodity prices fluctuate unpredictably according to local supply, so it is vital for poor villagers to enjoy access to inexpensive credit. Otherwise, they would be forced to buy and sell goods at the least advantageous times of the year.

Southern Patuakhali is populated by deep-sea fishermen who spend much of their lives in trawlers on the Bay of Bengal. They are notorious for taking multiple wives. According to the literal word of the Koran, a Muslim is permitted four wives, but most of the Bangladeshis I met frowned upon polygamy. "The prophet Muhammad married four times," a villager explained, "but for the purpose of giving low women dignity. People who do it here just have bad characters."

As for the fishermen: "Many of them lose their lives at sea," explained a Grameen manager. "They like to enjoy themselves when they come home."

A woman named Rohema, a self-described "number two wife," told me that her husband had married her for her looks. "If my husband dies what will happen to me?" she said. Her husband's sons from his first marriage were loyal to their birth mother, and Rohema feared that they might throw her out of the house. She had no children of her own. "That's why I joined the Grameen Bank. I'm keeping my own savings in the bank and taking loans."

"The house is in my name," she went on. "And all my deeds are kept at the Grameen Bank." Even with these precautions, Rohema did not seem to feel very secure.

In Patuakhali, Dipal authorized loans for fishing nets and boat purchases and seasonal trading. The problems faced by fishermen taking multiple wives could often be addressed with house loans. And since these women were always in danger of being widowed young, their livelihood depended, even more than in other districts, on their ability to support themselves. Dipal also distributed alum crystals for water purification in the south of Patuakhali because the wells, due to their proximity to the sea and the high water table, are often contaminated.

In Rangpur, Daiyan provided loans for low-investment technology such as threshing machines, and for inexpensive pumps to allow villagers to irrigate small plots of land. The villagers had requested these and other services. And because the members selected their own activities, and because credit could be transformed into any asset instantaneously —in Patuakhali, fishing nets; in Tangail, looms; in Chittagong, salt flats—Grameen did not have to recalibrate its program in each district. Credit is always a local resource.

When villagers requested investment advice, Yunus told his staff to reply: "The Grameen Bank has lots of money, but it has no ideas." Members had to come up with their own ideas. A great deal has been written about how the Grameen Bank has "transformed" people's lives, but in truth, Yunus has always maintained a fairly modest conception about what his bank can do for any individual villager. In short, not very much. Grameen can provide resources and information about things like health, sanitation, and child care. Beyond that, people have to help themselves.

Grameen's approach—focusing on the individual in need as the agent of change—is diametrically opposite to that taken by conventional development organizations, which typically see *themselves* as agents of change on behalf of those in need. This is one reason why large governmental or multilateral aid agencies typically follow a top-heavy *deductive* methodology, by contrast to the *inductive* methodology favored by Grameen (which Yunus has termed *action research*). The key distinction is the direction of information flow: Deduction moves from the general to the particular, induction from the particular to the general. Deduction begins with theories; induction begins with observations.

While deduction is a closed system, induction, or "action research," remains open: Because it is impossible to observe every occurrence of anything, it is impossible to prove anything through induction, which is precisely where its advantage lies in the unpredictable field of development. Following an inductive approach, one has to remain open to new information and experiences: an experiment or "project" is never complete, an argument never resolved.

Gigantic development projects in the Third World are usually conceived through a deductive process initiated in the First World, and are justified by economic theories rather than by prior performance in a similar milieu. Since everything in deduction rests on a set of premises, even tiny oversights at the outset can, in complex systems, lead to massive problems. In physics, the technical name for this is "a sensitive dependence on initial conditions." It is commonly referred to in Chaos Theory as the Butterfly Effect, and, among other things, it explains why, despite great technological advances, mankind still cannot predict the weather accurately beyond a couple of days.

It follows that before something is attempted on a large scale, it should be tested on a small scale. Logical enough, one would think; and yet, throughout Bangladesh and the Third World, one can point to hundreds of costly development projects that would have benefited from this simple advice. Yunus likes to refer to them collectively as the "graveyard."

One of the largest development fiascos in Bangladesh are Deep Tubewells. Since the 1970s, the World Bank has pressured the Bangladesh government to sink tens of thousands of Deep Tubewells (DTWs) across the country (each well costing between $12,000 and $30,000). In the early 1970s, before the price of oil escalated worldwide, these wells seemed invaluable for a nation that badly needed to modernize agriculture and had millions of acres of land that required irrigation.

Over the years, however, it became apparent that even with top-notch management it was extremely difficult for Bangladeshi farmers to operate these wells at a profit. The wells were costly to run; for efficient use, dozens of villagers had to share them. This meant they had to work out elaborate systems to channel the water to as many as sixty individually owned plots of land. The farmers also had to figure out how to divide up overhead expenses. Without an innovative management system, such as Yunus introduced in the Three Share Farm in Jobra, the farmers could not grow enough rice to offset the costs of diesel fuel or electricity, plus other farm inputs. And, of course, if these were typical villages, there would be local political interference, and countless feuds and clan rivalries that would only make matters worse.

Nevertheless, the wells were sunk by the thousands. And today, a great many of them have fallen into the hands of rich landlords, or fallen into disrepair, leaving the people of Bangladesh owing the World Bank hundreds of millions of dollars, with little development to show for their money. A study of a few hundred, or even a few dozen, wells would have exposed the problems.

Deduction requires great foresight. Induction is self-adjusting and better suited to problem solving because errors can be absorbed by the system.

Induction is also humble in that it resembles the way human beings learn—bit by bit, stumbling and correcting themselves as they go along. And as Yunus has demonstrated, the greatest advantage of "action research" is that, as you proceed with your research, you build an institution that becomes more and more adept at solving its own problems. *"Logic* is the study of ideal method in thought and research," wrote Will Durant in *The Story of Philosophy*. "[I]t is a dull study for most of us, and yet the great events in the history of thought are the improvements men have made in their methods of thinking and research."

No doubt, Yunus stumbled here and there on his many walks through Jobra. When, after four years in the village, he landed upon an intervention that seemed perfectly suited to the villagers' needs, he tried it out with a few dozen people, then a few hundred, then a few thousand. Along the way, he tinkered with his system until he got it running smoothly. In his 1973 landmark book *Small Is Beautiful,* the economist E. F. Schumacher provided an exquisite rationale for this approach: "There is wisdom in smallness," Schumacher wrote, "if only on account of the smallness and patchiness of human knowledge, which relies on experiment far more than on understanding."

Even with all its experimentation, Grameen would falter and scramble to right itself over the years. It would take Yunus more than a decade before he would generalize his findings in thousands of villages to all of Bangladesh and, ultimately, to many parts of the world.

32

Armed with Information

In 1986 and 1987, Grameen opened 170 branches, bringing the number to 396, and hired 2,000 more employees. During the two years, the bank disbursed 1.4 billion takas ($45 million), and its membership grew to 339,000 villagers, 80 percent women. In 1987, in recognition of his "outstanding contribution in rural development," Yunus was awarded the Independence Day Award, Bangladesh's highest civilian honor.

As the bank expanded, Grameen's system became the subject of a contentious debate within the development community. The most common criticism aimed at the bank was that its loans were used primarily for small-scale, low-yielding activities that would ultimately lead to diminishing returns for villagers. The criticism came largely from theorists outside Bangladesh, but Grameen's own managers were also concerned about borrowers not "scaling up" their activities. As one branch manager put it, "Bamboo is not going to save our country."

In 1986, the Bangladeshi government handed Grameen an opportunity to experiment with a new approach to scale up members' productivity. The Ministry of Fisheries was looking to unload a development project that had been a financial disaster: an eight-hundred-pond fish farm in western Bangladesh. Under government control, the ponds had fallen into the hands of wealthy individuals and the hatchery had been neglected. As much as 80 percent of each year's catch was stolen by organized poachers. Properly managed, Yunus felt the farm could be a "veritable gold mine" with the capacity of producing $1 million worth of fish each year. Research had shown that fish farms had the potential to produce many times their current average yields in Bangladesh. Yunus envisioned his staff turning the farm around and, over time, transferring management to thousands of Grameen members, who would then run the farm jointly and share the profits.

Back in 1981, the bank had begun experimenting with collective loans or "joint enterprises" to groups and centers to finance larger businesses. Loans of 50,000 to 100,000 takas were extended to centers for joint land cultivation, operation of power tillers, threshing and rice-husking machines, and power looms. But Grameen's early attempts to help villagers "scale up" their productivity were disappointing. Managing these enterprises required coordination and abilities many villagers had yet to develop. Unlike wealthier entrepreneurs, Grameen's borrowers could not absorb the costs associated with learning. And the mutual accountability that existed in a group of five dissipated when thirty people came together. More powerful members took over; poorer villagers were pushed aside.

In 1986, Grameen tried another tack: The bank's Technology Division was to take over the management of the joint enterprises until they began generating profits. Then, as villagers' management capacity increased, the bank would gradually turn the enterprises over to them. The fish farm would be the first major test of this approach. Yunus had two demands: (1) the government was to give the bank a twenty-five-year lease, and (2) Grameen was to have no interference from the Ministry of Fisheries.

The government accepted Yunus's conditions. He renamed the project the Joysagar Fish Farm and remarked that it was an unusual organization that hired someone as a bank manager and turned him into a technician in a fish hatchery. Yet in a country where three quarters of the population were malnourished, an organization that set out to alleviate poverty could not very well overlook a promising business venture that involved growing inexpensive, high-protein food.

Within seven years, half of the eight hundred ponds in the Joysagar Fish Farm were under joint cultivation by more than 2,000 villagers, who were producing fish worth half a million dollars a year. The farm was just about covering costs and Grameen's managers were confident that it would soon be turning a profit.

In 1988, Grameen opened 105 more branches, with branch numbers 500 and 501 issuing their initial disbursements on December 29, just in time to push the bank over the five hundred mark and exceed Yunus's forecast by one. During the year, the bank hired another 2,000 employees and added 150,000 borrowers, bringing the total to 490,000 (420,000 women). Grameen now had centers in more than 10,000 villages. Its disbursements for the year—1.3 billion takas—were equal to the previous two years combined.

Of the thousands of employees who joined Grameen in the mid-1980s, the individual who would rise fastest in the organization was M. Masud Isa, an expert in finance who had come from the Krishi Bank. Masud had been handcuffed by the bureaucracy in his former job. Yunus offered him the freedom to help develop a new package of information systems to manage Grameen's ballooning loan portfolio. At the time, the word going around the head office was "decentralize." Grameen needed to "shrink the head." The head office had to shed responsibilities fast— to zones, to areas, to branches. With power being distributed to 7,000 staff members, Yunus needed a source from whom he could expect accurate and timely field-level information. He needed someone who was direct, who would not tell him what he wanted to hear.

Masud fit the bill. Everything about him conveyed the impression of efficiency. His hair was cropped short; he had the dense comportment of a marine; and he wore a thin mustache that curled down around his mouth, camouflaging a well-controlled smile. His views on Islam were known to be quite conservative, and within the office some felt that this might prevent him from interacting well with women; however, a number of senior assistants in the data analysis units were women, and Masud treated them with the same professionalism he did his other subordinates. He seemed to accept his responsibilities with the utmost gravity; next to providing management with first-rate information, everything was secondary.

When I inquired about those responsibilities, Masud responded with the mannered patience of a scientist to a layman. "The entire qualitative aspect of the bank's operations are dependent on the Monitoring and Evaluation Department," he told me in 1992, shortly after he had been promoted to head M&E. "We fear sending money out without knowing where it's going. If you understand the quality of the operation—how many target beneficiaries are covered, for what types of activities they have taken loans, and what kinds of problems they are facing—then it is possible to ensure quality; otherwise it is not. If monitoring is effective, you can immediately rectify and respond to new situations. And if you can transmit your ideas to the field level, then the entire system works. There are three considerations: *volume, quality,* and *speed.*"

Masud had taken over M&E from Mortuza, who had applied for a two-year leave of absence. Some managers in the head office were worried that the void Mortuza left would be impossible to fill. A relative latecomer to Grameen, Masud was certainly smart enough for the job, everyone agreed, but he had no field experience, and in Grameen this was like a military officer never having seen active duty. But Yunus had faith in him.

By the early 1990s, Monitoring and Evaluation had grown into a department of forty data analysts and computer programmers whom Yunus referred to collectively as "the eyes of the bank." To me, M&E seemed more like Grameen's nerve center, absorbing and processing the information carried by thousands of bank workers each day as they returned from their center meetings with stacks of money and sheets of figures. After the bank workers tallied the morning's collections and disbursements, they passed them on to the branch manager, who totaled them to produce a series of weekly and monthly statistical pictures. (Each branch was its own profit center.) From there, the information was transported, usually by bicycle or public bus, to the area office, where it was manually collated and totaled, and then driven via motorcycle or a three-wheeled motorized vehicle called a "baby taxi" to the zonal office, where data from several areas were entered into PCs to be massaged into dozens of accounting and monitoring reports. (In 1993, Grameen began experimenting with computers in branch offices, but humidity and an unreliable electric grid make rural Bangladesh still computer unfriendly. The cost of battery backups is declining, however, and utilities are improving; still, Masud looks forward to the age of solar-powered computers.) In the meantime, the head office gets by with printed reports prepared each week in its zonal offices. And once a month Masud receives exactly twelve packages (today, the bank has twelve zones) each containing a single 3.5-inch floppy disk. "The information we receive through them is sufficient for us to very specifically and very minutely monitor and analyze the operations at the branch level," he explained.

M&E was central to one of Yunus's management techniques—fostering competition among the staff. Masud reported to him several times a day, providing information about the bank's sources and uses of funds —sometimes down to such particulars as fuel and telephone expenditures by office. Every manager in the head office consulted Masud before taking a major decision. He was tough to get hold of. Each time we scheduled a meeting, he was called away before we finished. I would try to snag him in Grameen's computer room on the fifth floor, where he could often be found enjoying the air-conditioning while poring over reports and scribbling figures on a scratch pad. Whenever I asked someone in the head office a question that required a numerical response, I was told, "Ask Masud," and more often than not Masud had the figure in his head, to two decimal places. If not, he only had to glance at the most recent computer printouts of Grameen's internal statements, which he kept in a three-inch stack by his telephone.

Masud would flip through them lovingly, as if they were a dissertation he had written. He knew them by heart—the way villagers know the Sixteen Decisions: Statement No. 1, disbursements and repayments by zone; No. 7, savings and share purchases by zone; No. 8, loanee analysis —"first-time loanees," "second-time loanees," "third-time loanees," and so on; No. 11, zone-wise totals for "irregular loanees," "difficult loanees," "group quitees," and "deceased members." (An "irregular" loanee was defined as one who paid her installments in unequal amounts; a "difficult" loanee was one who had not paid any installments for ten weeks.) Statement No. 17 showed activity in the emergency and disaster funds; No. 20 looked at month-to-month outstanding balances by zone; No. 21 ranked areas by cumulative disbursements.

In total, there were more than a hundred report formats, detailing everything from weekly meeting attendance to fuel expenditures by area to the number of packages of iodized salt each branch distributed each month. There were pages of key ratios and trend analyses. Masud could calculate the degree to which the monsoons affected repayment in, say, Patuakhali or Tangail. If a mullah in a particular area issued a *fatwa*— an edict in the name of Islam calling for the destruction of the Grameen Bank—and if the local area manager responded by maintaining a low profile for a month or two, then Masud would see this reflected in the "Comparative statement on plan-wise group formation vs. actual group formation" (statement No. 84, printed quarterly). Masud had fund-flow and income projections that took the bank up to the year 2005. And for every single category that Grameen kept count, separate figures were maintained for men and women.

If you asked Masud about a particular zone's or area's repayment rate, he would respond, rhetorically, "Which repayment rate? On-time repayment? Cumulative repayment? Post-52 weeks overdue? Post-104 weeks overdue?" Grameen's most often quoted repayment rate of 97 or 98 percent represented cumulative repayment dating to the bank's inception, he explained. This figure was certainly helpful to Yunus when he used it to bolster his case for banking with the landless, but it was easily misinterpreted. Masud cautioned me never to use it to gauge the bank's loan portfolio at any one time. He never would.

"If you calculate overdue as a percentage of cumulative loans disbursed," he explained, "then this percentage will always tend to be low since you are comparing a constant historical figure against a cumulative one which continues to grow." Grameen's donors and the bank's management preferred on-time repayment. "And repayment is also seasonal," he went on. "It ranges: one month it will be 100 percent, the next month 97, the next month 98, sometimes 92. And then there are separate loan product indices." And, of course, you could not fairly compare repayment in Rangpur, where the economy is always sluggish, with Tangail, just a few hours north of bustling Dhaka. You had to base your analysis on much greater detail.

The phrase Masud used most often to describe his objective was "total operational transparency." He would repeat it several times in a conversation. No other organization in Bangladesh has anything close to "total operational transparency," he said. "In the Krishi Bank," he commented, showing a touch of disdain, "it used to take three or four months to get field-level information."

"Warning signals," he went on. "We look for warning signals—indications as to why the policies that we are currently pursuing are not working, and how they need to be revised." To do this, Masud liked to say, "I am armed with information."

PART V

The World

As a reporter, I'm very conscious that the sensational or tragic or catastrophic political events occupy the headlines of our newspapers and the foregrounds of our minds. They loom up all out of proportion when they happen, but are quickly reduced to size with the perspective of time. This is true of most wars, revolutions, massacres, terrorist acts, famines, gluts, slumps or booms. We are only vaguely aware that something might be going on in the villages. One reason I took up this work was curiosity; after all, two-thirds of the people on this planet aren't just sitting on their hands. Now I'm convinced that it is the unconscious, obscure and overpowering drives of millions upon millions of ordinary individual men and women that is the real stuff of history. Modern heads of state, like Tolstoy's king, are history's slaves. It hasn't got much zing, but the biggest story of the late twentieth century could well be the sum of countless small decisions and actions by unnoticed, humble little nobodies out there in their villages.

RICHARD CRITCHFIELD, *Villages*

33

Credit as a Human Right

*U*ntil the mid-1960s, the terms *development* and *growth* were pretty much interchangeable. Both aimed at improving people's lives by boosting production, as measured by gross national product (GNP). Western development organizations, following in the tradition of the Marshall Plan, focused on massive investments in infrastructure: roads, ports, power plants, communications, and dams. The Marshall Plan had been enormously successful in the reconstruction of post–World War II Europe; however, in the late 1960s, this development model—the "growth model"—came under attack from economists who saw that, despite impressive growth rates, massive poverty persisted throughout the Third World. In many developing countries, far from triggering the promised "economic takeoff," growth-oriented policies had generated *maldevelopment:* Great wealth had accrued to urban elites, while millions of villagers continued to sink deeper into poverty.

Some economists began to feel that a focus on national indicators such as GNP obscured the real problems faced by poor people, and by the end of the decade, the "growth model" was being challenged by the "growth-with-equity" model. The new argument revolved around what to do first and how fast to do it. Some said it was possible to grow first and redistribute later, others felt that first wealth had to be redistributed, then growth would follow. Some economists pointed to the failure of the growth model to justify politically loaded approaches such as land reforms. With the shift from the "growth-as-panacea" framework, economists began looking more closely at the human costs of underdevelopment. With everything focused on GNP, it seemed poverty alleviation had been forgotten.

In the early 1970s, a small but growing number of development practitioners began viewing credit as a powerful tool, one that showed promise in untangling the "growth-with-equity" conundrum. Certainly, a development approach couldn't be accused of bypassing poor people if it placed money directly into their hands. "In the economic literature, credit has been assigned a docile, passive role as the lubricant or facilitator of trade, commerce, and industry," wrote Yunus. Economists either failed to apprehend its true nature, or were too busy focusing on growth to pay attention. "Credit is a powerful weapon, and anyone possessing this weapon is certainly better equipped to maneuver the forces around him to his advantage."

In Latin America, ACCION International, a Boston-based organization established in 1960 to combat poverty throughout the Americas, began providing support to nongovernmental organizations experimenting with credit. In India, the Self-Employed Women's Association, initially a trade union, established a cooperative bank in 1974 to provide credit and savings services to women denied access to commercial banks. In the mid-1970s, the Integrated Rural Development Program in India began providing credit and subsidies so poor people could acquire assets for self-employment. In 1981, Tulay Sa Pag-unlad Inc., based in the Philippines, began providing credit to women in metro Manila. In the early 1980s, the Indonesian government converted an ailing agricultural credit program into a successful banking network capable of extending small loans to millions of villagers. In 1984, USAID helped establish the Kenyan Rural Enterprise Program to generate employment through small loans using a group methodology similar to Grameen's. In 1986, the first full-fledged Grameen replication opened in Malaysia. Elsewhere, in Africa, South America, and Asia, dozens of other credit programs were getting started.

In 1986, Hernando de Soto, a Peruvian entrepreneur, published *The Other Path,* which became a runaway best-seller in Latin America and caught the eye of policymakers around the globe. De Soto had spent seven years exploring the sprawling "informal" economy in Lima, Peru. In *The Other Path,* he showed how a lack of supportive institutions, combined with governmental obstacles and corruption, prevented poor entrepreneurs from enjoying the full benefits of their creativity and industry. Like Yunus, de Soto believed that capitalism was fully compatible with poverty alleviation. Addressing his critics on the left, he argued that wealth disparities were not the result of free-market mechanisms but rather that the "poverty of legal institutions" made it impossible for the poor to make optimum use of these mechanisms: "As full participants, the poor can not only be the beneficiaries of economic growth, receiving the drops as they trickle down, but the engines of growth."

The designation "informal" economy was misleading, implying that this sector was marginal and not worthy of economists' full attention. In fact, hundreds of millions of people in the Third World made their livings in the "informal" or "hidden" economy, so named because their businesses, too small and numerous to measure, were often excluded from GNP calculations. According to ACCION International, in Lagos, Nigeria, and Bombay, India, the "informal sector" represented more than 50 percent of each city's employment. In Lima, Peru, where de Soto wrote, it accounted for close to 80 percent of furniture production, 90 percent of clothing production, and 85 percent of bus transportation. Throughout the developing world, estimates of the proportion of people employed "informally" ranged from 30 to 70 percent. (Did they warrant "formal" status?)

Yunus doubted whether the world could ever "formally" employ so many people. "With the ever-increasing size of the labor force," he commented, "it is quite unlikely that Third World countries can raise the investment to a level that will create enough wage employment to absorb the labor force." He saw only one alternative: self-employment. "There is a strong case for self-employment based on sound economic reasons," he wrote.

One particularly important advantage to self-employment, he added, was that it brought "women into the income stream without the usual sacrifices required under wage-employment situations." Here was a subject that remained something of a black hole in economic literature. If economists occasionally nodded to the reality of the "informal sector," they almost never paid attention to the most "informal" work of all: women's work.

"The international economic system constructs reality in a way that excludes the vast bulk of women's work," wrote the New Zealand economist Marilyn Waring in *If Women Counted.* "Women engaged in non-wage labor or in in-kind exchange relations have been defined as inactive. All those designated as housewives are also considered to be nonproductive and are classified in the economically inactive category. This grossly underestimates the nature and extent of productive labor in which rural women are involved as well as the actual number of women employed." "Policy measures are based on a *selective* understanding of economic stimulus," added Waring. "[F]rom the outset, the figures are rigged."

What, for example, did it mean when economists said that a country like Bangladesh had a per-capita annual income roughly equal to $200 U.S.? "If this figure . . . indicates that people are living on the quantity of goods and services that could be bought in the United States for two hundred dollars in a year, that poses substantial problems," wrote Waring. "If they were invited to do this in Manhattan, they would quickly die. Yet, if the data do not mean that . . . it is not at all clear what they are supposed to mean." The big problem, she added, was that the accounting systems that produced these figures "were used to determine all public policy."

About the time that the "growth model" was being most fiercely attacked, E. F. Schumacher wrote that the challenges facing the world required new economic paradigms: "The conventional wisdom of what is now taught in economics bypasses the poor, the very people for whom development is really needed. The economics of giantism and automation is a left-over of nineteenth-century thinking and it is totally incapable of solving any of the real problems of today. An entirely new system of thought is needed, a system based on attention to people, and not primarily attention to goods (the goods will look after themselves!). It could be summed up in the phrase, 'production by the masses, rather than mass production.' "

His criticism paralleled Einstein, who, in another context, said: "The problems that exist in the world cannot be solved by the level of thinking that created them."

During the heyday of Reaganism, the Grameen Bank started making its way into the mainstream Western press. Articles cropped up in such publications as the *New York Times*, the *Washington Post, The Economist*, and the *Toronto Globe and Mail*, with headlines trumpeting: "Bangladeshi Landless Prove Credit-Worthy," "Bank Lending to Bangladesh Poor a Trail-Blazer," "Barefoot Money Management," "Banking on the People," and "Turning the Tables on Banking."

In 1984, Yunus was quoted in the *Washington Post*, saying: "We will determine whether this is a freak institution having beginner's luck, as some people say, or whether we can make a profound change in the economic structure of the landless people." In 1986, *The Economist* declared: "The only bank in Bangladesh with well-behaved borrowers is the Grameen Bank." The following year, Yunus told the *New York Times:* "We are not doing any favors. We are in business."

In the United States, he was now working closely with a Washington-based citizens' lobby called Results. In 1986, Yunus was invited to testify before the U.S. Congress on a hearing devoted to "microenterprise credit." The following year, Results' director Sam Daley-Harris convened two telephone press conferences with Yunus and editorial writers from twenty-eight major American newspapers. A number of the journalists expressed skepticism about Grameen. How much of an impact could be expected from an approach that involved such small transactions? Could the bank be cost-effective? Could similar programs succeed without Yunus's leadership? The questions were roughly the same as Yunus had fielded for almost a decade, so he was well prepared. Within a year, editorials on the Microenterprise Bill and the Grameen Bank had appeared in one hundred newspapers across the United States. Throughout 1987, Results pushed the House to pass a bill that would make provision in USAID's budget for at least $50 million in microenterprise loans to poor people. In December, Congress passed and President Reagan signed a measure providing $125 million for microenterprise lending over two years.

That fall, the *Washington Quarterly,* a review of strategic and international issues published by the Massachusetts Institute of Technology, reprinted an essay by Yunus in which he argued that "credit for self-employment" should be considered a "fundamental human right."

"There is nothing inherent in the nature of credit that keeps it away from the poor," wrote Yunus. "Nonetheless, the poor have no access to credit institutions. The logic behind this practice has always been considered infallible: Since the poor cannot provide collateral, the argument goes, there is no basis for lending to them. If collateral alone can provide the basis for the banking business, then society should mark out the banks as the harmful engines for creating economic, social and political inequality by making the rich richer and the poor poorer."

Yunus anticipated his critics: "Those who refuse to accept credit as a human right are likely to quickly turn credit into charity in an attempt to show that credit does not help the poor. . . . Credit without strict discipline is nothing but charity. And charity in the name of credit will destroy the poor, not help them. Thus credit institutions must make sure that any loans get paid back in full, and in due time."

"If financial resources can be made available at terms and conditions that are appropriate and reasonable," he added, "the millions of 'small' people with their millions of small pursuits can add up to create the biggest development wonder."

Yunus's hope was that the United Nations would amend its 1948 Universal Declaration of Human Rights to incorporate "credit for self-employment" into article 25 (1), which reads: "Everyone has the right to a standard of living adequate for the health and well-being of himself and his family, including food, clothing, housing and medical care, and necessary social services, and the right to security in the event of unemployment, sickness, disability, widowhood, old age or other lack of livelihood in circumstances beyond his control."

"[C]redit for self-employment should not only be formally recognized as a fundamental human right," Yunus concluded, "it should also be recognized as a human right that plays a critical role in attaining all other human rights."

When I asked Yunus if he thought the United Nations would ever adopt his idea, he replied: "People are listening. But I don't know how to make it happen. The U.N. is a strange bureaucracy. It has to be formally moved somewhere and go through the process to become part of the system—and I don't know how to enter that system. But as I go along I feel more and more strongly about it. And also the world has demonstrated that it's an important issue. That's why Grameen is referred to again and again."

34

How Can You Go On with a
Situation Like This?

By 1987, Yunus had already begun preparing for Grameen's "Phase Three," which was to begin in 1989. IFAD, the Ford Foundation, and the governments of Norway and Sweden were eager to remain on board, but Yunus would need to marshal support from other donors as well. His plan was to double the number of branches to 1,000, and expand services to one million villagers.

He was seeking more than $100 million and he was seeking it on his terms. Among the "development set," Grameen was fast becoming the hottest program around, and Yunus had made it clear that if donors wanted in, they would have to change the way they did business. Donors were fond of referring to the Third World institutions they supported as their "projects." "Grameen is nobody's *project*," declared Yunus. "It's homegrown." And he planned to use his leverage to alter some of the rules in the aid industry.

The time was right. International aid agencies were under heavy fire for their past performance. In three decades, the "growth model" had been replaced by the "growth-with-equity" model and then by the "structural adjustment" model, and in many parts of the world (particularly in rural areas), based on measurements of general nutrition, the poor had gotten poorer. The World Bank, the world's leading development organization, had undergone a 360-degree turn in policy, saying first that free markets *alone* could not alleviate poverty, and then, during the Reagan years, that *only* free markets could alleviate poverty, and finally in the 1990s, that, *in addition* to free markets, special efforts were necessary to ensure that development reached the poor.

Doubtless, impressive changes had taken place during these decades. The Green Revolution had led to a doubling of food production in the Third World. School enrollment had also doubled; infant mortality had dropped by more than 50 percent and 2 billion more people had access to safe drinking water. However, throughout South Asia and Africa, and especially in Bangladesh, many of these improvements had bypassed the poorest villagers. Were the children of the landless in Bangladesh eating better and attending schools?

In the late 1980s, the criticism intensified. Foreign aid was attacked as a $60 billion-a-year industry populated by "jet-setting consultants" who "parachuted" into the Third World, offered instant expertise, and hopped on the next country to offer another "erroneous diagnosis." In her book *A Fate Worse than Debt,* Susan George accused the top international lending agencies, the World Bank and the International Monetary Fund, of pursuing self-interested policies that loaded Third World governments with $1 trillion in debt while failing to seriously address hunger and poverty. "Never before have so few been so wrong with such a devastating impact on so many," wrote George, "but it is unlikely that the banks will ever admit it."

In 1989, journalist Graham Hancock came out with *Lords of Poverty,* a devastating indictment of international aid. Hancock focused his attack on powerful "multilateral" agencies such as the World Bank and the United Nations, and "bilateral" agencies such as USAID and Britain's Overseas Development Administration. In his first sentence, he wrote: "This book is an attack on a group of rich and powerful bureaucracies that have hijacked our kindness." International aid, he went on, "is a publicly funded enterprise, charged with grave international responsibilities, that has not only been permitted to wall off its inner workings from the public view but that also sets its own goals, establishes how these goals are to be attained, and, in due course, passes judgment on its own efforts.

"Despite the fads, fancies, 'new techniques', 'new directions' and endless 'policy rethinks' that have characterized the development business over the last half-century, and despite the expenditure of hundreds of billions of dollars, there is little evidence to prove that the poor of the Third World have actually *benefited,*" wrote Hancock. "Year in year out, however, there can be no doubt that aid pays the hefty salaries and underwrites the privileged lifestyles of the international civil servants, 'development experts', consultants and assorted freeloaders who staff the aid agencies themselves."

Development workers who opted for two-year postings to a Third World country received numerous perks to minimize their "hardship," perks that mid-level bureaucrats back home would never dream of asking for, such as housing allowances, private schooling for children, extended paid vacations, travel allowances, and membership to clubs with subsidized alcohol, swimming pools, and tennis courts.

Before traveling to Bangladesh, I had always assumed that development work involved a measure of self-sacrifice. My idealized image of a development worker was a young engineer digging an irrigation ditch under a hot sun, earning $18,000 a year, when he or she could easily earn three times that amount back home. To be sure, this was not a very realistic image, nor would it be a particularly good use of talent—as if Bangladesh did not have enough people to dig ditches—nevertheless the picture evoked for me the spirit of Peace Corps–style work: people from other countries pitching in, learning from one another, getting their hands dirty.

In truth, development workers spend little time getting their hands dirty. Many have little desire to stay in a village for much longer than a few days, or a few hours. When they must go to the field, they travel in air-conditioned Land Cruisers. Otherwise, they stay in air-conditioned houses in Dhaka and work in air-conditioned offices. (In Bangladesh, once you've grown accustomed to air-conditioning, venturing outside in the heat becomes almost unbearable.)

The 10,000 expatriates in Dhaka behave like an occupying army. They race around in squeaky clean vehicles with their development agency's logos proudly displayed on the doors. They meet at clubs that do not admit locals. And for the most part, they confine themselves to a few posh neighborhoods—primarily Gulshan, Banani, and Dhanmondi— where the phones are reliable, the video shops stock an assortment of American titles, the grocery stores carry Frosted Flakes and Campbell's Soup, and the restaurants serve Italian, Thai, and Chinese cuisine. (For their part, Bangladeshis split into two camps: "collaborators" and "resisters." Yunus is clearly a resister.)

One consultant told me: "The thing that really saves us are the advances in technology. The satellite dishes. We can watch *The Simpsons*. So we don't have to invest ourselves in the local culture, which we choose not to."

There would be nothing terribly wrong with this attitude if this consultant were not receiving so much money from his government—in this case the U.S. government—presumably to do something useful *for* Bangladesh. Indeed, two of the best-kept secrets in development work are: how little investment in the local culture is required, and how lucrative it is.

Because the cost of living in the developing world is so low, expatriates can rent spacious apartments; hire maids, cooks, and nannies; travel extensively; and still save more than half their salaries. After just two years in Bangladesh, a couple employed by their government's foreign aid agency can return home with enough savings for a hefty down payment on a house in the suburbs.

In Dhaka, I didn't meet a single individual, expatriate or local, who disagreed with the charge that massive quantities of aid money were wasted each year. Nor did I encounter disagreement that Dhaka had far too many Westerners crowding the city's streets with their Land Cruisers and Pajeros, and draining its electricity with their air conditioners. When the power fails, as it does almost every day in some part of Dhaka, and a million Bangladeshis cannot turn on their single lightbulbs, there is little sympathy for aid workers who groan about the heat.

The most troubling aspect of all this is that, while many aid workers complain about the system that employs them (and often handcuffs them), few seem inclined to try to change it. In Dhaka, I visited the Canadian and Americans clubs on numerous occasions and was generally impressed by the caliber of the aid workers I met. (I did encounter my share of subpar specimens, however: One consultant told me that "Bengalis have almost a total inability to deal in the abstract; it might have something to do with Islam.") By and large, they seemed to be intelligent, competent people. But something strange happens to them shortly after they arrive in the Third World: They lose all enthusiasm for their work.

One afternoon, over beers at the Canadian Club, I asked four development workers why aid was such a muddled enterprise in Bangladesh.

"I don't know," began one. "We've got brains *galore,* but nothing seems to change."

"That's because 95 percent come for the money."

"We're here to offer technical assistance, but the last thing Bangladesh needs is technical assistance."

"The whole thing is driven by a cover-your-ass mentality. Nobody wants to break the news that it isn't working."

"The longer you keep the public in the dark, the richer you'll get."

"The bottom line is we've got too much money to spend."

"The bottom line is we spend it on ourselves."

"The bottom line is we shouldn't *be* here."

After a few minutes, the conversation degenerated into a vague discourse about government incompetence, the threat of global warming to Bangladesh, and, in general, the wretched state of the earth. Everyone shook his head woefully and downed his beer. Within five minutes, the conversation had turned to dinner plans: "Eight o'clock at Don Giovanni's?"

After my first few weeks in a village, I found myself occasionally taking out my wallet and examining my credit cards. I would stare at them with fascination while the bank workers chatted in the next room. At any time, I knew, I could escape the heat and the poverty, fly to Dhaka, pay $5 for a swim in the Sheraton swimming pool, and sit down to a Western meal with a cold beer and a copy of the *International Herald Tribune*. For me, as for all foreign aid workers, the "field" was something you prepared yourself for and endured for a limited time. We did not belong there.

But for Sabina and Saleha, and for the thousands of Grameen Bank workers, the "field" is home. Very few Westerners would be willing to accept the job of a bank worker. I know I couldn't do it. And yet, a Western consultant can earn in a *day* what a bank worker earns in eight months ($500 vs. $2 per day). Is this justified? Even allowing for a generous cost-of-living adjustment, the compensation is ludicrously out of proportion to the value of the work. And in the end, in Bangladesh, how much honest development work can be done with a computer and a fax machine in an air-conditioned office in the city?

I recalled a long walk I took one afternoon with Saleha, the veteran branch manager from Chittagong, in which I felt as if I were accompanying an old-time constable on her beat. Everybody knew Saleha. As she passed, villagers came out of their houses to ask questions, or to show her something new they had done with their loans. We had traveled to this village by bus (cost: five cents). The sun blazed down on Saleha's black *burkah* and handbag. She wore flimsy sandals (no *Teva* shoes here).

At one house, Saleha noticed a sick child and advised the mother to purchase medicine. Later, she dropped in on a woman named Khuki who had recently received a 25,000-taka family loan to expand her tailoring shop in the bazaar. Later we visited the shop. Above the entrance, the sign read: *Shima Tailors, Modern Sewing Shop, New Fashion.* The walls were freshly painted; the metal still shone on the light fixtures and overhead fan. Khuki had three sewing machines and a good stock of cloth for shirts and trousers. Saleha had first met her when she was a junior bank worker in the same branch ten years before. At that time, Khuki lived in a broken shack and had four children and a husband who was deaf and going blind. Saleha helped her into a group and authorized the loan for her first sewing machine. "Only God above knows how hard I worked to get where I am today," Khuki told me. But Saleha had a pretty good idea. As we left, Saleha commented: "This woman has great courage."

Farther along, Saleha paid a visit to a rickshaw driver who had quit the bank a few weeks before. Saleha knew that the man had sold his rickshaw to purchase medicine and couldn't repay his loan. She had since made inquiries on his behalf in a rickshaw repair shop. Now she advised him to speak to the proprietor about a possible job. Later that week, she visited him again and told him that if he would agree to repay his previous loan at the rate of 10 takas a week, in three months she would authorize a supplementary loan for another rickshaw.

This was development work. (Saleha's salary: $3.50 a day.)

In 1992, the *Toronto Globe and Mail* published an article with the lead: "After 20 years and $23 billion (U.S.) in foreign aid, the world has returned to Bangladesh to discover the monumental failure it has created."

Today, Bangladesh receives more than $2 billion of foreign aid each year. Aid constitutes 8 percent of its GDP and about 90 percent of its annual development budget. So much money—by 1995 more than $25 billion—had flowed into the country for so long that the political process had become grossly distorted. Aid figured into every government decision. And every country that provided aid had its own priorities: "You need to develop *civil aviation*," some said. "No, you need to develop *railways*. No, you need to develop *infrastructure*. No, *sanitation* . . ." Because the Bangladeshi government had to provide counterpart funds in order to receive each country's aid, government officials found themselves pulled in so many directions that they could not formulate coherent policies of their own.

Even if the politicians were inclined to resist the tugs of so many benefactors, their range of policy options is limited. Unlike its donors, Bangladesh is not permitted to protect its currency or markets, or subsidize its own farmers. It cannot do these things because it takes loans from the World Bank, and every poor country that takes loans from the World Bank must adhere to its current development model: "structural adjustment."

The policies of "structural adjustment" are designed to force the governments of poor countries to spend within their means, and to prevent them from interfering in the mechanisms of the free market. According to this model, bloated Third World governments must trim down, cut subsidies, turn over more and more economic control to private investors, and open borders to foreign investment. Then the free market will work its magic. Although these measures might cause pain in the short run, as the theory goes, they will pay off in the long run. (Of course, as the economist John Maynard Keynes observed, "In the long run we are all dead.")

Yunus was highly critical of these policies. He felt the World Bank was staffed by detached theorists and was still dominated by a "Reaganite inner core." Unlike many of the bank's critics on the political left, however, Yunus could not be casually dismissed as an ideological enemy. He had been advocating an entrepreneurial approach to development at a time when the World Bank was *progovernment* and *anti–free market,* and he continued to assert that most social problems were amenable to market-oriented solutions. But he felt that the economists of the World Bank had forgotten a fundamental tenet of market capitalism, an idea closely associated with Adam Smith's "invisible hand": Namely, that human beings (even economists!) are incapable of foreseeing the consequences of their actions beyond a very limited range.

Which is why he favored approaches that evolved from experimentation and direct experience, and why he felt that trying to cope with the diverse economic problems of Asia, Africa, South America, and Eastern Europe with a set of predetermined policies was arrogant and foolish. Yunus didn't even like to interfere in the affairs of his zonal managers because he felt *Dhaka* was too far away to appreciate their problems. How about Washington, D.C.?

Ultimately, he felt that the World Bank, the "flagship" of international development, was not well designed to alleviate poverty. In a 1993 speech in Washington, D.C., Yunus, the David of bankers, accepted a $2 million grant from the Goliaths, and proceeded to blast the World Bank for being guided by a "theoretical framework" that did not "assign any urgency or primacy to poverty reduction." He criticized the bank for continuing to pursue growth "single-mindedly" until it was "distracted by other issues" like hunger, women, health, and the environment. He said the World Bank remained conservative "at its core" because its analysts were simply "not hired to eliminate poverty." And he added: "This may require us to go back to the drawing board, to design the bank from scratch."

"If you keep on hitting that big wall called the World Bank," Yunus told me, "maybe it will begin being chipped away like the Berlin Wall."

Back home, he spoke bitterly about aid and went so far as to state publicly that Bangladesh would be better off if it had never received *any* aid, an extreme position even his closest colleagues would not take. "After $25 billion, you don't see any positive change in Bangladesh," he told me. "Poverty is wider and deeper. So what would have been different if we didn't receive that $25 billion? Would we be worse off or better off? And I say that probably a case could be made for both sides—and I would support that we would have been better off."

"The essential pattern of poverty has to be broken in Bangladesh," he added. "I think we can do it. Only the environment has been vitiated by all these policy complications—donors—recipients—experts coming from all over the world giving their ideas—the wrong ideas—the whole country turned into a graveyard of ideas and projects. But nobody turns around and says, 'Why is it in the grave?' You can almost mark the spot: 'Here lies idea number 634, project number such and such, initiated with such high hopes, which never worked, at a cost of $32 million.

"It's all here: half done, never worked, limping. And each time there's lots of excitement, all the experts saying, 'This is it. You can't go wrong with this.' You go to the graveyard. There are at least 552 projects of the same nature which failed. But nobody talks about them."

In December 1990, the military regime of President Ershad was overthrown by a peaceful uprising and an interim government was installed for three months until Bangladesh could hold a national election in late February 1991. Yunus challenged the interim government to dedicate itself to self-reliance and demonstrate the fact by accepting no foreign aid until the election. "Let's see how we can run the country," he told his fellow economists.

He was roundly criticized for making such a reckless suggestion. How could Bangladesh function without foreign aid? "People said there would be shouting in the streets. I said, 'I bet you the poor won't be shouting, because they don't see the money anyway.' "

"The temporary government could have forced the parties to make it clear to the electorate how they felt about dependence," he added. "But they didn't accept it."

Many people in the aid community in Dhaka felt that Yunus's statements about aid were arrogant and hypocritical. "I sympathize with his position," explained Richard Holloway, an English development worker in Dhaka who admires Yunus's work, "but I do worry about saying that and at the same time taking huge amounts of money from foreign aid. He says, 'We will use it properly.' I'm sure he will—compared to the rubbish that the government does with it. I fully support that. But slamming foreign aid in principle when he takes it himself? I find it difficult to stomach."

In truth, Yunus was not opposed to aid per se, although his public statements gave this impression. ("Yunus simplifies and goes for the *jugular*," commented one colleague.) In a 1995 speech in Oslo, Norway, he called for donor countries to *raise* their foreign aid budgets to 0.7 percent of GNP, the rate recommended by the United Nations. But instead of focusing on economic growth, he argued that foreign aid should be spent directly on poverty alleviation. It should not be channeled through government "projects," he said; it should be managed as investments in "social-consciousness driven" enterprises like the Grameen Bank, enterprises that fuse the goals of social programs with the performance edge of businesses.

"I have nothing against foreign aid," Yunus conceded when I pressed him on the question. "I'm interested in the quality of foreign aid. Today, the quantity has become the overpowering issue. Donors have to increase their aid budgets so they've become articulated agents for us, speaking in Parliament saying more and more aid should come to Bangladesh.

"I'm making a point. I'm saying if this $25 billion hadn't come, what would have happened to Bangladesh? So I say Bangladesh would have been better off. Then, everybody goes, 'Oohhh, aahhh, how can you say that kind of thing!' Then we have to go into details. Probably, we would have learned how to survive—because a nation just doesn't disappear from the face of the earth. The people find their way, they organize themselves. Probably, we would have been like Vietnam, struggling to do things for ourselves.

"Or, an alternative scenario is if this $25 billion hadn't come as aid; if it came as *investment,* I can immediately make a case that this country would have been better off. Today, we can't even get $25 *million* of investment, but we get $2 *billion* of aid. If we had $2 billion of investment, this economy would be booming."

Much of that $25 billion has been spent on large infrastructure projects such as roads, bridges, and power stations. Bangladesh is badly in need of these things. Some parts of the country, particularly Patuakhali and Rangpur, are chronically depressed because of poor infrastructure. At harvesttime, in northern Bangladesh, food often rots along the roadside while farmers wait for it to be transported to urban markets.

But Yunus did not feel that improvements in infrastructure constituted positive "developments" in and of themselves. He had a simple test: Did they bring direct improvements to the poorest 50 percent of the population? In many cases, after their roads are built, the consultants go home. Did the road help wealthy traders at the expense of poor ones? Did it cause a drop, or an increase, in local food prices? Did it increase the incidence of crime and prostitution? Only locals knew the answers to these questions. To understand if something as grand as a power plant could be called a true "development," Yunus felt, one had to observe how things changed, or failed to change, for the poorest 50 percent of the population.

"People talk about per-capita electricity consumption as an index of development," he explained in a 1991 speech. "[But] the bottom 50 percent don't even consume any electricity. If the electricity consumption increases a thousandfold, so what? If you want an index of development, I would take per-capita sets of clothing or food intake for the bottom 50 percent. If a person has one piece of clothing [and] you let her acquire another piece of clothing to change into, I'd say that is a tremendous development. If one who can afford one meal a day moves to two meals a day, that is development of the highest order."

He posed another question to foreign donors: If you're going to build a road for us, are you going to make sure we maintain it? "The government will ask for a road," he explained. "The road will be built and two years later they'll ask for more money to repair the road.

"Don't make life so easy for the government!" he demanded of the imaginary donor in his office. "Let them do the first mile. Make a condition: 'You must demonstrate to me that you're going to have enough money to maintain this road. If the road is not maintained, we're not going to talk about any more roads in the future.' Only then will the government become responsible."

35

An Expensive Way to
Transfer Technology

Why did foreign aid agencies finance projects that past experience showed would not be properly maintained? Why did they put successive generations of Bangladeshis in a position where they would be repaying enormous loans decades after the projects the loans had financed had ceased to perform?

I asked a friend of mine in Dhaka named Anthony Knowles, who had been working in development for two decades. Knowles had been a consultant on several projects financed by the Canadian International Development Agency, one of Bangladesh's largest donors, and had worked on many other projects throughout the world. Some had succeeded and some had failed. Of all the consultants I spoke with in Dhaka, he seemed to understand best the practical challenges in international aid, and he spoke from the point of view of one who sought to improve things.

"First, our system enlists by and large inexperienced professionals to take a two-year detour out of their normal career path to participate on a development project," Knowles explained. "Now, my stereotype is you've got four reasons why people go overseas. One is a young couple. It's a good time to save some money. Another group are people in a career—children under eight. They say, 'You know, this would be a good time to take a two-year detour out of our normal existence. The kids are still at an age where they can travel. Let's go and see the world.' The third group thinks God sent them. And then there are various personal reasons for going—one of which might be that you have a serious interest in development. But I would say that this group is only one fraction of the total."

"Then," he added, "we do things that are almost hard to believe from the uninitiate's point of view. For example, we moved into an idea of

Integrated Rural Development in the 1970s. That is: You can't just do one thing, you have to do a number of things. You can't just build a school and expect to improve the well-being of the population through education if the students are falling asleep from malnutrition. So now you'll also mount efforts to remedy food production and perhaps health care and perhaps build a mountain road that will give them access to other services. Hence: Integrated Rural Development.

"That attracted a lot of support and seems to stand up to common sense. But we're talking about a major intervention in a whole number of areas in a delicately balanced equation of rural life, in a village setting, perhaps under tribal leadership, perhaps under colonial leadership, which even complicates it further in terms of what people perceive about themselves or expect from government.

"So we march in. Now, if I were telling you that this is the situation you're going to try to intervene in, it would seem that you should really think about it as a team: you the doctor, you the crop specialist, you the civil engineer. How are we going to approach this? And ideally, it would be nice if a few of us had worked together before. It's like a basketball team. At least you go out for a few hours on the floor and throw the ball around, work out a few basic plays, have some fun.

"What do we do? We assemble teams of people who most often— and I know people will find this hard to believe—most often have never met each other. And meet for the first time after they arrive at the airport. So you get doctor so-and-so, plant pathologist, who's going to head up the agricultural crop part of the program. He's sixty years old. This is his first time overseas; it's a retirement post. He's been assistant deputy minister of agricultural for Saskatchewan and is waiting to cruise out of his career.

"Maybe also on the team you will have a couple of twenty-five- or thirty-year-old graduates in environmental science and they're going to work in his unit. A man who's sixty isn't of a mind to be going out to change the world. He's learned through hard experience that you live and let live and perhaps he's even been a bureaucrat all that time so his inclination isn't to think, 'How can I change the world?'

"The thirty-year-old is at the other end of the scale; he's looking at the same set of needs and saying to himself, 'Well, if we just change this or that, boy, we could really make things happen.'

"And then you've got to incorporate the engineer and the economist and so on. And if they have never lived overseas, then they're all going to go through their own personal adjustment processes—often with family, wives and children—that will at the very least distract them from what it is they're supposed to be doing. And so, already I've painted a picture you can see.

"And then we have all these expectations that in a very short time, one or two years, this team is going to have gone out and laid the foundation for a program that will be carried on by counterparts.

"You can go and talk to people who worked in the 1960s and the 1980s and the 1990s and you'll hear about the same things, finding the same faults, observing the same contradictions. And it's like you've just had déjà vu.

"Unfortunately, there is no systematic effort on the part of development agencies to say, 'Over time, we're going to build up a team of experience. So let's watch for the naturals and maybe build them up to the point where they can be team leaders and then, ultimately, out of the best of the best, bring in some officers that become your anchor men at head office.'

"Instead, the dynamic just repeats itself. Some groups turn out to have the innate wisdom to do the best possible thing in the circumstances; others are abysmally mismatched. There's all kinds of internal conflict in the teams and you wonder whether they yielded anything at the end of the day, except pay the bill for the consulting firm and everybody made some money."

"How much money?" I asked.

"I've been talking about this for ten or fifteen years," Knowles said. "For a round figure it's safe to say it's in the order of $200,000 a year to deliver a body in the form that we do it now—that is, with all the benefits, whatever salary the guy was getting at home plus 10 percent, probably, overseas allowance, some tax-free components, housing, and the agency overhead to implement all this.

"My point being, irrespective of whether it's $100,000 or $200,000, the classic experience is that the guy gets overseas, it takes him maybe the first half a year to figure out which end is up, find out how the country works, wait for his housing, which wasn't ready when he got there, wait for his wife and family to arrive, who came two months later because school wasn't out, go through the griping, 'Why did Harry get a 1,500-square-foot house and we only got 1,200 square feet? They got a new fridge and we didn't.'

"It's amazing how unprepared and perhaps what poor transferrers of technology North Americans are. And if a lot of effort wasn't paid to try to sort out whether the person has the right outlook, they can get there and find out they really can't stand living with cockroaches.

"Anyway, he spends the first six months sorting himself out, starts to see what this thing's all about, discovers that the project document is organized in a way that doesn't make sense. It says they're supposed to do this, this, and this, when in fact the research for the crops they're thinking about working with is not yet complete, so it doesn't make any sense to plant this year's crop because the trials aren't finished. . . .

"So he finds out that one of the original premises of this whole project might be off. Or, if he's a perceptive person, even though he was in plant agronomy, he starts taking an interest in the villagers and he starts finding out how people think. And he finds out that there's going to be a long process required here before these folks are going to take our suggestions, given that their survival may be dependent on it.

"And all of a sudden he starts to realize, 'Wait a minute, this thing's structured *backwards*. The sociologist and the community *animateurs* should have been here for a couple of years *before* we came in with this.' He starts seeing that this thing may have been patched together not necessarily entirely logically, and that's not surprising because it was patched together by somebody at the Ministry of Agriculture and a consultant who came out three years before.

"There are supposed to be mechanisms whereby the team does an inception exercise to revise those items that have changed. But in practice, if the inception team concluded that this project is not needed, I would suggest that the consulting firm management has no inclination to call up the government and say, 'Look, we've taken a look at this and we don't think this $5 million contract you've given us is really what should be done and we think we should come home and think this thing through.'

"No one I know has ever said that. They take the view, 'Look, right or wrong, they told us to do this, they gave us the terms of reference, we won the contract, keep turning the crank.'

"The local governments aren't usually so confident to step in and intervene. They're the happy dependent recipients of aid and hope to get more and wouldn't offend an aid agency by refusing a disbursement. And like any bureaucratically approved program, once the money's out the door, it's not acceptable to come back and say we want to change everything because everyone who was involved in the approval process would have to explain how they could have been so blind to approve it in the first place.

"At this stage in a project's career, you sometimes get dissension among teams and dissatisfaction. You don't get a lot of people resigning dramatically and refusing to work any further. The process is more one of gradual disillusionment: people working out their contract and then quietly telling you, 'These guys don't know what they're talking about.'

"So I've heard and watched individuals say, 'Well, at the very least I'm going to sit down and complete a study, a paper, whatever, so that these problems are documented; or perhaps more selfishly, I'm going to make sure when I go home at least I get a paper out of this because in my profession that's currency. I can't afford to waste two years and not publish.'

"So you busy yourself for the next six months doing something in focus that you've defined yourself, presumably that you think is a useful thing to do.

"Well, now we're down to only six months left in a two-year term and it occurs to the cooperant that he is leaving soon, and there's a lot of places he hasn't had a chance to see yet. And at the very least he's not going to think of new things to initiate because at some point before the last day you psychologically leave, and for many that's actually two or three months before they depart.

"So if we sum up the twenty-four months, how much productive contribution of talent and skill and transfer of knowledge occurred? At the very least we know these individuals cannot possibly work at 100 percent of their efficiency; they're hamstrung by cultural, language, and other differences, so they can only operate at a percentage of normal efficiency. Let's say it's 75 percent. Then it turns out that out of the twenty-four months, the time you actually were focused and could concentrate and work at your usual level is twelve months, maybe fifteen or eighteen months at most. And then weigh that against the $400,000 it took to field you for those two years.

"You have to stand back and say, 'This seems like an awfully expensive way for the developing world to try to transfer technology.' "

"In many respects," Knowles added, "the way we're trying to marshal our resources, financial and technical, and presumably transfer them to some recipient in need, is often done in what seems to me the most expensive and the least effective way."

I asked Yunus what role he saw for foreign aid workers in Bangladesh. "Very little," he said. "Things can usually be done better by local people. Most often the donor government wants to recover part of their money by creating employment for their own citizens."

"But there are many genuine places where you need some special knowledge and there's one guy who can come and help," he added, "but unless the receiving end is ready to take it, his contribution or her contribution is meaningless."

When dubious development projects are sanctioned, it is often because they benefit political constituencies whose support is crucial to the aid agencies back home. Seventy-five percent of the assistance Bangladesh receives is "tied aid," which means that the money returns to the home country, where it is paid to construction contractors, equipment suppliers, consultants, shippers, farmers, banks, and insurance companies. Tied aid is "donor driven," meaning that it is more responsive to the political and economic needs of the donor country than the development needs of the recipient. "If Holland has excess capacity in its machine tool industry or Britain wants to dispose of used telephone exchanges from Birmingham (two real examples)," wrote James J. Novak in *Bangladesh: Reflections on the Water,* "the aid agency will offer to give these items." He added: "The United States donates food aid largely because it is cheaper to give it away than to store it." Food aid that arrives just before harvesttime will depress the market for local food producers. "[But] God help the USAID director who recommends curtailing food aid. He will face the wrath of the U.S. farm lobby."

Of the 25 percent of foreign assistance spent within Bangladesh, more than one fourth goes to local consultants, indentors, businessmen, contractors, and government officials. Bribery is an important component of the aid machinery. "Donors deliberately accept or tolerate or promote this to get things done," Yunus told me. "They call it 'facilitating money.' They don't earmark it in their budgets but they will pay it as part of their contracts. Often there's a patronage game being played on both sides."

Because of such practices, critics of aid call it a "transfer payment from poor people in rich countries to rich people in poor countries." And Yunus believes that if ordinary citizens in the West knew how their money was being spent, they would be very angry. "Taxpayers allow this money to come to Bangladesh because they hope it will help Bangladeshis to lead better lives," he told me. "Bangladesh may be a poor country but not everybody in Bangladesh is a poor person. There are a lot of rich people—much richer than the taxpayer himself or herself. The money goes to that rich person, not to the poor person. If the taxpayer knew that, she would say, 'Sorry, I struggle to earn my money and I don't want to help that fat cat build another villa in Gulshan.' "

"In order to ensure that the poor person gets it," he added, "the address has to be written correctly. When you write your aid check, don't write just 'Bangladesh.' Because 'Bangladesh' means 'rich people in Bangladesh.' Write: 'The bottom 50 percent of the people in Bangladesh.' Then the aid agency has to find projects which benefit this bottom 50 percent."

In addition to the Grameen Bank, many other locally based nongovernmental organizations (NGOs) financed by international aid were doing just that job. In the past decade, these local NGOs, with their staff stationed in thousands of villages, had provided credit services, basic health care, education, and employment opportunities to millions of villagers in rural Bangladesh (although population growth had outstripped many of their gains). Most were fairly young organizations with modest budgets—tiny budgets in comparison to the infrastructure projects funded by international donors; however, a few had grown very large. The two usually spoken of alongside Grameen were the Bangladesh Rural Advancement Committee (BRAC) and Proshika—two organizations whose schools, credit, health care, and women's development programs had spread to thousands of villages. The dissemination of a simple and inexpensive oral rehydration solution for diarrhea by these and other NGOs probably saved more lives than any other single "development" in Bangladesh's history.

"The big three," as Grameen, BRAC, and Proshika are known collectively, had evolved separately, each under the charismatic leadership of an individual who was widely regarded as a "visionary." Although all had received large sums from foreign donors, each fought hard throughout its history to resist donor involvement in management. After years of struggle over the issue "who's in charge," all three had retained their independence and Bengali identity. Today, many believe that homegrown institutions like the big three represent the best hope for Bangladesh.

36

A Risk Taker

With foreign aid agencies on the defensive, Grameen was in a position to set conditions on its donors in a manner that no institution in Bangladesh, and perhaps the entire Third World, had ever done. "If you have to justify why Canada's aid budget is as big as it is during a time of recession at home," explained a Canadian donor, "or why the sewer system in Niagara Falls is not being fixed because so much of the taxpayer dollar is pouring into aid programs, well, you'd better be able to justify that by financing a winner. Grameen is a winner."

Three new donors agreed to provide funding for Phase Three. IFAD, the Ford Foundation, and the governments of Norway and Sweden were joined by the Canadian International Development Agency (CIDA) and two German agencies, Kreditanstalt für Wiederaufbau (KfW) and Gesellschaft für Technische Zusammenarbeit (GTZ). By 1988, the bank had commitments for $105 million. Yunus was wary of having to deal with so many agencies, each with different reporting requirements, so he insisted on a single consortium office, with one person to act as liaison with Grameen.

Negotiations were to take place in Bangladesh, not in donor countries. This meant that IFAD and the German agencies, which did not have offices in Dhaka, had to fly in. Donors were used to their recipients coming to them, not the reverse. "When the German economic counselor wanted to see us," recalled Muzammel, "we set up a meeting. And we waited and waited but he didn't show. I had told him that the meeting would be at our office. But it never occurred to him that there could be a meeting with a donor at the place of the recipient. Although I told him, it didn't register in his mind."

The Ford Foundation had helped assemble the consortium. Susan

Davis, Ford's representative in Bangladesh at the time, explained that, unlike traditional aid recipients, Grameen adopted a tough stance with donors. "They negotiated like a business," she explained. The bank's managers rehearsed presentations; they were highly disciplined and even secretive at times. "Grameen was very much at the lead of the revolt of the recipients from a highly ethical and principled position," she added. "They had a righteousness about what they were doing. They felt they were making sacrifices, and they wanted fancy consultants to work in the heat and rain alongside them. And donors were beginning to realize that if you wanted to build an institution you needed an organizational entrepreneur like Yunus. You couldn't design one and just go out and hire somebody."

One of the thorniest issues was the requirement that donors periodically conduct "missions" to review the bank's progress and recommend changes. Nobody in Grameen liked the idea of being "reviewed," especially not by consultants who knew comparatively little about life in rural Bangladesh. For Yunus, the word *mission* summed up everything that was wrong with aid: "People at the top talk about projects with, God knows, fifteen different missions, in the process spending $5 million on the missions before they get started with the project itself. Inception missions, identification missions, formulation missions, programming missions, preappraisal missions, appraisal missions, follow-up missions, and midterm missions. And while doing the missions they recommend more missions and they themselves come to do those missions."

Muzammel recalled, "We would say, 'This will be a *joint review,* not a *mission.'* But the greatest irritation to the donors was that they felt that whatever the missions recommended we had to abide by. We said, 'These are only recommendations; they are not mandatory.' "

"We had a program going," he added. "We said, 'If you want to participate in this program, you can join us, and if you don't like what we are doing, you can stop funding us. But you cannot touch our management.' "

Donors were not accustomed to such lack of deference and they often felt the sting of ingratitude. Joan Hubbard, the liaison officer representing the donor consortium, told me in 1992: "I find myself getting very frustrated with Grameen because of its attitude: 'We know best what's right for the Grameen Bank. We're not going to take any outside intervention. We don't need technical assistance. And multilateral institutions are all useless organizations which have only contributed to the horrible economic state of affairs in this country.' "

For his part, Muzammel had trouble hiding disdain for individuals he felt rarely accepted responsibility for their actions and were ridiculously overpaid. "I have never known any consultants who have ever been penalized for the disastrous failures of projects, for ill-conceived, ill-advised projects," he told me. "In fact, people have been rewarded although their projects have been disasters because they have come up with clever reasons for why they didn't work. And one thing they can always blame is the bureaucratic incompetence in the Third World."

When their projects succeeded, donors were more than happy to claim credit, he added, even when they didn't deserve it. "When I met the president of IFAD accidentally in the lift of a hotel in Burkina Faso in 1988," he recalled, "he was furious that, 'This guy's talking about Grameen Bank but he's not talking about IFAD. Has he got IFAD's permission to come to Burkina Faso?' Since IFAD funds Grameen Bank he thought that they would even control our movements. And then he wrote an article in a newspaper saying that IFAD experts created the Grameen Bank. Then Yunus wrote to him that the Grameen Bank had started functioning before IFAD was created and we would be happy to know the names of the experts who created Grameen Bank. So that ended there."

Muzammel recalled another example of donor complacence: "In September 1991, I signed a 10 million mark cyclone rehabilitation program with KfW. They sent an official and a consultant. It was their first visit. They were surprised that we just signed it. They were expecting a big party, a show, functions."

Muzammel shook his head and laughed.

" 'That's it?' they said.

"I said, 'Yes.'

"I said, 'If I were you I wouldn't have come. You should have signed it and sent it to me. I would have seen that it was signed and I would have signed it and sent it back to you.' They think there's going to be a lot of celebration. One consultant said, 'Don't you have any nightclubs in Dhaka?' He was expecting that the recipient would be organizing these sorts of things."

Yunus and Muzammel had almost identical views on the subject, but Yunus would soften the blow of his criticisms with humor. Muzammel would not. "He has these big theories about everything—and he's so self-righteous," one consultant told me in a disparaging tone. Muzammel would not have disagreed. And he probably wouldn't have minded being seen by a donor as prickly. His contentiousness served a purpose: As in the good cop/bad cop interplay, he tended to draw the resentment that donors would have otherwise directed at Yunus. By acting so cranky, he made Yunus's horse seem whiter.

Even so, Yunus's public statements, particularly those against foreign aid, caused resentment among other development practitioners. What was the good in denouncing foreign aid in general? Why oversimplify the issue? Governments were always threatening to cut aid budgets; all they needed was a good excuse. Did Yunus want to give them one? And why did he get to take the bow for everyone else? Other NGOs had been experimenting for years with education, health care, and innovative approaches to community development, as well as credit. Some had impressive success rates. Sure Grameen was doing great work, but why did Yunus have to come along and argue that credit was the key to *everything*?

This last point was particularly irksome to development theorists. They had labeled Grameen's system "minimalist" because the bank did not offer formal training in things like bookkeeping, inventory management, marketing or improving production methods. Without upgrading their skills, borrowers would soon see their returns plateau and then drop off, they said. Although Yunus was searching for new ways to help villagers boost their productivity, publicly he held that credit was, in itself, sufficient to bring about an immediate and profound change in poor people's lives.

But if credit alone was enough to help the poor, did that imply that all other development organizations should stop in their tracks and switch to providing small loans as well? And what would happen to other programs when their donors, seeking "winners" for themselves, inevitably began to display a reluctance to finance anything *other* than Grameen-style loans?

They would get very upset, of course. Mary Houghton, one of the Chicago bankers who had helped Yunus in the early 1980s, and has since visited Bangladesh as part of a number of donor missions, explained: "The reaction of the development community to Grameen went from disbelief to *rage*. They got so upset that Yunus would come in and say that it was so simple.

"Yunus's leadership style is to assert that if people had the will to cause change to occur, by and large, it would occur. He says it's absolutely possible to eradicate poverty with will. He does it with a kind of sales charm that people don't expect from a Bangladeshi—they don't expect that sort of repartee. But people rarely speak to *anyone* who asserts that things are that simple. And they grew suspicious that Yunus was lying about Grameen's performance, hiding information. They would quarrel about the way he defined his delinquency ratio or the amount of subsidy he received. At best, they offered grudging respect for the organizational quality of Grameen."

However, Houghton felt they had a point. "Yunus makes development sound attractive to people who aren't interested in it, and he has forced the industry to raise its standards," she explained. "But his effect has also been to persuade an enormous field to shift to minimalist credit. And economic development *isn't* as simple as he publicly states. When poor entrepreneurs move past one relatively simple profitable activity, they usually can't connect with markets and don't have enough management capacity to run a larger business. In addition to a loan, there's got to be some kind of intervention that connects people to markets and adds management talent. And very few organizations have figured out how to do that on a cost-effective basis at scale.

"Of course, before Grameen came along, no one had figured out how to do *credit* on a cost-effective basis at scale."

In 1989 and 1990, the bank expanded operations to ten zones, hired 5,000 more employees, opened 280 new branches, and added 380,000 members, bringing the total to 870,000. By the end of 1990, the bank was extending $8 million in new loans each month. It had built more than 90,000 houses.

In 1989, the Bangladeshi government offered Grameen another opportunity to diversify, this time into agriculture. The government was looking to unload thousands of deep tubewells (DTWs) at a fraction of their cost, the same DTWs that had proved such an embarrassment to the World Bank. Grameen's donors were decidedly against the bank getting involved with DTWs. Unlike the Joysagar Fish Farm, which Grameen leased from the government for a relatively modest sum, the cost of purchasing and operating so many DTWs could run into the tens of millions of dollars. *Nobody* in Bangladesh had been able to turn a profit with these wells, donors argued.

Yunus countered that Bangladesh had tens of thousands of these resources and they were underutilized and neglected. Somebody had to try to figure out how to make them work, he said. Bangladesh needed to grow more food.

As mentioned, the problems with DTWs were formidable. To be financially viable, a well had to allow farmers to produce high enough yields so that they could cover the costs of fuel or electricity and pay for farm inputs and maintenance expenses. In order to do this, a DTW had to irrigate an area close to its full "command area," in the neighborhood of forty or fifty acres. Because land holdings in Bangladesh are so fragmented, this required the cooperation of dozens of villagers. Getting them to work together, modernize their farming techniques, share water, and synchronize their planting was extremely difficult.

In the Three Share Farm, Yunus and his students had overcome these problems. But could Grameen do the same on a large scale? In Yunus's mind, the question was simple: Could Bangladesh afford to waste resources? Many of these wells were sitting idle and rusting. Additionally, if Grameen got involved in agriculture, Yunus felt that it would be able to use its leverage with the government and international development agencies to address some of the problems faced by small landowners in Bangladesh. "Here, the individual farmer has no voice," he told me. "Grameen cannot be ignored."

In the fall of 1989, the United Nations Development Program sent a "mission" to Bangladesh to investigate the possibility of funding Grameen's DTW operations. The mission was coordinated by Henry Jackelen, a senior technical adviser for the United Nations Capital Development Fund (UNCDF). In his report, entitled "Assessing the Ability of Grameen to Diversity," Jackelen concluded that the odds of succeeding with the DTWs were not in the bank's favor, but that given Grameen's track record "of succeeding against formidable odds," it deserved "the benefit of the doubt."

In his conclusions, Jackelen took a novel approach, by looking at Grameen not as a bank or social-development program, but as a "modern, sophisticated corporation." Grameen was a "risk taker," he wrote. The bank's "corporate culture" was characterized by an ethos of pride —the "Grameen Man" held his head high like the "IBM Man" of old. Its decentralized management and information systems had more in common with Sony or McDonald's than with other banks in developing countries. And its rate of expansion had "little, if any, precedent in private development efforts." The decision to embark on this "massive diversification" into DTWs was another example of Grameen's "entrepreneurial" style, and any donor that chose to participate in the project had to accept the risks.

That year, Grameen assumed control of several hundred DTWs. It soon hired 2,000 employees to manage the Grameen Agricultural Program

(GAP). The essential premise of the Three Share Farm remained unchanged: Grameen would manage the wells and provide all farm inputs in exchange for a third of the crop; the remainder would be split equally among cultivators and landowners.

If GAP succeeded, Yunus felt it would provide an enormous boost to tens of thousands of small landowners, especially in Rangpur, where there was little industry. In addition, GAP would dovetail with the credit program: The crops grown by GAP could be sold on credit to borrowers, who could process, transport, and resell them at a profit. "What I'm doing is preparing a huge marketing network," Yunus told me, arms spread wide.

Two years later, the UNCDF and the government of the Netherlands provided Grameen with $14 million for GAP. Yunus also raised funds from USAID. By 1995, however, Grameen was still experiencing widespread problems with its DTWs. On top of all the other complications, the bank had encountered unexpected political opposition and problems with staff supervision. But the most serious setback was that the government had changed policy in midstream. Rather than continue to try to make all of its DTWs financially viable, the government allowed many to remain badly mismanaged. While GAP struggled to try to cover its costs, in neighboring areas the government sold its water at half the market price. As a result, villagers felt that Grameen was trying to cheat them. "Here we are asked to rent at a commercial rate," complained Yunus. "And everyone goes around saying that Grameen is a big monster." He shook his head in frustration. "I don't know. We'll keep on chipping our way through on trips to the field."

Along with the donors, several of the bank's senior managers now voiced regrets about Grameen having gone into agriculture on such a large scale. Yunus never said so much, but one staffer told me, "If Yunus had never gotten involved in agriculture, he would be a happy man today."

37

A Great Strategizer

In March 1990, CBS's *60 Minutes* broadcast a segment on the Grameen Bank. A few weeks later, the *New York Times* ran an op-ed piece by Yunus under the headline "Credit as a Human Right." That summer, CBS rebroadcast its Grameen segment. Articles on the bank were surfacing in such publications as the *Financial Post,* the *Wall Street Journal,* the *Los Angeles Times, The New Republic,* and *Fortune, Time,* and *Discovery* magazines. That September, Yunus was asked to testify before the U.S. Congressional Subcommittee on International Economic Policy and Trade, which was debating how to administer USAID's $75 million microenterprise program.

Back home, Grameen now had a presence in more than 20,000 villages, almost a third of the nation's total. In the 1991 election campaign, every political party in Bangladesh, except the Muslim fundamentalists, had claimed an association with the bank. When Grameen was in only 5,000 villages, *The Economist* had cautioned that it would be in danger if it grew much bigger. "It is already a political force. The more powerful it is, the harder it will be for the government to resist taking it over. . . ." "Takeover by the government," warned *The Economist,* "would destroy [the] Grameen Bank."

Yunus took pains to avoid any connection with individual political parties. "We have the whole spectrum of political views within the staff of Grameen Bank," he told me. "The moment you take a political position, you have opposition from within." Staff members were expressly forbidden from discussing politics with members. With Bangladesh's history of factional brawling and military coups, the risks were too great. Years before, management had introduced a policy of transferring bank workers and branch managers every two to three years. This enabled the staff to gain experience in different parts of the country and prevented them from developing vested interests or becoming involved in local politics.

(As head of administration, Dipal coordinated the movements of thousands of staff members, each of whom hoped to be posted as close as possible to home. Many found the transfers excessive; some complained bitterly, particularly when managers used the policy to punish subordinates. One bank worker I met had been transferred after only six months in a branch because he had not purchased a bicycle from a friend of his area manager. He had recently moved into a house with his wife and baby boy when he received notice of his new posting. "If your manager says the sun sets in the east," he told me resentfully, "then you say it sets in the east." Abuses of this sort would soon pose serious problems for the Grameen Bank.)

While Yunus avoided overt references to political parties, when given the opportunity to speak publicly he openly criticized governmental policies that he felt did not foster self-reliance or participatory democracy. He seemed to enjoy shaking up corrupt or slack institutions and he was particularly disdainful of the Bangladeshi middle class and urban elite, whom he felt had largely abandoned the task of helping the poor. "Yunus is never afraid to speak his mind," Muzammel told me. But in a country that receives so much foreign aid, his international profile has lent him a certain immunity. Few politicians were eager to provoke a public confrontation with the founder of the Grameen Bank. They preferred to hitch their wagons to his star.

One way Yunus used his leverage was to gradually shift ownership in Grameen from 40 to 75 to more than 90 percent landless. (Today, the bank's board of directors contains thirteen seats; the government still retains three seats; Yunus, as managing director, is an ex officio member; the remaining seats belong to nine Grameen borrowers, elected every two years by their peers.)

But if Yunus was bold, he was also careful not to criticize public figures by name. It was in his interest to provoke thought, not anger. Indeed, with Grameen large enough to begin linking the many microeconomies of its villages with the macroeconomy of Bangladesh, it needed friends to help enact supportive national policies—and the right person to act as a liaison with the government.

One perceived threat to Grameen's survival, typically uttered in low tones, as if words might lend it substance, was: What if something happened to Professor Yunus?

Since his days in Jobra, critics had been calling Grameen a one-man show. Some still did. Now, in his mid-fifties, Yunus was working harder than ever. He spent months outside Bangladesh each year, attending conferences, giving speeches, sitting on boards of directors for organizations around the world. How long could he keep up the pace?

Muzammel was concerned: "He's getting older. He's looking tired. He's traveling too much, but he won't cut back. He loves it." Yunus's wife, Afrozi, told me: "He's got a tremendous amount of energy—sometimes I find it amazing. Perhaps he's losing a bit of it. But not a lot. When he needs to, he can still run." (Although she added that she usually woke up at 6:00 A.M., a half hour or even an hour before her husband. "Sometimes he tries to get up before me," she said with a laugh. "He doesn't like that I get up before him.")

Yunus was in his office shortly after 8:00 A.M. each day. He had cut down on field visits and gotten into the habit of taking catnaps in the afternoon. For years, he had been withdrawing from the day-to-day operations of the bank, although he still dominated all discussions of strategy. The head office supervised fund flows, recruitment, and monitoring activities, but just about everything else was handled at the zone, area, and branch levels. Unless a serious problem cropped up in a zone, the head office did not intervene. Yunus felt that if Grameen were to survive it would have to evolve into a loose federation of independently managed zones. "A mega organization can collapse in one day," he told me. "It becomes too dependent on personality."

Despite his efforts to spread power among his staff, some felt that Yunus's presence still prevented top managers from blossoming. "Doctor Yunus is always in our minds," Nurjahan told me. "Even when he is out of the country we know he will return and see our work."

Was Yunus like the proverbial "big tree" that does not permit things to grow in its shadow?

The thought troubled him. As a teacher, he had encouraged his students to think for themselves. As a banker, he had created an institution predicated on the belief that human beings have the capacity to solve their own problems. Now, at the top of that institution, he wondered how much he kept others from reaching their full potential. "Because I'm sitting here, they stand with respect at a distance, looking to me to hear what I have to say, and I nod and they go. But, if I was not here, they would probably make the decision just like that."

"Could Grameen survive today without your leadership?" I asked.

"There are needs for different kinds of people at different stages of life. I was the mother. People came crying to me, I said, 'Don't worry, I'll take care of it.' But that phase is over."

"An institution is an institution," he added. "It will have its own life cycle."

"Grameen will remain strong without Yunus, but perhaps its ability to innovate will be curtailed, because he is totally fearless," Muzammel explained. Nurjahan added, "Grameen will run fine, but the staff's enthusiasm may wane. There's a lot of work we do outside our job descriptions, and that may be lost."

Among Grameen's donors, there was no consensus on the issue. "Yunus is the vision of the Grameen Bank and he carries the message to the rest of the world," explained Joan Hubbard. "The system's not going to collapse without him but its visibility is going to diminish substantially. And if the visibility diminishes, what is the effect on the program itself?" Brian Proskurniak, an official of CIDA, countered: "Grameen has reached a point where it is a very strong, dynamic institution standing alone from Yunus. The institution almost certainly will survive him."

One of the main reasons for his confidence was an individual named Khalid Shams, who joined Grameen in 1990 at Yunus's urging and immediately assumed the post of deputy managing director. Khalid displaced Muzammel as Grameen's number two man. Yunus had consulted with his senior managers before recruiting him. "There was no hesitation," he said. "People were relieved."

Khalid was a rarity. He had been a civil servant for a quarter century, and was widely regarded as a man of unimpeachable integrity. Tall, thin, and scholarly-looking, he wore glasses with thick black rims and spoke in a voice so calm and so low that, when I transcribed our conversations from cassette, I had to replay passages many times to catch his exact phrasing.

It was worth the effort. His well-considered English, spoken with a soft British accent, was a pleasure to listen to. For emphasis, Khalid liked to drag out the vowel sounds of certain words. When I asked him how the older managers had accepted him, he replied: "They took me in very graciously," giving "very" a full two seconds. He had an exacting mind. When he quoted a statistic, he always provided the source. If Yunus enjoyed turning ideas upside down and Muzammel liked to pull them out of a hat, Khalid was passionate about reducing them to manageable units. He would organize his extemporaneous thoughts in point form and then number each point.

He had been fascinated by the Grameen Bank for more than a decade. In the early 1980s, while working with the government's Management Training Center, he had often dispatched young trainees to rural areas to gain experience. When his students came back from Tangail, they told him about an unusual banking project they had seen. Khalid decided to investigate for himself. Three years later, when Yunus needed a sympathetic government official to join IFAD's appraisal mission, he thought of Khalid Shams. Yunus then asked him to help design Grameen's training institute. A few years later, Khalid left government for a position with the Asian and Pacific Development Center in Malaysia, which was then exploring the feasibility of replicating the Grameen Bank in Southeast Asia. In the meantime, Yunus had embarked on a purposeful search to bring in someone with impeccable credentials, elite connections, and strong fund-raising ability. He challenged Khalid to come back from Malaysia and "get his hands dirty." According to colleagues, it was the 60 Minutes segment on Grameen that finally pushed Khalid over the edge.

Yunus told Khalid that Grameen needed a strong interface with the government. "Whether one likes it or not," Khalid commented, "the government is a key actor in a country like this. You can't bypass it. You have to deal with it."

"Yunus is a great strategizer," he added. "He was thinking ahead. And I thought that it would be a tremendous opportunity to do something meaningful and relevant in the context of Bangladesh. I felt that Grameen had, by now, developed an operating system that could have an impact on the macroeconomy as a whole.

"My friends were divided. But I decided to make a clean break from government and join."

"Could Grameen survive today without Yunus?" I asked.

"Grameen was something very innovative," Khalid replied, "and you need charisma to do something new. But now its strength comes from something else, and essentially that is 'action research'—learning from experience. A body of knowledge relevant to life in Bangladesh underlies all of Grameen's work. The operating system at the branch level is something that has become very well defined. You now have, one, a set of applicable skills, two, a set of motivations, attitudes, and values which can be internalized through training and experience on the job. And, three, this is reproducible from one branch to another. And Yunus is not doing it."

"Yunus was able to get a few key people to support him," he added. "So charisma was important initially, but now it is a professional operating system. Institutionalization has taken place. Yunus has shown the way. Pardon the comparison: Columbus discovered America, but once he established the track, other ships could follow."

These days, Khalid refers to his former employer, the government, as the place where he learned "how not to manage development." He recalled the finance minister's reaction when he first mentioned the Grameen Bank to him. "He said, 'One thousand takas? Two thousand takas? It will take hundreds of years.'

"People in Bangladesh who are responsible for policy-making still do not have a perception of the strategic importance of Grameen as a development model," Khalid explained. "There have been so many development experiments here," he added, stretching the word *so* to ten letters, "that people have become quite cynical."

He shrugged and dropped his voice.

"It's going to be a slow process given the present macropolicy. Because if that doesn't change, the impact will not come quickly. You see, poverty alleviation and the development of disadvantaged people are political questions—and unless there is political will to cope with the situation, you'll not see much of an impact."

38

An Intensive Care Unit

Shortly after Khalid arrived, word reached the head office from the Rangpur zone that default was spreading out of control. Thousands of borrowers had stopped attending center meetings. Delinquent loans had jumped from 5 to 16 percent during the year; by the following year they would reach 25 percent. Grameen was faced with its second major repayment crisis—this one ten times larger than the one that had struck Tangail six years before.

Problems in Rangpur had been festering for three years. During the summer of 1987, colossal monsoon rains caused rivers to overflow dams and embankments. By the time the monsoons stopped in August, flooding had damaged 2 million homes. Rangpur, situated at the junction of three rivers, was hit hardest. Of the 80,000 Grameen borrowers in the zone, more than half lost major assets, 30,000 saw their homes partly or entirely destroyed, and 170 members or their children were killed.

Until 1987, Rangpur had been one of the bank's top performing zones, with a close-to-perfect loan recovery. By the end of the year, normal bank operations were in complete disarray. Flooding had reached a peak of eight feet, submerging houses for days; disease spread; borrowers lost livestock, poultry, food stocks, plantations, and household possessions.

Immediately, the bank responded by sharply expanding the housing program, which had been scaling up gradually. In 1987 and 1988, the bank extended 50,000 house loans. Then, in 1988, Bangladesh was struck with another massive flood, this one coming at the worst possible time: when crops were standing. The staff had never faced successive disasters of such magnitude.

After the floods, installments were suspended for weeks, and, in some cases, months. After relief agencies departed for the second time in late 1988, the Rangpur zonal manager began putting pressure on his staff to increase repayment. Like Tangail, the staff's initial response was to get tough, and, like Tangail, this approach only alienated borrowers. The situation quickly deteriorated.

In the head office, older managers began urging Yunus to replace the Rangpur zonal manager before the zone was beyond repair. As always, Yunus was reluctant to intervene in a zone. He asked the manager if things were under control and he replied that he expected the situation to improve.

Eighteen months later, it had worsened. Finally, in September 1991, the district was hit with another severe flood. With thousands of villagers terribly affected, at the annual conference of zonal managers, Rangpur was designated an "intensive care unit." Any staff member who needed a rest would be given the option to transfer to another zone. The zonal manager was to be replaced and the new manager given the power to overturn all rules and initiate any programs he saw fit.

Yunus asked each zonal manager around the conference table how he would tackle the situation. The best response came from Mohammad Shah Alam, a squat, bull-chested man with a boisterous laugh. Shah Alam was the bank's number one troubleshooter. He had been one of the bank's first area managers and Daiyan called him the best manager he had ever worked with. "Shah Alam is very dedicated," Daiyan said. "He knows how to motivate people and he has excellent ideas—very simple ideas."

As zonal manager of the bank's Dhaka district, Shah Alam had fought off political troubles; in Sylhet, Bangladesh's most conservative area, he had battled religious fundamentalists; in Patuakhali, he had responded to floods that set back thousands. In 1987, when aid organizations asked the bank to help distribute relief to flood victims and Yunus was reluctant to associate Grameen with any form of charity, Shah Alam came up with the idea of a revolving Disaster Fund within each center. Relief would be distributed by Grameen on the condition that members voluntarily replenished the fund when they were back on their feet. The next time disaster struck, each center would have access to the Disaster Fund for their own relief. Yunus was impressed.

Now, he challenged Shah Alam: "Are you ready for Rangpur?"

Shah Alam accepted. His first move in Rangpur was to disburse emergency food loans to 18,000 villagers. "No member shall pass a single day without eating," he vowed. "If this happens, I'll take my branch managers to account."

Next, he spent two months in meetings with staff members and borrowers, listening to villagers' problems, and inviting suggestions, following the original example set by Yunus in Jobra. He designed a dozen new forms for data collection. And he urged borrowers to bring their husbands and wives to meetings. At these meetings, he discovered that many villagers were extremely angry with the bank. They had been insulted by the staff. Some bank workers had even threatened to jail borrowers in the branch unless they repaid their loans. One woman said that when she told her bank worker that her baby had died, he responded: "It's none of our business. You have to pay the installments."

Having been recruited by the thousands in the mid- and late 1980s, the majority of bank workers did not know how Grameen had handled similar problems in Tangail. Faced with insistent demands for repayment from the zonal office, they repeated the old mistake of "loan adjustment." In some cases, they extended supplementary loans to villagers who were so desperate they immediately spent the money on food. Once again, staff members had lost touch with the borrowers, and, once again, the borrowers, fearful of the bank, had grown secretive. "People would lose their capital and not say anything," recalled branch manager Nurul Huda. "Then they'd sell their labor to make the payments. Some borrowed from moneylenders. Eventually, they just dropped out."

Shah Alam listened as the villagers vented their frustrations. He traveled from branch to branch, visiting centers. He explained to the members that the bank had rotated its staff and reversed its policies. "The past is over," he told them. "It cannot be changed. But what do you need now?"

Borrowers, especially newer members, had never recovered assets from the first major flood, almost four years back. Immediately, Shah Alam froze interest on their old loans and introduced a variety of new loans for rehabilitation, food security, and capital, land, and livestock recovery. Taking Yunus's idea, he linked the credit program with GAP, and gave members the opportunity to buy large quantities of food when the price was low, which they could resell at a profit later in the season. He devised a ten-day training program to "reconfirm" problematic groups and centers, and made 90 percent of the funds in the Group Fund immediately available for disbursement (under normal conditions only 50 percent is available at any one time).

He made a promise to all members: If they attended three months of consecutive meetings and each week repaid one taka on their old loans and deposited one taka in the Group Fund, they would become eligible for capital recovery loans. If they repaid their capital recovery loans in two years, they would again become eligible for general loans. "If a villager comes to us with a problem or idea," Shah Alam told his staff, "we must try any program that can help them. We must say, 'If you think you can profit, then we will help you to do it.' "

One problem brought to his attention was that many borrowers had been forced to mortgage their land to purchase food. In most cases, poor villagers never regain control of mortgaged land. Even if they can save enough money to repay the mortgage, wealthier villagers are able to fight their claims and hire lawyers who will keep their spurious cases in court for years. In response, Shah Alam instituted a program in conjunction with GAP, which had extensive experience with land transactions, to release the mortgages on behalf of Grameen borrowers.

Many of the poorest villagers were wary of drawing more money from the bank. The bank, in turn, was worried about extending cash loans to people who were so poor they were likely to immediately consume a portion of their loan capital. "What do you do with a borrower who is close to the point of starving?" Khalid asked.

What Shah Alam did was to institute a program of loans-in-kind. Rather than cash, he offered villagers inexpensive foot-operated pumps (called treadle pumps) that could be used to irrigate small plots of land for rice, vegetable, or tobacco cultivation. The pumps were repayable after two harvests. For income generation, he made available manual threshers, repayable after four harvests. He introduced loans for stocking potatoes and pumpkins and wheat. However, the most popular program of all was the "goat loan."

In this arrangement, a borrower received a she-goat on credit in exchange for the goat's first two kids. Goats grow fast, are immune to climactic hazards, and are readily disposable in local markets. By listening to villagers, Shah Alam learned that locals had been trading goats in a similar fashion for centuries. One goat was valued at 500 takas, two kids at 600. Grameen's return was 20 percent—the same as on its general loans. If a goat died, the bank replaced it; if it was stolen, it was the member's responsibility.

"A goat loan?" commented Khalid. "Who ever heard of a goat loan? And today, if you are staying overnight at a branch in Rangpur, you can't even sleep because of these goats bleating throughout the night."

In his first two years, Shah Alam had distributed 35,000 goats and 15,000 treadle pumps and provided capital recovery loans to 30,000 villagers. His objective was to ensure that all members had enough capital to return to work. It would take many years before Rangpur's borrowers had recovered to the point where they would be able to resume payments on their old loans. But Shah Alam wasn't looking that far ahead. The statistic he cared about most was rising steadily. By mid-1994, he explained, voluntary attendance at weekly meetings had climbed above 95 percent. "Everyone is saying that the manager of Rangpur has the lamp of Aladdin," Shah Alam told me. "But it's not the lamp of Aladdin. It's realistic programs."

39

Two Cyclones

One morning in March 1991, Yunus discovered a letter on his desk informing him that the staff had registered a trade union. He was shocked. He summoned his senior managers. Grameen had more than 12,000 employees. A union petition required the signatures of one third of the staff. How could he have remained completely in the dark?

Yunus was badly shaken by the news. Trade unions in Bangladesh are highly politicized and belligerent. Even people on the political left in Bangladesh are fearful of the tactics employed by powerful trade unions. "In this country, a union is a terrible thing," Yunus told me. "It means that people will start standing around telling you how to run your show. And they will try to do it with force—with violence."

Maheen, who considered herself a supporter of labor rights, commented: "I had very contradictory feelings, because I've always thought of unions as good things. But a union could destroy the Grameen Bank."

This union had been registered as an affiliate of the Bangladesh National Party, which had won power in the national election only a few weeks earlier. Suddenly, an organization that had remained studiously apolitical for a decade found itself bound to a single political party.

For the first time in two decades, Dipal recalled seeing his former teacher looking beaten. "I would drop by his residence at night and find him sitting back, slumped, looking very tired," he told me. "But the next morning, he would be standing with that stiff back again, with a list of suggestions for everyone."

Yunus quickly circulated a letter to the staff officially acknowledging the union and reminding them of the bank's humanitarian objectives. He urged peaceful dialogue.

Within weeks, the union organizers had signed up thousands more employees. Yunus's heart continued to sink. For years, bank workers had grumbled about low wages, frequent transfers, slow promotions, and management abuses. In response, management had instituted an ombudsman system in each zone. But this halfhearted measure had proven ineffective because each ombudsman reported to the zonal manager rather than to an impartial authority.

Yunus regretted not having taken the staff's complaints more seriously; now it was too late. Union organizers had a shopping list of demands and they were pressuring management to act quickly. Yunus could not stomach the thought of being bullied by a group he regarded as political opportunists. But he knew that, under no circumstances, could he afford to alienate the staff. Everything in Grameen depended on the regularity of the bank workers' visits and weekly center meetings. A union could stop the heartbeat so easily.

Six weeks into the crisis, on the night of April 29, 1991, Bangladesh was hit with its worst disaster since its independence: a cyclone that killed 139,000 people overnight. By 2:00 A.M., the winds in the Bay of Bengal reached 235 kilometers per hour, creating a twenty-foot tidal wave that decimated offshore islands and drove the Indian Ocean eight miles inland—transforming the coastline between Chittagong and Cox's Bazaar into a vast saltwater swamp.

The few hundred cyclone shelters, scattered along the coast and offshore islands, were not nearly adequate for the millions of Bangladeshis who live within a few miles of the sea. Many villagers, worried about the theft of household belongings and fearful of traveling with their children, decided to remain at home or sought shelter in local schools or in the concrete houses of wealthy neighbors. Maximum-level storm warnings are not uncommon in Bangladesh—the country gets hit, on average, by sixteen cyclones each decade. Since most storms lose force or change direction before reaching land, many villagers stay put and hope for the best. "If you don't stay in your house there's no saving it," a villager told me. "And I've got four children. If I go out with them in a storm, isn't that taking the road to death?"

When the tidal wave hit, tens of thousands of villagers were drowned. Stronger villagers scrambled onto the roofs of houses and schools; some climbed trees and pulled themselves onto the tops of cement latrines. Parents tied themselves and their children down with saris and *lungis,* while sheets of corrugated tin sliced through the air. "The sky was red, like fire," recalled a villager who had been pulled from the water onto the roof of a house. "The rain burned my skin; it was bitter and salty. I was shivering with cold. The wind was blinding; I couldn't even recognize someone three feet away."

By morning, the wind had abated but a light rain persisted. The land was inundated. Huts were flattened; trees were scattered like toothpicks. The muddy water was littered with planks of wood, beds, pillows, palm leaves, crockery, animal carcasses, and human corpses. Helicopter photographs revealed a shoreline littered for fifty miles with death.

"We found babies in the weeds of ponds, washed up alongside cows and uprooted trees," a schoolteacher told me. "The bodies were bloated. The eyes were swollen. Mothers walked around half naked, covered with any cloth they could find, crying, 'I can't find my son.' My husband and I helped bury twenty bodies in one grave. Most of the dead were women. One was clutching her baby to her breast. They couldn't release her arm. I still see her in my dreams. Then the illness began."

When the storm struck, the Chittagong zonal manager, S. M. Shamim Anwar, was in bed in his residence on the fourth floor of the zonal office. "I thought the building would be destroyed," he recalled. "The wind was shrieking. Windows shattered throughout the city. Communications were dead."

Shamim was one of the bank's most experienced and best-liked managers. He had joined the Grameen Bank Project as a bank worker in Jobra and had managed the second oldest branch. Shamim had the distinction of being the only Grameen staff member to have held every major rank: bank worker, branch manager, program officer, area manager, and zonal manager.

Shamim set out the following morning to contact his area managers, but transportation was hindered by hundreds of fallen trees. When he finally got through, he suspended all normal bank business indefinitely and instructed staff members to visit their borrowers and list their most urgent needs.

At the Dulahazara branch, located twenty miles north of Cox's Bazaar, bank workers had spent the night huddled on the dormitory floor, wrapped in a blanket and surrounded by shattered glass. At 6:00 the following morning, the branch manager, Sridam Chandra Das, left the office with his senior assistant. "We went from house to house," he explained. "The members were huddled together in the rain. We asked about the damage and urged them to find out about the other members and let us know what had happened to them. I returned to the branch and decided that everyone should visit one or possibly two centers. We each ate a little rice and one egg and then everybody left to go to the centers closest to the sea."

M. Shah Jahan, a bank worker, recalled: "I saw more than forty human bodies floating, and hundreds of carcasses of cattle, goats, and sheep. I felt sick. As I went to visit my members, I was thinking: 'What has happened to my family?'

"Except for the high roads, everything was under water. The mud was filled with broken objects and tin. It was easy to cut your feet. I hired a boat. The first man made me pay, but another person offered me a ride for free. I was able to track down fifty members. In one family, a house had collapsed on top of three people.

"I told every borrower the same thing: 'You have to find the strength to gather yourselves and start again. The Grameen Bank will do its best to help you.' I told them that there weren't going to be any collections, but that they should continue to attend the meetings to keep up their strength. I told them the bank would soon give them more loans. On the way back to the office, I helped place some more bodies in a mass grave.

"At the branch, the area manager had left instructions to send a report of the damages to the area office. Many bodies had not yet been found. Each of us resolved to work harder and to visit each member individually.

"After the water receded, we continued to come around each day. We inquired about their health. We advised against eating fish for the time being and drinking any water, including tubewell water, without boiling it first. Most people had diarrhea and needed water purification crystals and oral saline solution. Many members cried, 'How will we live? Our homes are lost. Our cattle are lost.' I tried to tell them that they could recover."

"You know, the government didn't visit them," Shah Jahan said. "Their relatives couldn't come. But *we* came. And the members told us that our words were as important as our loans."

A week after the cyclone, Shah Jahan traveled to his own village. "It was badly affected, but my family was unharmed. Our house was half destroyed and our crop was ruined. I stayed with my parents a few hours and then returned to the branch."

On May 1, the second day of cyclone "Gorky," officials of the newly elected government were away from their offices because May Day is a national holiday in Bangladesh. In Chittagong, the military was in disarray. The airport control tower and several runways were damaged. Helicopters had to refuel in Dhaka because local fuel supplies had been contaminated by saltwater.

Torrential rains continued for a week, hampering relief efforts. Stormy seas made it initially impossible for trawlers to reach offshore islands with supplies. Meanwhile, villagers suffered from untreated wounds and severe diarrhea. The Red Cross estimated that, if relief didn't arrive imminently, up to 4 million people faced starvation.

Thousands of farmers waded through knee-deep water to salvage potatoes, gourds, and peanuts. Soon, the crops were piled up along roadsides. The food quickly perished and a brief glut was followed by a drastic shortage. The first wave of relief supplies were dropped from low-flying planes into a foot of saltwater; a third were damaged or destroyed. Profiteering was rampant. In many areas, the price of rice doubled, kerosene tripled, the cost of hiring a boat quadrupled, and the price of nails went up ten times.

The head office gave Shamim free reign to handle the situation as he saw fit. The first priority, he determined, was food; second, supplemental loans to purchase medicine and items such as matches, paraffin, plastic sheets, and water bottles; and third, shelter.

Immediately, he authorized the disbursement of millions of takas throughout the zone to distribute rice, dal, potatoes, salt, molasses, water purification crystals, and oral saline solution. He sanctioned thousands of supplemental loans so members could purchase other supplies. He suspended all normal rules for house loans. Any member who lost her house was immediately eligible for a fifteen- to twenty-year mortgage of up to 15,000 takas.

He coordinated efforts with other relief agencies and set up Disaster Funds in affected centers. As in Rangpur, the staff advised members that all food and supplies given by the bank were not charity, but a loan from their own Disaster Fund. "You'll take the supplies when it's raining, and replenish them when it's sunny," explained the bankers.

Shamim also suspended holidays until further notice. Union leaders, angered by this action, directed the staff not to work on Friday, their day off. Only a few complied.

Yunus traveled to Chittagong to survey the zone. "At one branch," Shamim recalled, "a woman with her child at her breast said to Doctor Yunus, 'She is not sucking my milk. She is sucking my blood. I have been hungry for two days.' " Shamim clenched his fist and hammered his desk. The government had responded ineptly, he said. "They were stupid. What did they do? They dropped relief from the air. So the strongest men got it. They didn't give priority to women and children." Most of those who died, both before and after the cyclone, he added, were women and children. The bank had no branches on the islands where most of the deaths occurred, and the staff had continually warned villagers to heed storm warnings. In the end, fewer than one hundred borrowers and family members lost their lives. The damage, however, was enormous.

In the months following the storm, Shamim disbursed 14,000 house loans. "The members helped each other rebuild their houses—it went fast." In branches close to the sea, installments were kept on hold for a few months. In areas where the damage was less severe, members were able to return to work in four to eight weeks, although their fields were useless until the monsoons washed out the salt. After two months, the staff informed borrowers that it was safe to eat fish. One unexpected by-product of the tidal wave was an abundance of fish in inland rivers and ponds.

One fourth of the district's forestry had been destroyed, so the staff distributed saplings and—Shamim's idea—seeds for quick-flowering plants. "It gives people courage when they see things begin to grow again," he explained.

He continued to spend his days traveling between branches. His two main concerns were: Would the "survival of the fittest" mentality that had taken hold in the days following the disaster weaken group and center cohesion? And would the massive relief effort—involving the government, hundreds of NGOs, private Bangladeshi citizens, religious organizations, and dozens of foreign aid agencies—foster resentment against the bank? (Everybody else was giving away their relief; Grameen made it clear that its help came in the form of a loan.)

But Shamim discovered that he had underestimated the villagers. "The members' unity actually increased after the storm," he told me. Villagers who owed large sums to their Group Funds were surprised when their group members permitted them new loans. "The members allowed those who were most badly affected go first," he added. "Even villagers who did not like the bank before, became supporters after the cyclone." They saw how the bank workers visited the members over and over, he explained, and they knew that long after the other relief agencies had departed, the staff of the Grameen Bank would still be coming around.

At Grameen's head office, the cyclone had temporarily wiped out management's concerns about the union until two weeks after the storm, when a dozen union members decided to stage a lockout. When the head office staff arrived, they discovered the gate to the bank's compound locked. Grameen happened to be in the midst of its second International Dialogue Conference, and visitors from twenty different countries also arrived at the office only to find the entrance sealed.

The union representatives demanded to speak with Yunus, who had been at his desk since early morning. Yunus sent word that under no circumstances would he meet with them. In frustration, the union members tried to rush the office, but they were blocked by senior officers inside who had also arrived early to work on the cyclone relief effort. The police were called and the union members forced to disperse. Yunus felt betrayed. "How could they be so irresponsible?" he said, shaking his head. And he wondered: How could Grameen continue to exist with this union?

For weeks, Dipal had been quietly investigating the union. He was suspicious of the speed and stealth with which organizers had mobilized the staff. How had they kept management in the dark? It didn't make sense; so many people were involved. He reviewed the names on the petition. Had these people understood what they were signing?

He sent officers to ask them. Some replied that they had never signed the petition. Dipal dispatched more investigators. Is this your signature? they asked. Some said yes, some said no. How many were authentic?

Within a few weeks, Dipal discovered that thousands of the signatures on the initial union petition had been forged. After collecting statements to that effect from hundreds of employees, he contacted the registrar of trade unions and presented their declarations. Reluctantly, the registry office rescinded the fraudulent petition. Shortly thereafter, a court canceled the union.

Dipal and Khalid quickly went to work establishing a staff association that would operate independent of management to address grievances. Dipal met with employee representatives and drafted new rules designed to curtail managers' power to discipline subordinates. The head office introduced a new package of benefits and expense allowances and modified its transfer policy. All efforts would now be made to post staff close to home. As a precaution, Grameen changed the designation "bank worker" to "center manager." By law, employees in managerial and supervisory positions cannot form trade unions, and Dipal felt that every staff member in the bank was in a supervisory position. "Dialogue is a soft way to achieve a hard objective," he added.

"The association is something that should have been started long ago," Maheen told me. "We shouldn't have waited until the union blew up." Khalid concurred: "It's surprising that for so long no union was registered. Grameen should have anticipated it." The bank was lucky, he added. "The union would have divided the staff. But at the topmost political level it didn't get support. That has to be said in favor of the people at the top."

"In 1991, the Grameen Bank was hit with *two* cyclones: one internal and one external," commented Dipal.

Which was the greater threat? "We can deal with natural disasters," Maheen told me. "The cyclone made life difficult for borrowers in Chittagong. But by destroying the staff discipline, a union could destroy the bank. Everything depends on the bank workers going to the center meetings regularly and doing their work systematically."

"No cyclone could cause the collapse of the Grameen Bank," she added. "But all it would take would be *one strike.*"

40

If I Had to Become a
Businesswoman

The bridge we crossed had been reconstructed months before, but the remains of boats still lay scattered along the riverbank. As yet, no one had gotten to work repairing them. The newspapers reported that an engineer working on the bridge had neglected to move his crane, and the wind had transformed the steel claw into a demolition ball. Nine months after the cyclone, I was traveling south from Chittagong to the Grameen Bank's Dulahazara Branch along a road a few miles east of the Bay of Bengal.

Outside the city, except for the occasional electric tower lying on its side and what appeared to be a disproportionate number of coconut trees at forty-five-degree angles, I could detect few traces of the storm. Everywhere, houses had been rebuilt and new bamboo fences erected. The bazaars every ten miles or so looked as ancient and weatherworn as bazaars everywhere in Bangladesh. The shops did not appear to have been blown asunder and hastily rebuilt. Testing the dust on their merchandise, one might have guessed that no wind had stirred in these parts for decades.

I was traveling south to interview Grameen borrowers about the cyclone. However, after a bank worker introduced me to Oirashibala Dhor, the village peddler, I found myself spending all my time talking with the Hindu widow about her "business of bangles" and her struggle to build a two-story house and find a husband for her daughter.

Oirashi lived across the road from the Dulahazara Branch in a newly built L-shaped house surrounded by a bamboo fence. In back of her house was a vegetable garden; up front, eight coconut trees encircled a yard so tidy the dirt appeared to have been smoothed by hand.

When the cyclone broke, Oirashi and her daughter, Nonie, had sought refuge in Oirashi's father's mud house, which was shielded from the wind by a grove of old trees. Both houses stood on high ground, so the water did not reach them, but Oirashi's bamboo and straw hut was blown apart. She managed to salvage her merchandise and the gold jewelry she had saved for Nonie's dowry.

In the morning, Oirashi and Nonie saw the damage caused by the storm. "We saw the dead bodies being brought in, in boats," she recalled. "We watched them the whole day. We said our thanks to God that our lives were spared." The loss of their house and possessions would post-pone Nonie's wedding for at least five years.

Weeks later, Oirashi received a 15,000-taka house loan from the bank. A laborer built a new house in twelve days. Oirashi saved a portion of the loan to live on for a few months. "How could I sell my jewelry?" she said. "People had lost their houses. Some didn't have food. How would it have looked?"

The entrance to Oirashi's new house is four feet high, but inside there is plenty of headroom. When I entered, Oirashi immediately apologized about the darkness. She had saved money by forgoing windows. To the left, a bamboo partition separated the sleeping area from the main room; to the right, another doorway led to a small extension that served as her kitchen. A prayer altar stood in the corner. On the wall hung a calendar featuring a photograph of the beach at Cox's Bazaar, Bangladesh's sea-side resort twenty miles south. Beneath the calendar, Coke and 7-Up bottles were suspended by braided ropes made from blue, yellow, and pink plastic bags. Above, in a rafter, Oirashi stocked bamboo, tin, and wood—preparations for the future. The bamboo door fell open against the wall. When she left for work, Oirashi secured it with a bicycle chain and a padlock and tied the key to her sari.

She unrolled a mat and called out to a small boy, who ran to fetch a bowl of puffed rice and molasses. The boy had to push himself through a crowd of children jammed three feet deep at the door; the kids blocked the sunlight, and, no doubt, reminded Oirashi of the absence of windows in her house. So she picked up a stick and tried to shoo them away, but she just sent them into fits of laughter. They bolted and returned seconds later, blocking even more light. In the evenings, I was told, these same children often packed into this house and, by the light of a kerosene lamp, Oirashi would tell them strange and scary and often hilarious tales, complete with all manner of sound effect and facial expression.

The consensus was that she had inherited her storytelling ability from her father. Before 1947, he had been a well-to-do partner in a gold trading business and Oirashi had memories of him returning from

Oirashi in front of her house

"long voyages" to Burma with his pockets full of "huge gold coins."
When Partition set Muslim-Hindu antagonisms aflame and millions of
Hindus fled from East Pakistan across the border to India, Oirashi's
father, a Hindu, elected to remain behind. One morning he discovered
his partners gone. They had fled to India and taken all the gold. "Then
we became poor," Oirashi said.

At twelve, Oirashi was married. "I was carried to my in-laws' house. I
didn't see my husband until after the wedding. At first I was scared of
him. I used to hide. But then he showed me love and I came to love
him." Her husband had inherited enough land to live on and together
the couple enjoyed what Oirashi described as a dozen "sweet years." She

gave birth to two daughters, Renu and Nonie. Shortly after the birth of her second daughter, her husband died. Initially, Oirashi told me that he died of "Frozen Satan's Gout," or pneumonia. However, when I asked other villagers about "Frozen Satan's Gout," they laughed and reminded me that Oirashi was famous for her stories. On subsequent visits, I inquired again about her husband's death, and each time she modified the cause: from pneumonia to epilepsy and, finally, to ghosts. "He would be fine all day, and then at night he would have a fit and faint. This went on for nine days and then suddenly one night he died. It was ghosts." I let the subject drop, waited a week, and brought it up again. This time Oirashi said that nobody knew the real cause of her husband's death. "We used to give a drop of this, a drop of that, some leaves and other remedies, and then if the patient still got worse, we said the ghosts got him."

Oirashi had no sons, and it soon became clear that her value in her husband's family had greatly diminished. Her husband's land had been registered as a gift from his father, which was easily revoked. Since she had no hope of retaining ownership, when her in-laws began fighting over the land, she decided there was no point in lingering. "If I had to become a businesswoman, I would rather do it in my home village."

Back home, she built a small hut on her brother's land, which she soon had to vacate after he sold the land. She returned to her father's house until she was able to build herself a hut on another brother's land. In the meantime, she started a business making puffed rice, which she quickly abandoned because she couldn't stand the heat from the fire. She tried husking rice but found it a poor use of time. "All that processing for such little money." But on her rice rounds, people used to ask her to bring them other things, such as cosmetics and gold earrings. "So I decided to try that. But after I sold the gold, it became discolored and people complained." The gold maker—her cousin—had been adding impurities. When her uncle found this out, he beat his son. "I forgave him," Oirashi said. "He was a drinker." Nevertheless, she resolved not to work with gold anymore. "I quit that business and became a peddler."

Years passed. It came time for Renu to marry. To pay for the wedding, Oirashi borrowed several thousand takas from a moneylender. From that point on, her loan began draining almost all of her income. Soon her suppliers, believing she was overextended, refused to sell her merchandise on credit. Customers complained about her poor selection. "It was the hardest time of my life," she said. "My financial system had completely collapsed. If I told you the whole story, you would *faint.*"

Meanwhile, she worried about Nonie, who was now in her early teens.

Unable to send her to school, Oirashi approached the nurses at an American missionary hospital seven miles away. She had heard that the hospital staff often hired teenage girls as mothers' helpers and trained them as seamstresses. Perhaps she could secure Nonie's future this way. After a dozen bus trips, she met Shabbatra, a Bangladeshi woman working at the hospital, who agreed to hire Nonie.

With Renu living with her husband fifteen miles south and Nonie living at the hospital, Oirashi grew lonely. After a year like this, she decided to leave her village—a highly unusual step for a Bangladeshi woman. She rented a house across the road from the hospital, where she could visit Nonie every day.

Here she found the vendors more accommodating, and her sales began to pick up. Soon a divorced sister came to live with her. Oirashi found a new husband for her sister and, eventually, their parents and one brother decided to join them.

After Nonie landed a job in the hospital craft shop as a seamstress and returned to live with her mother, Oirashi decided to build a new house for the two of them. Her new brother-in-law permitted her to build one on his land, but after a few months, he sold the land and again Oirashi was forced to dismantle her home. She asked her parents for a small plot of land, but they believed land should be passed only to sons. Hearing of her difficulties, Nonie's former employer, Shabbatra, offered to lend Oirashi 2,500 takas. "It was pure luck that she gave me this loan," Oirashi said. "Finally, I built a house on my *own* land."

She paused and wrinkled her brow. "And then the cyclone came and blew it down!"

Oirashi began laughing so hard that she had to hold herself. Following her lead, the children fell into hysterics. A half-dozen adult villagers, who had joined them, were holding their stomachs. "The whole village laughs at my house troubles," Oirashi said, still laughing. "I've had even more houses than businesses." She caught her breath. "But my life isn't over. And for my daughter's wedding I'm going to break this house down and build one more. It will be my final house. And I hope I die in it."

In 1986, the Grameen Bank opened its 265th branch near Oirashi's village. As soon as the peddler heard about the bank, she resolved to join. "I saw the potential immediately: If I could put more money into my peddling business, my sales would increase."

Although Oirashi had no trouble selling bangles to strangers, when it came to approaching someone as official as a bank manager, she balked.

So she convinced her friend Pushpobala, who was not shy at all, to go see him.

"Pushpo was funny," Oirashi said. "She used to talk so much—so much—but without listening."

The bank manager had already recruited some women from Oirashi's village, but their groups had disbanded. Now, the manager thought the same women were approaching him again. "He sent back a message saying he'd already been humiliated in this village. So I sent Pushpo to tell him that we were different people and we promised not to humiliate anyone. But when Pushpo went there, he told her to come back again— to test her. He thought, 'If she comes three times, she's serious.'

"But Pushpo wasn't so good at arranging her words. She told us that the manager had agreed to come over right away. So we laid out the mats and waited. We waited all day. Then Pushpo said she wasn't *absolutely* sure he said he would come. So I sent her back. This time, she told the manager she wouldn't leave without him. So the manager said, 'She's serious.'

"My old house had a lot of windows, because I love windows. When the manager began explaining to us about the bank's regulations, others came over. At first, not many wanted to join. Afterward, when they saw that we were improving, they said, 'Please take me.' I was the group chairman, so I was the last one in my group to get a loan. The mother always eats last.

"First I borrowed 2,000 takas, then 3,500. I went on and on. Then I got 4,000, then 4,500. Now I'm on 5,000, with two installments left."

41

Oirashi's Final House

Walking under a blazing sun along a path a mile from home, Oirashi called out to another peddler in the distance: "Hey, come with me. You'll sell more things." The woman waved back. "I used to be the only peddler around here," Oirashi said. Now many other people take loans from the Grameen Bank and do this type of work."

"Has it hurt your business?" I asked.

"A little, perhaps," she said. "But these people have to eat, too. It's not just me. Besides, don't animals go in herds? And do they come back without eating?"

In five years, Oirashi's business had grown steadily. Her best customers—other Grameen borrowers—had more disposable income than ever before. "These days people often buy presents for no special occasion," she said. "A woman may buy a surprise for her daughter or a brother might buy a bangle for his sister."

In five years, she had saved a good portion of her daughter's dowry, but Nonie was now in her mid-twenties and relatives worried that her wedding date might never arrive. Oirashi was moving things forward as fast as possible, although she would not abandon her plan to find a *ghor jamai* (a husband who agrees to live in his mother-in-law's house). She didn't want to be separated from Nonie again; she didn't want to grow old alone.

A decade after Renu's wedding she was still repaying the loan she had taken from the moneylender. Before the cyclone, she had planned to take a house loan and build an expanded house for her daughter, son-in-law, and herself. Her new plan was to pay off her present mortgage as quickly as possible—perhaps in as fast as five or six years, drawing on Nonie's salary from the hospital—and then take out another mortgage.

Oirashi peddling

Oirashi had told me that one of her brothers in Chittagong owned a television set. "If he can afford a television, why doesn't he give you more help?" I asked.

She seemed put off by the question. "Why should I take money from him? I'm a peddler."

Indeed, since moving to Dulahazara, Oirashi had gained a reputation as an excellent businesswoman. Vendors in the local bazaar treated her with deference. Few people in the area consistently purchased more goods; and they competed for her business, offering discounts and short-term interest-free credit. But Oirashi preferred to pay cash; she didn't like to be tied to one supplier.

In the villages, she maintained good relations with her customers. A successful peddler had to mix well with everyone: "When people speak angrily, you can't let it get to you. You have to make it water." Since half her customers purchased goods on credit, she was constantly in the position of having to remind them to pay her back. She tried to be as delicate as possible. "Sometimes people tell me, 'Come back another time, I'm facing poverty.' What can I say?"

"With so many customers, how do you remember what everybody owes you?" I asked.

"This has become a way of life," she replied. To make her point, she began rattling off the items she had sold that morning. "So far, one face cream for 40 takas, one hair clip for 24 takas, one Tibet Snow Cream, one plastic red bangle . . ."

On her collection stops, Oirashi would usually receive a portion of the money owed and then sell more merchandise on credit. In this fashion, she was constantly turning over her accounts receivable. She didn't charge her customers interest; this was a cost she had to absorb for doing business with them. Things ran smoothly as long as her sales were high enough to cover her merchandise costs and her living expenses and the weekly installments on both her general and house loans. In good times, Oirashi was able to accumulate materials for her new house and save for Nonie's wedding.

It was when sales dropped off that Oirashi's membership in the Grameen Bank became most critical. As a member of the bank, she enjoyed easy access to other noninstitutional credit sources, such as relatives and neighbors. Since everyone knew she received a regular infusion of money each year and could borrow interest-free from her Group Fund if necessary, villagers did not worry about advancing her small sums when she ran short. As a member of the Grameen Bank, Oirashi was seen as a low credit risk. And villagers knew that there would be times when they could count on her for a small loan.

Occasionally, customers who owed money would give her the runaround. When all else failed, Oirashi resorted to her trump card: sympathy. One morning, after trying for ten minutes to extract a few takas from a woman who had not paid her for two months, she finally said: "Look, you know I have no husband. You know I have no sons. How will I be able to eat if you won't give me my money?"

The woman eventually remembered that her husband had hidden some money inside the house. She emerged with a 10-taka note. But before the peddler departed, the woman purchased a small hair clip for 8 takas—on credit.

"Was that the truth? Do you have trouble eating?" I asked.

"To tell you the truth," Oirashi said, with a grin, "I don't eat very much."

That evening, as the sun painted the western sky with streaks of henna and the smoke from cooking fires filled the countryside, Oirashi sat on a stool in her front yard detailing her plans for Nonie's wedding. Nonie sat on a cane mat ten feet away cutting vegetables and chatting with two cousins. "I have a few boys in mind but I'm not sure about them," Oirashi said. "The one I like best works in a tea stall. But I prefer independent men, even if they have only small businesses. Maybe I'll try to help him open a business. It's good to stand on your own feet."

Nonie raised her eyes from her work only to converse with her cousins. She could certainly hear her mother, but her face betrayed nothing. Oirashi could have been discussing the weather or the number of earrings she'd sold that day. My translator guessed that, after so many years, when the subject of her wedding came up, Nonie felt embarrassed, although she added that she was also probably a little bored with the subject. She understood the feeling. She and Nonie were roughly the same age. And although middle-class, university-educated women in Dhaka have more control over their choice of husbands, their parents still have the final say. Ever since she completed university, my translator explained, the subject of her wedding had been a daily topic of conversion at home—with her mother beginning to sound more and more like Oirashi.

Later, she asked Nonie if all this talk of sons-in-law made her uncomfortable. "Why should it?" Nonie replied. "My mother has struggled all her life for my sister and me. When she is ready, I will abide by her wishes."

When I asked Oirashi if she had prepared Nonie for marriage, she said that mothers and daughters never discussed such matters. "When the time comes she will have her grandmother and sister to ask. It's a very embarrassing issue." On one occasion, I offended Oirashi by asking if she ever looked for a son-in-law on her peddling rounds. "Of course not," she said. "How could I? If I did, people would speak ill of me. They would say, 'She's trying to pick up a husband for her daughter in every village.' "

At home, however, she went on endlessly about her plans to find a good son-in-law. "These thoughts obsess me," she told me. "Everything will have to be ready with the house before I bring him. I've already collected some of the wood and tin and I know a good laborer. I also paid 200 takas to a holy man to find out the exact measurements for the house. It should be eighteen arms in length and ten in width. I don't know if I'll be able to afford beds, but I'll buy some small benches for the main room. I've already started building one myself."

"How big will the house be?" I asked.

"There will be one main room; three sleeping rooms, two downstairs and one upstairs; and two verandas, one at the front and one at the back. The kitchen will be off to the side." Oirashi glanced at my pad as I noted her description. She tapped my arm, picked up a stick and traced a picture of her house in the dirt.

"Like this."

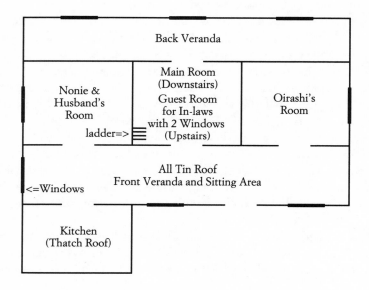

"When will you build it?" I asked.

"I don't know," she said. "When I can, I will."

PART VI

The Future

Maybe our great-grandchildren will go to museums to see
what poverty was.

MUHAMMAD YUNUS

42

The Golden Boat

(Two years later)

"We've moved from Mach one to Mach two."

That was how Muzammel described the changes Grameen had undergone since our last conversation in mid-1992. Grameen had exceeded all growth projections by a country mile. In late 1991, the bank had surpassed one million borrowers; in 1994, it surpassed 2 million. Annual disbursements had leapt from $130 million in 1992 to $385 million in 1994. In early 1992, Grameen was extending $12 million in loans each month; by early 1995, the figure was $40 million. Grameen had raised credit ceilings and introduced several new types of loans. In 1994, many borrowers were working with three times the money they had been working with in 1992. "We now see that what we have been promising all along about poverty alleviation is really possible," Yunus told me. "And you don't have to inch your way all along."

As the demand for credit escalated among older borrowers, the bank had responded with family loans, seasonal loans, technology loans, second house loans, machine leasing loans, tubewell loans and land purchase loans. And borrowers were now permitted to take out more than one loan simultaneously. Suddenly life was very complicated for the staff. In 1992, bank workers had time for frequent afternoon visits with borrowers; two years later, it was not uncommon to find them working on their ledgers by candlelight. "Before we were selling soda on the sidewalk and we had a little cup for our money," Yunus said. "But now we have a big department store and we're still putting our money in a cup. We need cash registers and more counters so that people can pass through quickly."

The bank had also departed from its traditional organizational thrust, although not from its original objective. Beginning in 1992, it began to curtail branch expansion. Previously, Grameen had focused on horizontal growth—establishing new zones, new areas, and new branches. The new focus was on vertical expansion—concentrating on existing borrowers and trying to devise new systems to move them out of poverty as fast as possible. "We're increasing the horsepower to give each borrower a better lift," commented Yunus.

The shift had come in response to events in 1991, Grameen's toughest year, when, in addition to the cyclone and the union threat, management had been confronted with repayment problems in Rangpur, serious setbacks with GAP, and a new government that acted unpredictably and, in Yunus's view, irresponsibly. Shortly after its election victory in 1991, the new government had awarded itself a 25 percent salary hike. Since Grameen followed the government pay scale, it was obliged to follow suit. To meet the new salary costs, the bank raised its interest rate four points, from 16 to 20 percent, after consulting with borrowers around the country. To compensate villagers for the higher charge, the bank reduced the mandatory contribution to the Emergency Fund.

Then the government announced that all agricultural loans under 5,000 takas were waved due to flooding the previous year. Yunus felt that a government so dependent on aid had no business forgiving its loans, and he feared that Grameen borrowers would expect their loans to be forgiven, too. But Grameen's portfolio consisted almost entirely of loans under 5,000 takas. For months, bank workers had to placate villagers. Three years later, resentment still lingered.

Back in 1986, Yunus's optimistic scenario had Grameen reaching 1,500 branches by 1993 and 3,000 branches by 1999, with "saturation" occurring in 2010 at 6,000 branches. After 1991, he quickly put the brakes on. "How big can we get and still maintain quality?" he wondered. By mid-1993, Grameen had slowed branch expansion down from a high of 140 per year to less than 10 per year. "Now it's like a ship on the ocean," Yunus told me. "We've turned off the engine. But we're still coasting. And we're saying to branch managers, 'Look at the quality of the work you're doing with the borrowers you already have.' "

The branch managers did just that, and after conducting some market research, they reported that members had requests for all sorts of additional services. Within a year, the sidewalk stand had turned into a department store. "Before we were taking one woman and supporting her enterprises," Yunus said. "Then we saw there were other members in her family who could use loans. Can we take her as the representative of the family?" But husbands were beyond the bank's direct influence. "Would a woman be oppressed by her husband after he got the money?"

Yunus worried. "Perhaps it would be better not to give this loan. So we said, 'Let's find out.' "

Grameen introduced the family loan, with a ceiling of 25,000 takas (about $625), more than three times Bangladesh's per-capita annual income. "Then," added Yunus, "since we used to have small seasonal loans during the dry season, we thought, 'We've tried a family loan, why not expand this loan?' The moment we moved from single-person, single-purpose to family loans, other loans became easy for us to accept. They were consistent with what we had already done. A husband, brother, or sister could use the money, too. Anybody who wants to run a business—go ahead, run a business. Then we wondered what should be the ceiling for a seasonal loan? Everyone suggested that it should be equal to the general loan.

"So now if the general loan has a ceiling of 10,000 takas and the seasonal loan is 10,000 takas, a member can take up to 20,000 takas, and on top of that, up to 25,000 for a housing loan. That brings them to 45,000 takas. Then with the tubewell loans and the other loans, it's 50,000 takas.

"And we see that they can handle more money than we ever *imagined.* If you go to the oldest areas, you'll see people are talking about 40,000 takas or 50,000 takas and they're not worried about paying it back. So after all these years of preparation, they now have the capacity to use that money. And not only that. After carrying so much money to villages and bringing it back again, we see a capability build up for our organization as well."

According to the bank's research, it took a borrower between ten and fifteen years to cross over the poverty line. This meant that most of the 1.5 million villagers who joined Grameen between 1989 and 1994 would still be below the line by the year 2000. Yunus was not satisfied with this. "We're saying, 'Can we make it shorter?' And now we believe that by the tenth year, or maybe by the seventh year, a borrower can be out of poverty."

But crossing the poverty line was not enough, he added. After that, there was the vital issue of sustainability. Most of Grameen's borrowers had not been landless a generation ago; similarly, someone who crosses over the poverty line this year can drop below it next year. While it was not within the bank's power to reach all of Bangladesh's poor, it was within its power to strengthen the positions of existing borrowers. This was no small achievement considering that Grameen's clientele represented 10 percent of the nation's households.

"Again it's like a ship," said Yunus. "We've picked up 2 million marooned families. Now the job is to take them as far as they want to go. This ship will not abandon them at any stage even if they become the 2 million *richest* families in Bangladesh. We're not going to drop some off, pick up more, and go back. They *own* this ship. You cannot ask the owners to disembark from the ship.

"And to those who raise the question, 'What about the others who are marooned?' I say, 'You know what to do: build another ship.'"

Grameen's disbursements attested to the villagers' capacity to handle money, but the figures said little about the bank's own financial viability. As a rule, bank analysts are not terribly interested in the statistics on which Grameen prides itself most: its volume of customers and disbursements. Two million small, short-term loans are much more costly to manage than a few big, long-term loans. Indeed, Grameen's annual report, which lists more than 400 different types of businesses initiated by borrowers, along with the number of men and women who took loans for each business, would be a commercial banker's nightmare.

Bankers care more about the average loans outstanding and the costs and revenues associated with a loan portfolio. But in this area, Grameen is fast gathering strength. From 1992 to 1995, operating income increased from $19 million to $60 million. Grameen reported small profits in five of the seven years between 1989 and 1995; however, analysts were quick to point out that the profits were not "real" because the bank had received grants and low-cost loans from aid agencies. Was Grameen a real bank? No, said its critics. Without subsidies, it couldn't cover its costs.

"A variety of people come here and they say they wanted to see a *bank,*" Yunus told me in a lighthearted tone, a tone that nevertheless conveyed annoyance. "All of a sudden, when I start talking, they say, 'Well, this is not quite a bank.' I say, 'It depends what you mean by a bank. I think this is a bank.' So they say, 'Oh, you are *more* than a bank.' I say, 'Well, that's what you think, but we think we are *just* a bank. And every other institution that you see that calls itself a bank is *less* than a bank.'"

Of course, Grameen *was* more than a bank. On another occasion, Yunus had told me: "We do a lot *more* than a bank, but when people come to judge us many say, 'Look, it doesn't add up.' I say, 'Give it time. Most businesses don't add up in the first days. We can show you the gap is closing. But don't be so mechanical that you lose sight of the big picture. After eighteen years, it's still a learning process, and learning has a cost. We say, allow us that cost.'"

From the point of view of operations, Yunus felt Grameen had already made important strides toward sustainability. Neither villagers nor branch managers were conscious in their day-to-day affairs that the money they received came from donor agencies. Grameen treated each branch as a separate profit center. While the head office received subsidized funds, it lent money to branches at 12 percent interest. The branches then lent the funds to villagers at 20 percent interest; this gave each branch an 8 percent "spread" to cover operating costs. At a certain point, typically after four or five years, outstanding loans reached a level where a branch began turning a profit.

The challenge for Grameen's head office, then, was to use its "spread" —the difference between the 12 percent it charged branches and the cost of its own funds—to cover all administrative costs, including the accumulated losses in newly established and as yet unprofitable branches.

This had long been a top concern among donors. At some point, they felt, Grameen would have to stand on its own. It was a sticky point. Yunus grew resentful when observers focused too long on Grameen's bottom line. "A donor doesn't mind spending $10 million on a relief operation and never looking at what happened to the money," he told me. "But the moment they give $10 to this organization, they want to bring in the most experienced bankers from their countries to find out whether we look like a bank and are behaving like a bank."

At the same time, Yunus was adamant that Grameen not be perceived as a "special project" or "NGO"—a nongovernmental organization, the generic term applied to the thousands of nonprofit concerns working to develop Bangladesh. "The Grameen Bank is a business enterprise on a sound economic base," he explained. "Special projects, after a while, disappear. Management must never forget that it is a profit-making business enterprise owned by the poor."

Yunus said he looked forward to the day when Grameen's board of directors would vote to distribute profits in the form of dividends to its shareholders—the 2 million villagers who, by the mid-1990s would control more than 90 percent of the bank's paid-up share capital.

When he spoke this way, some felt that he was losing his sense of perspective, or perhaps dreaming. After all, what "legitimate" business receives such heavy subsidies? And then there were Grameen's accounting procedures, which did not conform to international standards. No, these things proved that Grameen was not a bank. It may be a wonderful social program, but it was not a bank. In the "real world," critics said, given the *true* cost of funds, Grameen could not survive.

Ultimately, Yunus viewed financial viability strictly as a management problem that required time to solve. If the bank were to switch from weekly to biweekly installments, for example, administrative costs would fall by a third. If it switched to monthly installments, they would fall even more. What prevented the bank from taking these steps? Only time. First borrowers had to become more adept at investing their loans. With revenues rising and costs falling, it was inevitable that the curves would cross.

In the early 1990s, some of Grameen's donors felt that the bank should consider raising its interest rate again in order to boost revenues. Microenterprise banks in Latin America charged interest well above the commercial bank rate. In 1992, one such bank in Bolivia, BancoSol, part of the ACCION International network, set out to prove that it was possible to be a bank for poor people and turn a profit in just a few years. To do this, BancoSol charged an annual interest rate more than 25 percentage points above the regular commercial bank rate. Some felt that it was unjust to charge poor people so much for credit; others observed that, even with the high interest charges, BancoSol's customers still found it advantageous to take loans. And, as a profitable business, BancoSol would not have to depend on donors to grow. Rather, it could attract investors by promising double-digit returns. In a world with a billion people living in what the World Bank termed *absolute* poverty, everyone agreed that donor funds were insufficient to meet the enormous credit requirements of the poor. Venture capital, on the other hand, is virtually limitless.

Charging 30 or 34 percent interest, some donors argued, Grameen could immediately cover its costs, and the additional charge to each borrower would be minimal—only a few takas per week. On principle, Yunus rejected the idea. He didn't believe that poor people should pay more for credit than rich people, especially in Bangladesh, where the poor had proven themselves far better credit risks than the rich. Yunus was not pleased that he had already been forced to raise the interest rate to 20 percent from 16. Even if the difference between 20 percent and 30 percent represented just a few takas per borrower per week, he preferred those few takas to remain in the villagers' hands. A few takas bought a meal of rice.

Should the donor consortium run dry, Yunus was confident that he could raise funds elsewhere. What neither he nor the donors anticipated was the effect of a precipitous rise in disbursements coupled with a sharp curtailment of branch expansion. In 1993, despite the lingering effects of the cyclone and the ongoing problems in Rangpur, Grameen found itself in a stronger position than ever before.

In 1993, when Grameen's agreement with the donor consortium expired, Yunus felt confident enough to turn to local money markets for financing. Grameen borrowed 3.5 billion takas (about $88 million) from the Bangladesh Bank at the bank rate. At last, Grameen had entered the "real" world of financing. (Individual donors still supported the housing and workshop programs, and other nonbanking initiatives such as the Joysagar Fish Farm and GAP.)

Still seeking less expensive funds, Yunus began negotiations with the Japan-based Overseas Economic Cooperation Fund (OECF) for a $211 million long-term, low-interest loan. But a change of government in Japan forced OECF to postpone its decision and, in 1994 and 1995, Grameen turned again to local money markets. The Bangladesh Bank increased Grameen's credit line to nearly $150 million, and Grameen later raised an additional $125 million through bond issues. Despite the higher interest costs, the bank continued to report small profits.

"As it stands, Grameen has made it," commented Brian Proskurniak, a representative of CIDA, in 1994. "They have a measure of self-sustainability that would allow them to continue without added contributions. Of course, if they wish to grow at a much quicker pace, they will require more funds. But the short answer to the sustainability question is: It's already been done. They have already succeeded."

Masud, for one, was not surprised. To him, it was elementary: "All profitability depends on is increasing the volume of the operation without proportionally increasing the volume of support services, so that the per-unit cost continues to fall. If you can expand and maintain quality, then you can be financially viable."

But Masud did not envision mere "viability" for Grameen. In ten years, he projected annual revenues approaching $200 million and profits of $20 million. In the past, however, Masud's estimates had been rather conservative.

For Grameen, of course, success had never been measured by the bottom line, and while some celebrated the bank's accomplishment, others worried that it was disbursing too much money and, on occasion, missing its target. Top managers argued the issue continually. A few were particularly concerned about the situation in Tangail, the zone in which disbursements had risen most precipitously.

Nurjahan was troubled that too many villagers in the upper levels of the bank's eligibility range were being recruited there. "I have already conducted one investigation and sent the information to Doctor Yunus," she explained. Masud had a different concern, which he dubbed "credit pyramiding." With loans coming at different times of the year, it was now possible for a member to use the proceeds of one loan to make the payments on another. Unless borrowers were careful to keep "separate pockets," they could get into trouble. Credit pyramiding was impossible to detect in its early stages; the only way to identify the problem was to curtail disbursements.

Which is exactly what Masud had recently done. "Tangail had small overdues," he told me. "All of a sudden they started giving loans without looking back, and very fast those overdues vanished. How did this happen overnight? I'm sure some members have adjusted old outstanding dues with new money. That's risky. So immediately it was screwed down and tightened. We'll observe them to see how they perform. If the loan quality is good, then shrinking their funds shouldn't affect them drastically. Maybe some of the loanees will be disappointed but under no circumstances should we let them lend money indiscriminately."

Shamim Anwar, the manager who supervised the Chittagong zone during the cyclone, worried that the bank was departing from its well-tested practice of increasing loans in small increments. "In Tangail, what's happening is an emotional thing, a great fervor for profits," he told me. "It's dangerous. You have to build steps for people. If you know you can carry five kilograms, you can handle six or seven or eight, but what if I put *fifty* kilograms on your back?"

"People tell me that I'm very conservative," he added. "I admit it. But if they fail, then what? They're worse off. Then repayment habits get spoiled. And once this happens, it spreads like a virus."

Not all managers shared this opinion. "In Tangail, they are doing something very dynamic," Daiyan told me. "If they're constantly criticized, they will lose their confidence." Without a doubt, Tangail was a banking experiment on a different order of magnitude, he argued, but hadn't the Grameen Bank begun as a bold experiment? And Dipal commented: "Remember, some members in Tangail have been taking loans for *fourteen* years."

"When you're driving a car on a very fine highway in second or third gear," added Khalid, "you need to push to the top gear. This has not been done suddenly or in an amateurish way. There have been a lot of discussions and a lot of experimentation. And we have seen that quietly some profound changes have taken place."

43

One Thousand Doctors

For years, managers in Tangail had been clamoring for higher loan ceilings. With so many conflicting views among the staff, Yunus was not sure what to do. So he left it to his zonal managers to decide. In the meantime, he wondered if the bank might not benefit from an outsider's view of its most prosperous zone. After more than a decade, how far had borrowers in Tangail really come?

The opportunity arose one day when Yunus was speaking with David Gibbons, a Canadian-born professor of political science, who had founded one of the first and most successful Grameen Bank replications, Amanah Ikhtiar Malaysia, which today has close to 40,000 borrowers. Gibbons had expressed an interest in studying the long-term impact of Grameen loans. He felt that definitive research had yet to be conducted on Grameen's oldest members. He proposed a one-year controlled study, working in conjunction with his wife, Helen Todd, a journalist, to examine ten-time women borrowers in Tangail.

One of Gibbons and Todd's findings confirmed something the bank had long suspected. In Tangail, many borrowers were using their loans to lease and purchase land. Although the returns were higher than for other activities, Grameen officially opposed loans for land acquisition or leasehold because the staff feared that members would try to acquire land from poorer villagers. What Gibbons and Todd found was that many older members simply lied on their loan proposals and did it anyway. But contrary to expectations, most of the land leased by Grameen borrowers came not from poorer villagers, but from wealthier villagers, who were underutilizing the land. Poorer villagers had been hurt slightly, not because bank members had exploited them, but because the increased demand for land inevitably drove up the price.

Grameen's clientele had always been defined by the fact that they

Muzammel, Yunus, and Khalid talking to Grameen Bank replicators

lacked the one asset villagers covet most: land. By introducing the seasonal loan, Grameen gave landless villagers the opportunity to invest in land and substantially increase their incomes. But with the potential for higher returns, came higher risks—especially from flooding and droughts. "We're a little worried but there is no major apprehension," Khalid told me. "A lot of new checks and balances have been introduced."

Gibbons and Todd's most important findings emerged when they contrasted Grameen borrowers with a "control" group of women, comparable in age, who could have joined the bank ten years earlier but did not. Among the nonmembers, they found women contributed 25 percent of household earnings, while in Grameen households, income generated by women (or through women's access to credit) accounted for 54 percent of total family earnings. In addition, Grameen families had higher child immunization rates and contracted out their children for work at one fourth the frequency of nonmembers. Grameen children were taller and heavier for their ages and, remarkably, even fared better than the national average. According to standards established by the World Health Organization, every child in the study remained underweight; however, using a standard classification of weight-for-age, Gibbons and Todd reported that Grameen children suffered "first-degree" malnutrition, while the children of nonmembers suffered "second-degree" malnutrition.

Perhaps their most significant finding was that, compared with 18 percent of nonmembers, 58 percent of the Grameen borrowers had crossed over the extreme poverty line (defined as an annual income sufficient to provide each family member with a daily intake of 1,800 calories). Of the 42 percent of Grameen borrowers who failed to cross the poverty line, fully 60 percent had experienced a serious illness in the family—most commonly tuberculosis, typhoid, jaundice, and gastric ulcer. Grameen loans prevented these families from becoming destitute, but they were insufficient to overcome their crises.

"This was a very powerful revelation for us," recalled Khalid. "Gibbons very sharply pointed out stories of people who spent thousands of takas on simple injections or antibiotics and people who died in childbirth. We always knew it was there but we didn't realize it had so much impact."

Without access to reasonably priced health services, illness would continue to erode the incomes of hundreds of thousands of villagers.

"Is it possible for the Grameen Bank to administer a health program?" Yunus asked Khalid.

Grameen had grown too complex for Yunus's liking. He had dubbed 1992 the "Year of Reorganization" and proceeded to break up the bank's components into separate legal entities. Grameen established the Krishi (Agricultural) Foundation, to manage the DTWs; the Motsho (Fisheries) Foundation, to oversee fish farms; and, later, a foundation called Grameen Uddog (Initiatives) to manage other businesses. The bank had earlier established the Grameen Trust, a not-for-profit company, to support Grameen replications and poverty research throughout the world. The Trust also provided Yunus with a political escape hatch. Here, he could experiment without having to conform to government banking regulations.

If the bank could not manage a health program, what prevented the Trust from doing it? "But how to make it operational?" asked Khalid. "You need barefoot doctors going around convincing people that they need sanitary latrines, telling mothers who are expecting that they'd like to give them some basic prenatal and postnatal services. In addition, we would also need a full medicare package—for common things like an ear infection or a chest cold, pneumonia or bronchitis.

"Doctors should have offices, as well as mobile clinics. And the idea was that if any Grameen Bank member wants these services, she'll subscribe to the health insurance program, pay a premium, and, in addition, pay a token fee for prescriptions—say one taka. We'd provide small laboratories to do routine tests—blood, urine—and supply medicines at cost. Those who are not Grameen members who are poor can have access to these services but they pay a higher rate. And a rich person can come and avail himself of these services, but he pays at the market rate. And our expectation is that this will pay for all the expenses."

Grameen's experimental health program was launched in 1993 in seven locations. Each health center was attached to an old branch with close to 2,000 borrowers. Each health center had one doctor, three paramedics, and a half dozen field-workers trained to provide basic health care information. The initial fees were as follows: Registration cost 3 takas. The premium for members was one taka per week (2 takas for a very large family); for nonmembers it was 10 takas per month. Each doctor visit cost 2 takas. Grameen members who elected not to purchase health insurance paid 10 takas per visit. Nonmembers without insurance were charged based on ability to pay.

In the first few months, the staff had identified a number of problems with the plan. But by far, the biggest obstacle was simply the villagers' resistance to the concept of insurance: paying for something they hope they will not need.

After two years, only a few villagers in each branch had signed up. Participation was increasing, but slowly. Management began debating whether the health insurance premiums might be better handled as an invisible charge rather than a cash payment. "Instead of trying to collect it every week at the meeting," Khalid explained, "we could charge it to the Group Fund where they have enormous savings—provided the group agrees."

"If we do that, I think this health program can take off," he added. "It could bring about an almost revolutionary change in the health scene. We could hire a thousand doctors—one per branch."

44

The Luck of Manjira

The path to Manjira's house was lined with mango groves and rice paddies. The branch manager traveled by bicycle to deliver the message. It had come from the head office, relayed via the Rajshahi zonal office to the area office, and then to Manjira's branch.

She was half-expecting the manager's visit. At the most recent meeting of the bank's board of directors, Yunus had brought up the subject and put the question to her and each of the other eight members who sat on the board. Grameen had been awarded the King Baudouin International Development Prize from the Belgium monarch, to be presented in Brussels, Belgium, in April 1993. And because the prize was awarded to the bank and not to him personally, Yunus explained that it would be fitting for one of the board members to accompany him on the trip.

Who would be interested in visiting the king's palace in Belgium and accepting an award on behalf of all the borrowers? As the question went around the boardroom table, a few of the villagers explained that they could not be away from home for a full week; a few said their husbands would not permit them to make the trip; some worried about having to travel in an airplane; and everyone was anxious about having to eat in the presence of the King and Queen of Belgium. A vote was held and Manjira Khatun, the representative from the Rajshahi zone, was elected. It wasn't a final decision, Yunus explained. He would contact her within a few days to confirm the decision.

After the board meeting, Yunus sent a fax to the king's staff explaining that the Grameen delegation would comprise Manjira Khatun, Grameen Bank borrower and board member; Nurjahan Begum, principal of the bank's training institute; and himself.

In a few days, he received a reply from the king's staff, expressing concern that a village woman might be uncomfortable in Belgium. Yunus reassured them that everything would be fine. "This award was given to the Grameen Bank," he reminded them, "and the Grameen Bank is owned by village women."

Now, on the porch of Manjira's house, the manager relayed the news. "Are you sure you can go to Belgium?" he asked.

"Yes, I can go," Manjira replied.

"You know, you might not be able to eat rice."

"Yes. I know."

"Belgium is a cold country," he added.

"They told me it was," Manjira said.

The manager arranged for Manjira to travel to Dhaka accompanied by her brother. From the moment she boarded the bus, her mind was spinning. "I kept worrying about how I would present myself to the king," Manjira told me when I visited her a year later. If the king asked about her life and her relationship with the Grameen Bank, she would have to speak precisely and eloquently. So for hours, she reflected upon her life.

Manjira had grown up in a family with twelve children. Her father, once a relatively prosperous farmer, was forced to sell off most of his land due to legal disputes. At seventeen, Manjira was married to a man studying to be a legal clerk. She gave birth to two sons while working to help pay her husband's tuition. Years passed. When she was pregnant with a third child, her husband lost his job. Angry and humiliated, he sent her back to her father's house. Soon, Manjira heard from a neighbor that he had remarried; when she confronted him, he denied it. When the child was born, she went to the house where he lived with his new wife to inform him that he had another son. He demanded that the children remain, so Manjira remained as well.

From that point, her husband began to beat her mercilessly. After months, a friend finally implored Manjira to leave. "Better to beg than live in a butcher's house," she said. Manjira returned to her father's house with her baby boy, still hoping that her husband would change his ways. By then, her father had become a poor man and did not want her home. She and her son were treated as outcasts. Her son was forced to eat after all the other children. Manjira earned her meals working in the houses of other villagers.

Several years passed until one morning—a Saturday morning, recalled Manjira—when her seven-year-old son fell ill with a severe case of diarrhea; the following day, he died. Devastated, Manjira stopped working.

For three months, she ate barely enough to stay alive. "I couldn't function. I was waiting to die," she told me. She remained in this state until her brother grabbed hold of her one day and yelled: "Your son is gone, but you're still alive—and you have to take care of yourself."

Manjira went to work as a tailor's assistant, earning 5 to 7 takas a day. When the Grameen Bank opened a center in her village, her father urged her to join. Manjira didn't want to get involved with loans, but her father persisted. When she received her first loan of 2,000 takas, she purchased a sewing machine. Before long, she gained a reputation as a high-quality stitcher. Over the next four years, her earnings climbed from 50 takas to more than 250 takas a week. Eventually, she had to hire an assistant to keep up with demand. In her fourth year, she applied for and was granted a 20,000-taka mortgage to built a house of brick and tin. When the bank held elections for board members, Manjira was selected to represent her center. In the zonal election, she was chosen to represent more than 100,000 borrowers in the Rajshahi zone.

As her bus approached Dhaka, Manjira wondered if she should tell the king her saddest memory, a day five years before when her son had asked for some ice cream. "It cost only one taka but I didn't even have one taka to give him," she said. "Then the next day, he got sick and died."

At the bank's head office, Yunus and Nurjahan took Manjira shopping for a sweater, a shawl, shoes, and socks. Previously, Manjira had worn only sandals; these shoes had small heels. She practiced walking in them immediately.

On the airplane, Yunus watched carefully for signs of discomfort. Nurjahan showed Manjira how to use a fork and knife and explained how to use the airplane lavatory. Shortly before landing, Manjira asked Yunus: "How should I greet the king when I meet him?"

"You catch the king's hand and take it smartly with your two hands and wish him well," Yunus replied.

The plane arrived in Brussels in the morning. The king had sent a car to pick up the passengers and take them to the Hilton, where they were booked in suites on the twenty-second floor. "My room had five telephones," Manjira said. "There was even a phone in the bathroom. In my whole life I had never received one telephone call."

"One wall was made of glass," she continued. "When I looked out, I could see the whole city. I watched the cars. Brussels is very clean. There was no mud to be seen anywhere."

Manjira had not eaten much on the plane, so that night Yunus took her to a Bengali restaurant for dinner. The next few days were filled with visits. Each time, when someone asked Yunus about Grameen, he replied, "What can I say? She borrows the money, she repays it. Ask her."

Then Manjira stood up. "I explained everything—about the centers, the branches and zones, and the 1.5 million borrowers."

Manjira was invited to tell her story to a university audience. She spoke of her problems with her husband, of her son's death, and the eight years when she subsisted on one meal a day. "God gave me hands and legs and eyes," she told the students, "so why couldn't I earn anything just a few years back? I couldn't save a single penny. I couldn't even buy my son an ice cream for one taka. I could do none of these things due to a lack of money."

After the lecture, a Belgian woman holding a tray approached Manjira.

"Mrs. Manjira, orange juice?" she said.

"*Na,*" Manjira said.

"What is *na?*" the woman said.

"In Bangla, *na,*" explained Manjira, "in English, 'no.' "

Then the woman said, "In English, 'water.' "

Manjira responded, "In Bangla, *panni.*"

"In English, 'mother'?"

"In Bangla, *ma.*"

" 'Father'?"

"*Pita.*"

Nurjahan overheard the conversation and commented to Yunus: "You've brought Manjira here for seven days—she'll know English by the time she returns home." Then Yunus asked her, "Are you learning English and teaching her Bangla?" Manjira replied, "Yes, it's my luck."

"I was so happy," she added. "I was so excited that I could understand a few English words. But when they spoke in sentences, I couldn't get it."

The day came to meet the king and queen. As Manjira entered the palace, she noticed her reflection in the marble floor. "Then I felt a little dizzy," she said. There were several men in the room but nobody wore a crown. Everybody seemed to be paying attention to one man in a dark suit. Manjira asked and Nurjahan explained that he was the king. "He was dressed very simply. I thought, 'Why didn't he wear something fancier?' "

When King Baudouin greeted her, she took his hand in her two.

Manjira Khatun

"You have come from a long way," the king said. "You have great patience." He inquired whether Manjira was happy to have come to his palace.

"I'm happy to accept this honor on behalf of my 1.5 million Grameen members," she replied. "All of Bangladesh is proud. I thank you, your queen, and your government."

"You must be a very happy man to live in a palace like this," she added.

"I know you, Manjira, have suffered a great deal," replied King Baudouin. "The poor people suffer. But even the King of Belgium has pain." He added, "I have heard that you follow sixteen decisions." Manjira said yes and recited them for him.

The queen greeted Manjira with a kiss. Nurjahan was astonished. "If it had been me, I would have been stunned. But she simply returned the kiss. The queen was quite impressed."

Afterward, Manjira saw that Yunus was laughing to himself. "When I asked him why," she recalled, "he said, 'You gave a beautiful answer.'"

The reception two days later was attended by three hundred guests.

"We had to walk through three large rooms, and in each room I had to shake hands with *everyone.*"

During dinner, Manjira sat next to the Bangladeshi ambassador. Yunus recalled: "Manjira was not eating anything. Everybody inquired, 'Why are you not eating?' and Manjira said, 'I'm not very hungry. I'll just nibble at something to keep you company.' She was worried that if she tried to eat it would be a big mess. People asked her questions and then the ambassador became the interpreter.

"So here at the table is the ambassador, the interpreter, and she, the main speaker. And she did it so naturally."

After the presentation of the award and check for 4 million Belgian francs, Yunus gave a speech. Then the king said to Manjira, "You have come from so far away, let us take a photograph together."

"The king had never gotten a chance to talk with a woman from a remote village in Bangladesh," Yunus said, "a very poor person who couldn't give her son one taka to buy sweets before he died. When she told him about that, it shocked him."

At the press conference, the reporters directed questions at Manjira while Yunus stepped back and acted as interpreter. "She was all over the press, big pictures all over the TV." That night Manjira could not sleep. "I knew I would have to tell the story, so I memorized everything."

Before returning to Bangladesh, the three took a trip to Holland, visiting Amsterdam, the sea shore, and a tulip garden. The king had given Manjira a book of photographs and some spending money. I asked her if she bought any souvenirs in Belgium. "If I could afford to buy things in Belgium," she replied, "would I be a member of the Grameen Bank?"

Back in Dhaka, she was besieged with questions from journalists and the bank staff. "I didn't even have time to eat. It was like when someone returns from the Haj." In her village, the attention was even more intense. "For three days, I told my stories all day long." Neighbors, even local elites, crowded onto her porch and invited her to their homes. They inquired: How did you know what to say and how to behave before the king and queen?

"Sometimes I wonder myself where I get my ideas," she replied. "I don't know where they come from."

Was it thrilling to meet the king?

"Yes, but it would have been more enjoyable if the king understood my language," Manjira said. "How long can a person speak through another person?"

Inevitably, one villager asked: From among all the Grameen Bank members in Bangladesh, how were you, Manjira, selected to meet the King of Belgium?

"I'll say this," she replied. "I'm certainly not the only member who joined the Grameen Bank, took loans, and worked hard. I was very lucky."

45

An Infinite Amount of Work

The boat trip to Patuakhali was as peaceful as I remembered, the bus journey every bit as chaotic. Little appeared to have changed in two years. A high-voltage tower downed in the 1991 cyclone still lay on its side. The shops by the ferry crossing stocked the same assortment of biscuits, cigarettes, candies, and fruit. Across the muddy river, the buildings in town were perhaps slightly more weather-beaten, but not noticeably so. The familiar sound of rickshaw bells still filled the winding roads. I noted one change: In two years, the price of a ride to the Dibuapur branch had gone up 2 takas.

A number of shops in the bazaar were gone. The rickshaw driver explained that the government had ordered them dismantled to widen the road. I asked about Hasina, the young girl who ran her father's restaurant. He said the family was forced to close their business and move away.

The Dibuapur branch, freshly painted with a sky blue wash, shone in the late morning sun. Inside, the bank workers sat at their desks behind rows of red and green ledgers. I recognized only one of the bank workers; everyone else had been transferred.

Sabina Yasmin smiled when she saw me. "If you had come a few months later," she said, "you would not have found me here."

Here many things had changed. Sabina's husband had gotten a job in a district thirty miles away working with BRAC's credit program. He was home only two days of the week. Now, in addition to work, Sabina had to manage the household alone.

The branch had grown by seven hundred members. Disbursements had soared. Where she used to collect 2,500 takas at a meeting, Sabina now took in more than 7,000. "I have much more paperwork," she explained.

"Are you worried that the new loans may be too large?" I asked.

"I don't see a problem," she replied. "I go to the houses. I know what they do, what their husbands do, what their sons do. They're investing the money, not eating it. Besides, not every member receives a large loan."

"The economic structure is gradually improving," she added. "At one time, not one member in each center would have a house with a tin roof. Now more than half do. Some have received house loans, but others have built houses on their own. They have a few chairs, better pots and crockery, their children are wearing better clothes. Eighty to 90 percent of my members now eat three times a day. And 25 of my 260 members have electricity. None had it two years ago. Now the Grameen Bank has to place even more stress on education, health, and family planning."

Sabina's ambition was to become a branch manager, and she hoped that when she received notice of her transfer, it would come with a promotion. "If my education were higher, by now, I would already be an officer." She hoped that the zonal manager would post her to a branch near her husband's office. "The kids will be disappointed having to move," she said. "But they're kids. They'll make new friends easily."

"How much longer do you think you'll do this work?" I asked.

"I don't know. I still love it. I have a lot of patience—you need a lot of patience to work in the Grameen Bank. I find it has even helped me as a mother. I explain things to my children and my husband the same way I explain them to my members. Not only has this job helped me to develop my country, but it has helped me to develop my family."

"Do you often get frustrated or angry?" I asked.

"I get angry when I'm hungry. When I'm hungry, if anyone speaks to me, I get angry."

"There must be a lot of angry people in Bangladesh."

"Yes, and it's because of anger that poverty increases. In anger and without thought, people sell off their assets and their land."

"Sometimes I do get tired of the fieldwork," she added, after a moment's thought, "but I still have the spirit. Perhaps in a few years, I'll lose it. I haven't yet—it's only been ten years."

I remembered that the first right turn off the high road led to a winding path that emerged from the overgrowth by the side of Aleya and Ansar's house. The house had recently been painted with a dark stain to protect it from termites. Out front, the mud court seemed deserted; there were no boys playing outside.

Aleya came out of her house holding a baby girl. Her daughters waved through the windows. They didn't seem surprised to see me. "The men are in town," Aleya explained. "They went to the fair for the Bengali New Year."

Aleya looked the same. "You look well," I said.

She smiled, "God has also kept you well. We thought about you after you left. All the others received photographs, but we didn't."

"I'm very sorry," I said. "They must have gotten lost in the mail."

I inquired about her baby girl, Minara. She was a year old. She was dressed in clean shorts and a T-shirt. "In the same year I married off one daughter and gave birth to another," Aleya said. "I prayed for a boy, but it wasn't written on my forehead. Still, I won't have any more children."

"Where is *apa?*" she asked. (*Apa,* literally "sister," referred to my previous translator.)

"She is in Dhaka studying for her exams," I said.

Aleya invited us in and left to prepare some food. While she was in her kitchen, Ansar returned from the fair with presents for his daughters: pieces of molasses candy, a little clay pot, a plastic deer, and two whistles. His ten-year-old daughter, Tamina, filled the clay pot with puffed rice. The girls inquired about the fair. It had music and plays and small shops and a Ferris wheel, their father explained.

"Girls can't go?" I asked.

"There's no rule that says they can't go, but there are too many men," Ansar said. "There may be fighting."

Minara slid down the front steps, picked herself up, and began walking, or tottering, toward the cow shed. I was surprised. She appeared too tiny to be walking already, although I knew she was a year old.

"Congratulations on the birth of your daughter," I said to Ansar. "How did you feel when she was born?"

"I felt happy," he said. "With a healthy child, I have to be happy. If it was a boy, I would have been elated."

Minara had been born at 11:00 P.M. "My wife ate her dinner, and then the pain came," recalled Ansar. "There were no problems. Some people take a lot of time, but she took only half an hour. It took three days before she was on her feet again."

Suddenly, Tamina ran to pick up Minara, who had wandered near the edge of a pond about thirty feet from the house. "She didn't use to go near the pond," Ansar commented. "Now she likes to play with water. Other babies the same age here don't walk as much. You can see that in just a few seconds she was down the stairs and at the pond."

Aleya returned from the kitchen and exchanged her tray of biscuits, puffed rice, and tea for the baby. She covered Minara's head with the edge of her sari and began breastfeeding.

"I have to put up a fence," Ansar said to his wife.

I noted the electric meter on the wall and the lightbulbs suspended overhead. "A lot of things have changed since last time. We have electricity. My daughter got married. I did some repairs on the house. Also my father died. You spoke with him. He was seventy-four."

"How did he die?"

"He had lung cancer."

"Did he suffer much?" I asked.

"No," Ansar said. "He didn't even know he had cancer. It was very sudden. He died a week after the doctors discovered the tumor, before my daughter's wedding."

Aleya and Ansar had saved for five years to pay for Halima's wedding. Now they were putting money away for the marriage of their second daughter, fourteen-year-old Rabeya.

"How is your son-in-law?" I asked.

"He knows his business and he's also good-looking. Up to this point everything is fine."

"Everybody in the family feels sad because our daughter is not here," Aleya added. "She usually visits once a week. But after a while, she won't come as often."

Aleya handed Minara to Tamina and went outside to do a few chores. This year, in addition to an 8,000-taka general loan, she had taken a 5,000-taka seasonal loan. The couple owed 2,000 takas on their original 10,000-taka house loan.

"Do you have any complaints with the bank?" I asked.

Ansar thought for a moment. "The interest for the house loan is too high," he said. "The house loan doesn't generate any income. Also the Group Fund tax is too high. And even when other banks forgive loans, Grameen Bank never does."

Ansar looked out the window at Aleya collecting straw by the cow shed. "My wife is very hard working," he commented. "Starting from the cooking in the morning, she does an infinite amount of work. That's why she's so thin."

"When we were very poor she had to work all the time," he added. "Now things are not so bad but she's still in the habit."

"Will there be a time when she works less?" I asked.

"Yes," Ansar replied. "I hope so."

• • •

In two years, Aleya (poor) had also given birth to another child—her seventh. Her husband had discovered her birth control pills and thrown them out. When I came upon her, she was sitting on the mud stoop with her sister-in-law, Fatima. Her one-year-old boy, Selim, was asleep in her arms. Aleya looked tired. The baby appeared unhealthy. His stomach seemed swollen and his head appeared unnaturally large for his body.

A nurse in Bangladesh had explained to me that babies often die of malnutrition because their parents fail to recognize the signs in time. "When the baby becomes anemic," she explained, "its complexion lightens and its body becomes swollen as fluid collects under the skin because the walls of cells begin leaking. This looks to mothers initially like a beautiful, fat, light-skinned baby. Only when the hair turns red, and the skin breaks out in ulcers do they try to do something. But at that point it's very difficult to turn it around. You have to pump food into the stomach and the stomach rejects it. The child's body is racked with terrible diarrhea."

It was impossible for me to say if Selim was this poorly nourished. But the contrast with Minara, the same age, was unmistakable.

Aleya's husband sat on a stool by the side of the house cutting strips of bamboo. Occasionally, he stared in my direction, but he did not speak or budge. When I tried to ask him a question, he waved me away.

"My bank worker was upset with me last time because I told you about my problems," Aleya said. "He yelled, 'Why did you tell him everything? He's going to go home to America and tell everyone.'

"I said, 'Why shouldn't I? It's my life. They should know that when the Grameen Bank gives us money, we must pay the installments. Some people can do this easily. But a very poor person like me, with a low income and high expenditures, can barely save anything. Sometimes, it's a great hardship to pay the installments.' "

Aleya had taken a 5,000-taka general loan and 4,000-taka seasonal loan this year. (Just two years before, the bank's maximum loan was 8,000 takas.) After my last visit, Aleya had had to borrow money from an uncle to make her interest payment. With her next loan, she repaid her uncle and purchased another cow, which died. "I have had bad luck with my cows," Aleya said. She quickly added that the cow that wouldn't produce milk later produced two calves. "So I have three now," she said. "But I would have had five if the other cow hadn't died."

Another of her sons had grown big enough to earn an income as a daily laborer, Aleya said. Her livestock generated a small but steady income. With the seasonal loan, she had leased a small plot of land.

However, because her husband was unable to farm it, she had to hire a laborer, and this cut into her profit.

"Now we eat in the morning and in the evening," she said. "Sometimes we eat three times a day—not very often. The children have some new clothes. But other people in the bank have done much better than I have. Some have built new houses and bought rickshaws and shops."

Fatima cut in: "I heard that the head of the Grameen Bank went abroad and was given a lot of money." She pointed to Aleya. "But did she receive the benefits?"

"The poor never benefit," Fatima said, answering her own question.

"Before I didn't even have pillows," Aleya countered. "Now I have some. And I have two quilts."

"Okay," Fatima said. "We know the Grameen Bank is good." She turned to me: "But this family is in trouble and it's hard for them to pay the installments. And there must be many people in the same situation."

"Not everybody can have their hopes fulfilled," Aleya said. "But I've been a member for only four years. So if Allah permits, I hope to improve more."

On my way back to the branch office, I passed Aleya (rich) carrying a water jug to the well. I mentioned that I had just come from the house of Aleya (poor) and her son looked ill. "It takes a long time for poor people to improve themselves," Aleya said. "It's slow, slow, slow."

"Can you speed it up?" I asked.

"No," she said. "These people have about ten mouths to feed."

At the branch, I asked Sabina about Aleya (poor).

"She was quite poor," she explained, "but she's come up a bit. The other Aleya has been a member for eight years. She's only been a member for four years.

"But watch. In the next three or four years, she'll continue to improve."

46

She Turned Her Face to the Light

The Patuakhali zonal manager had contacted the area manager in Barguna to arrange accommodations for my translator and me at Begum Rokeya's branch. I wondered if Rokeya had given birth to a son or daughter. A letter with photographs sent after my previous visit had gone unanswered. She would have made good use of the bank's new loans, I was sure. Perhaps, in the intervening period, she had even built a new house.

The afternoon before my scheduled departure, I returned to the office to find the zonal manager sitting at the manager's desk wearing a somber expression. "The area manager from Barguna contacted me this morning," he told me. "The member you wanted to visit at the Gourichanna Branch, Rokeya, died last month."

"Begum Rokeya?"

"There are two Rokeyas who are members in the same village," the zonal manager said. "The area manager is new, so he does not know her personally, but he said he believes the woman you wanted to visit is the one who died."

"How?"

"From diarrhea. From bad food or water."

"The road is in poor condition because of the storms," he added. "Do you still want to leave in the morning?" After a discussion with my translator, I said yes. The zonal manager explained that the bus departed at 6:30 A.M. from town.

The early morning sky brought no cheer. An hour into the journey, our bus got stuck in mud and the driver instructed all male passengers to disembark and push. When we arrived at the river, the ferry was out of

The river crossing to Barguna

commission. Along with twenty other people, we removed our footwear, waded into the muddy water, and climbed aboard a flimsy sculler for the quarter-mile crossing. Hopefully, a bus would be waiting on the other side.

In the boat, a man sat on the gunnel across from me, holding a briefcase close to his chest, and watched the clouds uneasily. Two minutes after we pushed off, a light rain began to fall. Suddenly, passengers began shouting at the oarsman to row toward a Mississippi-style riverboat docked a few hundred yards away.

As we slipped alongside the steel deck, several passengers quickly jumped onto the riverboat; a few held the boat steady while others helped pull young and old and bags safely aboard. Then the oarsman made a beeline for shore. The sky turned black and an explosive wind and rain descended on us; it seemed to me like a flash hurricane. "Look at the waves," said the man with the briefcase. "Our boat might have capsized."

Forty minutes later, the sky had cleared and the oarsman returned.

• • •

We reached the other bank just as a full bus was preparing to depart. Somehow, the driver found room for an additional twenty passengers. In a half hour, we arrived in Barguna.

Since leaving Dibuapur, I had been thinking about Rokeya. When she established her center, she taught all the other women the Sixteen Decisions. She knew them cold. She told me she never washed her crockery in ponds and drank only tubewell water. She was also aware that the wells in Barguna were not completely safe; after floods and heavy rains, when surface water contaminated wells, she purified her family's drinking water or boiled it. Of all the Grameen borrowers I'd met in Bangladesh, she seemed the most conscientious about safety. Could the area manager have been mistaken?

The Gourichanna Branch stood along the path to Rokeya's village. On the way to meet the branch manager and drop off my bag, I caught sight of Rokeya's husband, Alum, sitting in his tea stall. He waved me over. "You'll understand that I'm feeling a little sad," he said as I sat down. "Begum Rokeya died six weeks ago."

"I'm very sorry," I said.

"I have remarried," he said.

I nodded.

"Taslima won a government scholarship," he added. "She found out nineteen days after Begum Rokeya died." Alum smiled faintly. He handed me a plate of biscuits and a cup of tea. He would accept no payment. "Come visit the girls this afternoon," he said. "They'll be home from school."

"I will," I said. "How is your baby?"

"She is growing well," he said. "She is clever like her mother—not like her father."

"What's her name?"

"Sonia. Amena and Taslima named her."

If I hadn't spotted Rokeya's sister-in-law, Parveen, hanging laundry on a clothesline, I would have passed right by the house. It was hidden behind a stack of hay and a garden filled with young trees—banana, papaya, coconut, and guava.

Parveen invited us into Rokeya's house. Alum's mother and nephew were inside, along with Alum's new wife, Zakir. "Rokeya was holding my hand when she died," Parveen said. Without prompting, she explained what had happened.

Seventeen days into the month of Ramadan, Rokeya had not once broken her fast (from sunrise to sunset). On the eighteenth morning, she felt fine. In the early afternoon, she took a bath and tended to her cows. When a brother arrived to accompany her to her father's house for a visit, Rokeya said she was feeling too weak for the six-mile walk. "She thought it was because of the fast," Parveen said. A few hours before sunset, Rokeya vomited and began experiencing cramps and diarrhea. "Taslima and Amena told her to eat something. According to Muslim law, if you get sick, you *must* break your fast. But she didn't."

When Alum returned from work and saw Rokeya, he borrowed a bicycle and raced to the pharmacy to purchase rehydration solution in both oral and intravenous form. "If we had known her diarrhea was so severe, we would have taken her to the doctor immediately," Parveen said. "We didn't imagine that it would become so serious so suddenly." The girls tried to feed their mother but she was too weak to eat. When Alum returned, he tried to administer the oral saline solution, but Rokeya couldn't swallow it. "We tried to inject the saline solution into her arm," Parveen said, "but after midnight, it wasn't going through any longer."

The next morning, the scheduled day for Rokeya's center meeting, all the members came to her house. "The children were crying," Parveen said. "Her husband was crying. Several women helped bathe Rokeya and wrap her body in the burial cloth." Three hundred villagers gathered for the funeral. A prayer was said and Rokeya's body, carried on a thin pallet with a black cloth draped over it, was placed in the ground and covered with banana leaves and earth.

Tears filled Alum's mother's eyes as Parveen spoke. "My daughter-in-law loved taking care of her family," she said. "When her children left for school, she used to walk with them all the way up to the main path."

"Would you like to visit Rokeya's grave?" Parveen asked.

I nodded yes.

Parveen led the way a few hundred yards to a mound of earth hidden behind a line of trees. The mound was covered with branches and twigs to keep away dogs and other animals. Muslims do not believe in marking graves with elaborate headstones. "They buried her near her son," Parveen said. "In such a way, that her son is next to her lap."

Fifteen minutes later, Taslima entered the house swinging a new school bag with a patch featuring the logo from the Barcelona Olympics. Amena stood behind her, now a full head taller. The girls, eleven and fourteen, wore green-and-white school uniforms. They had grown beautifully. Amena looked more than ever like her father; Taslima was the image of Rokeya. "My father told us you had come back," Taslima said.

Taslima and Amena

"It would have made Begum Rokeya happy to see you." The girls excused themselves to change their clothes. Taslima returned holding two-year-old Sonia.

The baby was tiny, like Rokeya, but her bright eyes scanned the room watchfully. "Taslima is the only one that Sonia will let hold her," Parveen said.

I asked Amena if they had received my letter. She went upstairs and retrieved three photographs, faded from the humidity. "My mother looks very nice," Taslima admired. "What a smile."

"Congratulations on your scholarship," I said. "How did you win it?"

"I took a special exam," Taslima said. "My best friend also took it. She's smart like me. But she didn't get a scholarship because she gets nervous during exams."

"A few hundred people took the exam," Amena said proudly. "But only five or six won the scholarship."

"What was on the exam?"

"English, Bengali, social studies, science, and mathematics," Taslima said. "And I wrote a composition about jute."

"What sorts of math questions did they ask?"

"Percentage problems, order of operations and brackets. It was a three-hour exam split into two days. I finished the math part in one hour."

Taslima had earlier won a wristwatch when she came first in another school competition. This scholarship, awarded by the government, covered tuition expenses for grades six and seven.

"I had a feeling I was going to win it," Taslima said. "I told my mother. She would have been happy, but I got the news nineteen days after she died."

"Do you know what kind of work you'd like to do when you're older?"

"After I pass my B.A.," she replied, "I would like to become a magistrate. I think I would enjoy that job."

Amena, who had been whispering with Parveen, left the room to speak with Alum's new wife. Zakir would not sit in the front room with us or speak to me. "Sonia has a bit of diarrhea," explained Parveen. "The girls are worried that their stepmom will forget to give her her medicine.

"Amena was angry with Rokeya," she added. "Because Rokeya never told anyone when she felt sick. Just before she died, she took her father to the doctor. She took good care of everyone else but wouldn't allow anyone to take care of her."

Amena returned while Parveen was speaking. "We were right by her side when she died," Amena said, "but she didn't even say anything to us."

Suddenly, Alum's nephew shouted something from the door and Zakir ran out of the kitchen and handed him her largest *dah,* the hooked blade that villagers use for kitchen cutting. He ran off. Taslima passed Sonia to her stepmother and the girls and Parveen ran behind several houses to an open field where two groups of villagers were squared off across a rice paddy, twenty-five yards apart, shaking sticks and knives and yell-

Rokeya's youngest sister, Parveen, the author, and Taslima

ing threats. Taslima jumped right in. "Look at those puny knives," she yelled.

"One of them tried to have an affair with a woman," she told me. "He couldn't even write her love letters."

"Illiterate fools!" she shouted.

Back and forth, the villagers cursed one another's treacherous husbands, shiftless sons, and sluttish daughters. After half an hour, the groups disbanded, with nothing resolved. The dispute, over a plot of land, had flared up dozens of times over the years. On this occasion, Alum's brother had sparked it by plowing a field that had been contested in a court case. A few months earlier, Rokeya had been threatened by a member of the other clan for permitting one of her cows to wander onto their land. Days later, Rokeya's ten-year-old sister, also named Parveen, was playing in the same field when she was hit with a rope by one of the · men from the rival faction. Alum filed a complaint with the police and Taslima went with him to court. Nothing came of it, except that in court Taslima was extremely impressed by the "beautiful speech" of the officials. "I told my father that I wanted to study to become a magistrate," she said. "I told him, 'From now on, you can save money by feeding me only dal and *khud* [inexpensive food].' "

"As a magistrate, how would you settle this dispute?" I asked.

"I'd find some compromise," Taslima said. "It's not serious enough for jail."

Alum kept a notebook in which he recorded the significant events of his life: his marriage, the birth of his daughters, the birth of his son, the death of his son, the death of his brother, the birth of his daughter, the death of his wife, and, finally, his second marriage. Late one evening, he showed it to me by a kerosene lamp at the table in the front room of his house while Zakir prepared a dinner of rice and green beans and, in my honor, chicken.

At first Alum didn't want to remarry. But everybody said it would be for the best. Who would take care of the household and Sonia while he was in his tea shop? Amena would have to quit school. And who would take care of Rokeya's businesses? She had two cows and twenty-one chickens and a large garden. Alum had received 3,000 takas life insurance from the Emergency Fund upon Rokeya's death. But Rokeya had borrowed a total of 9,500 takas this year, more than half of which was still outstanding. Like many Muslims, Alum believed that the dead cannot enter heaven until their debts are repaid. The women from Rokeya's group had offered to accept his new wife as a replacement member, provided that she was a trustworthy person. Zakir had a good reputation. Her first husband had divorced her, but only because she gave him no children, Alum said. "When I saw her, I didn't want to marry her because she wasn't very beautiful," he added. "But then I was told that she's a fine woman. And I didn't need a face, I needed a whole person."

"She knew what she was getting into," he continued. "After we got married, I took her upstairs and told her all about Begum Rokeya. After hearing this, she said, 'I'll try to live up to her memory.' The day after we got married, she took over the responsibilities of the family. Since then, things have run smoothly. She loves my three daughters. When they go to school, she gives them their umbrellas, bags, and spending money.

"She told them: 'Because I'm your stepmother, no matter what I do, people will gossip. So please behave in such a fashion that no one has any opportunity to speak badly about our family affairs. You still have a lot of growing up to do. You have your studies to attend to. And you have to get married. We must think of these things.' "

"She and Amena have a good relationship," Alum added. "With Taslima, it's not as good. She's still very sad. But a few days ago Taslima told me, 'If we overlook her shortcomings, she'll overlook ours.' "

Alum let out a long sigh. "This death has been such an upheaval."

"You must be very proud of your daughters," I said.

"I am. When they go to school, they walk brightly and they speak softly. I'm going to educate them so they can reach their full potential as human beings."

Zakir served dinner. "Rokeya planted these vegetables," commented Alum.

After the meal, Zakir collected the bowls and brought Alum some *pan*. He asked my translator what she had studied in Dhaka. Engineering, she told him.

"Do you have any idea what it takes to become a magistrate?"

On the way back to the branch the next morning, we bumped into Minara, the woman whose husband repaired radios and who would not permit her to join the bank. Minara invited us into her house. Her husband, Hanif, was home. Minara had given birth to another daughter. Hanif had changed his mind about the Grameen Bank and was now hoping for a spot to open up soon in one of the nearby centers.

That evening, I spoke with the branch staff about Rokeya. They were watching her center closely for signs of trouble. "It's as if you had four bamboo poles supporting a house and one of them collapsed," explained Jainal Abedin.

"Her husband was devastated," added Shamsul Huq. "Alum is a man of laughter and stories. He's quite a kidder. When he and Rokeya used to quarrel, he would come and tell us, 'Do you know what your member did today?' After her death, he cried and cried. For a while, people thought he might go crazy. He told me, 'My family is finished. Begum Rokeya was the one who drove the family. I was there in name only. How will we carry on?' "

"His new wife seems very nice," he added, "and capable."

"Did Rokeya die of cholera?" I asked.

"We don't know," said Shamsul Huq.

"Whatever she had, she didn't get proper treatment," explained Jainal Abedin. "They brought the medicine only when it got serious. She thought she was feeling sick because of the fast."

"You must have been greatly saddened," I said.

"We were," explained Shamsul Huq. "Rokeya was very special. She had great enthusiasm. New things excited her. She wanted her children to reach a high level. And she often advised other members who weren't well off how they might do better. She was careful with her words—she worried about hurting people's feelings. And she had a special trust and instinct for the bank. She turned her face to the light."

47

Struck by Lightning

The most noticeable change about Oirashi in two years was that she had taken to wearing sandals. She looked the same, as did her house, although all her decorations had been re-arranged and she had planted more coconut trees. Nonie was still working at the hospital. She was still unmarried. "Maybe in another year or two," Oirashi said. "I've had some complications." Four months earlier, a scandal had caused her to quit her center.

It was a complex affair involving the capture of a fugitive, a missing 1,059 takas, a wedding drum, and an age-old feud. It all started when Monwara, a woman in Oirashi's center, received a 10,000-taka house loan, paid two installments, sold her house, and fled to Cox's Bazaar. Oirashi had warned against sanctioning the loan because Monwara's husband had been conspicuously absent in recent weeks. The tea stall gossip was that he had found a job in town.

Although Oirashi was no longer the center chief, hers was still the dominant voice, and now, over the objections of the new center chief, Tamunidash, the members turned to her. Oirashi advised them to withdraw 2,000 takas from the Special Savings, which was typically used for the upkeep of the center house. With eight men, she took a bus to Cox's Bazaar to track down Monwara. The following evening, the makeshift posse returned with the fugitive. Oirashi returned 941 takas to the center and produced a list of expenses, covering meals, snacks, and bus fare for nine people, gifts for the families that put them up for the night, and, most important, bribes to locate Monwara.

Like all villages in Bangladesh, Oirashi's is comprised of kinship clans whose members tend to be loyal to insiders and mistrustful of outsiders. In addition to these familial alliances, three major factions predominate in Oirashi's village: two Hindu castes denoted by the historical occupations of "gold workers" and "daily laborers," and Muslims. Oirashi, a member of the gold worker caste, called Bonic, maintained good relations with local Muslims. The daily laborers, the Jugis, who were in the majority, did not like the Muslims. Of the forty women in Oirashi's center, thirty were Jugis, including Tamunidash, the center chief. And by the time she finished with them, they were convinced that Oirashi had swindled the center.

"You're the oldest member," Tamunidash said. "Everybody used to respect you. Why didn't you discuss it with us? You spent too much money."

Oirashi said she had taken a day off from her peddling to save the center thousands of takas. And she added that the whole affair could have been avoided if they had listened to her about Monwara in the first place.

"How could you have spent 1,059 takas in one day?" Tamunidash said.

"If I did something wrong," Oirashi said. "I'll wear a sign on my back and walk around the village."

"It wasn't your money to spend," Tamunidash said. "We should never have placed our trust in Bonics and Muslims."

"I brought you into the center," Oirashi shouted. "I formed the groups. I received proper training. You know nothing about the rules of the bank."

The bank worker tried to calm things, but he was young and a little timid and he did not know the history behind the feud.

"Jugis are famous for their stupidity," Oirashi yelled.

Tamunidash countered with a lethal insult: "Your face is black."

Ten Muslims and Bonics sided with Oirashi, the other thirty sided with Tamunidash. Tamunidash warned Oirashi to watch out for her safety the next time she went peddling. Several women insulted the peddler. Oirashi, badly shaken, walked out.

Tears flowed down her cheeks as she related the confrontation. "I've been a member of the Grameen Bank for seven years," she said. "But it took only five minutes to get into trouble with my center."

"I'll wait for my death but I'll never go back," she added. "To be humiliated is like being struck by lightning."

Although Oirashi had stopped attending meetings, she continued to send her installments. "I won't be any trouble to the Grameen Bank," she told me. "If you ask me to go to the branch office and wash everybody's clothes, I'll do it. I still give the salute when I pass the bank workers. It's because of the bank that I've come this far. It was my intention to remain a member for the rest of my life."

Four years of payments remained on the 15,000-taka house loan Oirashi received after the cyclone. She had borrowed a total of 10,500 takas this year and had begun carrying more expensive merchandise—brassieres, blouses, and children's clothing. Her sales had gone up, although she was not sure by how much. Nonie had won an award for "faithful service" from the hospital and had gotten a raise. Things were looking up before the scandal broke out. Now, unless she returned to the center, Oirashi would not be able to take out any more loans.

"I should have just let the bank worker handle the situation when Monwara fled to Cox's Bazaar," she said, regretfully. "Now I don't even like to pass the branch office because it makes me feel so sad."

The following Sunday, I attended Oirashi's center meeting. It had rained all night. In the morning the paths were slick. As the women entered the center hut, Jugis, Bonics, and Muslims alike grumbled about the weather. There were a few salutes but no slogans chanted.

After the initial conflict, the Dulahazara branch manager had tried to smooth tensions. He visited Oirashi and Tamunidash at their houses, called a special meeting at the branch office, and rotated bank workers. When these actions failed to help, he threw up his hands. "It's frustrating having to deal with so many uneducated people," he told me. Oirashi wished that the first branch manager, Selim, was still in charge. "If Selim were here, this problem would have been solved," she said. "He wasn't afraid of anything."

Inside the center house, the bank worker collected the money without ceremony. For the third consecutive week, Irani, one of the women who'd sided with Oirashi, had failed to pay her installment. Her group members refused to cover it. Most of the women cursed Irani, but Tamunidash cursed Oirashi.

"Talk to Irani's son," the bank worker said to the group chairman. "See if you can reason with him."

"How can I speak with Irani's son?" she replied.

"Then ask your husband to speak with him."

"He would beat him up."

"Is your husband a woman?" the bank worker said.

"Once, Irani's son threatened to stab someone over nothing," the woman said.

Tamunidash sat in the first row. "It's all because of Oirashi," she said.

"Oirashi took the center's money and didn't tell us that she was going to use it to get Monwara back from Cox's Bazaar."

"Liar," shouted a woman from the group behind her.

"It's the responsibility of the group chairman to collect all the money and give it to me," the bank worker said.

"We've paid her installment for two weeks," the chairman replied. "We can't keep doing it. We're not rich."

"If she doesn't pay, we won't be able to give you new loans."

"Fine. Then we won't take new loans. Before the Grameen Bank came along, were we surviving?"

"Don't be so hotheaded," the bank worker said. "You'll have to speak wisely to get your money from Irani."

To me, he commented: "You're watching the Grameen Bank in action."

When I dropped by Oirashi's house the following day, she immediately said, "I heard what Tamunidash told you."

"You've walked with me," she said. "You've seen how people love me. God may not have given me wealth, but he gave me the gift of people's favor. Anyway, I had to get all forty signatures to take out the money. Everybody knew what it was for."

"They resent my status," she added.

"What was your relationship with Tamunidash before the feud broke?" I asked.

That was when Oirashi told me the story of the wedding drum.

It happened three years before when a cousin of Oirashi's was getting married and the bride's father had asked her to arrange for the rental of a wedding drum. A neighbor, named Bihari, who overheard the conversation, stepped in and said he would be happy to take care of the drum. "He's the kind of man," explained Oirashi, "who, if you give him 5 takas to buy something for you, will spend 4 takas on himself and buy you something for one."

Soon Bihari dropped in on Oirashi to explain that he had rented a drum for 1,200 takas and needed the money to pay for it. (He neglected to add that he had rented it from his brother-in-law.) Oirashi said that she'd already found one for 800 takas. Bihari was enraged. "I spent two days searching for a drum," he said.

"I told you not to get one," Oirashi said.

"Your cousin is going to have a wedding with no drum," he exclaimed. "I'll see to that."

Bihari went to threaten the man from whom Oirashi had rented her drum. Oirashi dispatched her cousin to head him off. The two men came to blows. A crowd surrounded them. Finally, the union chairman, a local political official, was called in to settle the dispute. First Bihari, then Oirashi, spoke. The union chairman ruled in Oirashi's favor and scolded Bihari for wasting other people's money. He left humiliated.

Now, Oirashi told me that Bihari and Tamunidash were cousins. "Ever since that day, they've wanted to get back at me," she said. "They finally found a way."

On rainy afternoons, Oirashi frequented the smoky tea stall across the road from her village. She was the only woman I ever saw inside the tea stall (except my translator). The men called her "mother-in-law." The proprietor, Motalleb Shaudagar, had heard the story of the feud more times than he could count. "They have given her grief beyond all imagination," he told me. "She should never go back."

Oirashi sat across a wooden table from me, beside another friend, a local school teacher named Monohor Ali Babul. Monohor was the largest Bangladeshi I had come across. Next to Oirashi, he looked like a giant. He was an important ally. Recently, a bandit who assaulted a bank worker with a knife had the bad luck to run into him. Monohor picked the man up by his neck—so the story goes—and carried him all the way to the police station.

Oirashi was angry about how her bank worker had handled the affair. "He caved in to the majority," she said. "A stronger person would have considered both sides and judged according to right and wrong. But he was afraid of rocking the boat. If he had scolded them right away, they would have gone soft."

"His head is not right because he's not married," she added. "He can't keep his mind on his work."

Everybody broke out in laughter.

"The bank will soon see that it will be very difficult to keep those members together. In my time, even before the bank worker arrived, I had all the money organized and the books in line. I used to tell the women not to wear lipstick or nail polish to the meetings. Now they've lost their discipline."

Monohor shook his head. "What can you do?" he sighed. He looked at me. "She used to be very strict. I think the other members resented her for being so tough."

"Also that business with the drum," added Motalleb.

"It took them three years to get back at me," Oirashi said. "Like a calf, the first year they're on their legs wobbling around, the second year they're on strong legs, and the third year they grow horns and get *nasty.*"

"They threatened her," Monohor said, "but they won't do anything."

"Without the support of my comrades in the tea stall," Oirashi announced, "I wouldn't do anything. Not even if Khaleda Zia were behind me."

The men laughed.

"But if you don't go back, how will you build your house?" I asked. "How will you find a husband for Nonie?"

"Even though I need the bank's money, I will never return to the center," Oirashi declared. "If a tiger has no meat will he eat straw?"

The morning I was to return to Dhaka, Oirashi was waiting for me in front of the tea stall/bus stop. "What will you do now?" she asked.

I told her that I was returning to Dhaka to interview Professor Yunus and some other people in the head office. "Tell him that Grameen Bank should cut back on its seasonal and rehabilitation loans," Oirashi said. "I walk around a lot so I see a lot of people. If the bank just stuck to the general loan, people would be able to manage their activities more efficiently." She laughed. "Then I'd be able to sell them more jewelry!

"Also tell him about the slogan—Discipline, Unity, Courage, and Hard Work—because there's none of that here right now."

Every villager I met in Bangladesh had asked me if I was married. When I replied that I was not, they would sigh and look upon me with great pity. I would quickly pull out a photograph of my girlfriend and explain that we *might* get married one day. Oirashi would not settle for "one day." She wanted to know when.

"I can't say. Maybe soon."

"When is 'soon'?" she pressed, smiling.

"Maybe in a year or two," I said, laughing.

"How will *I* know?" she said.

"I'll write to you."

Oirashi made me promise to inform her of the day of the affair and to send photographs. She would do the same for Nonie's wedding.

"How much does it cost to take an airplane from America?" she inquired.

"Fifty thousand takas," I said.

"Will you return to visit me after I've built my house and married my daughter?" she asked.

"I can't say."

Later that month, a cyclone was reported heading for Cox's Bazaar. The government issued a maximum-level alert, but a day before the storm was to hit the coastline, it lost force and turned south toward Myanmar. A few hundred people were killed and several thousand houses damaged. I paid Oirashi a final visit. The storm had not touched her house.

She had almost finished repaying her previous loan but nothing had changed in the center. "I was planning to take out a 7,000-taka general loan this time," she said. "But because of those turncoats, I won't be able to fulfill my dreams."

48

The Price of the American Dream

Since receiving the King Baudouin Development Prize, Yunus had won two other major international awards: the 1993 CARE Humanitarian Award, presented in Washington, D.C. by U.S. Secretary of State Warren Christopher, and the 1994 World Food Prize. He had also been invited by President Clinton to the White House.

When he accepted these awards and addressed audiences of development economists and dignitaries, Yunus typically reiterated the points he had been making for years. ("I'm like a preacher saying the same thing over and over and over," he told me.)

His five major themes were: (1) credit should be accepted as a fundamental human right; (2) self-employment should be preferred over wage-employment as a faster and more humane way to combat poverty; (3) women should receive top priority in development efforts because they are most acutely affected by poverty and they are the primary caregivers to children; (4) the concept of "development" should be redefined as an action that brings about an identifiable, positive change in the lives of the poorest 50 percent of the population; and (5) the "conceptual vagueness" of development theorists should be replaced by sharp and immediate attacks on poverty.

Although no country had formally accepted credit as a human right, its importance as a development tool was now widely accepted, while Yunus's other ideas continued to influence development thinkers and hundreds of microenterprise programs around the globe.

In the summer of 1995, within a one-month period, the World Bank announced two decisions that leaned toward Yunus's thinking. In July, it launched a drive to raise more than $200 million from international donors to finance Grameen-style microloans for poor people; and, in August, after a decade of planning, it canceled a controversial $1 billion hydroelectric project in Nepal, which many argued was far too expensive for the country. The decision, reported the *New York Times,* was a sign that the World Bank's new president planned to be "more cautious in financing big infrastructure projects."

In recent years, microenterprise networks such as ACCION International in Latin America, Credit and Savings for the Hardcore Poor (CASHPOR), in Southeast Asia, and Women's World Banking, based in New York, had sharply expanded operations. Small credit programs had also been established in many countries under the aegis of the World Council of Credit Unions. In 1989, USAID had launched a five-year development program called GEMINI (Growth and Equity through Microenterprise Investments and Institutions). One of the products, an impressive 1994 publication entitled *The New World of Microenterprise Finance,* edited by Maria Otero, of ACCION International, and Elisabeth Rhyne, coordinator of the GEMINI project, surveyed and contrasted microbankers around the globe and challenged them to make their institutions financially viable. Only by reducing their dependence on donors, they argued, would microbankers be able to mobilize the investment necessary to provide ongoing access to credit for hundreds of millions of poor people.

For the time being, many still looked to donors, including the Grameen Trust, which had recently embarked on a campaign to raise $100 million to support Grameen replication programs worldwide. The stated goal: to reach 7 million poor families, or 35 million people, by the year 2003.

Meanwhile, microcredit programs continued to sprout up across the United States and Canada. The Association for Enterprise Opportunity (AEO), a trade organization established in 1991 to support microenterprise development, listed, in 1995, four hundred members across the two countries, almost double the number it had two years earlier. Yunus was enthusiastic about the number of people who had focused, or recently refocused, on credit as a development tool. When I asked him if he believed Grameen-style credit could alleviate poverty on a large scale in the United States and Canada, given the substantial social and economic differences between Bangladesh and North America, he replied: "If credit is a key to a door, I'm not worried whether it's an aluminum door or a bamboo door. As a concept, that applies in general. How heavy the key should be depends on what kind of door you're opening."

It was an attractive metaphor, but it also left out a great deal of information. Years earlier, Yunus had said so himself. Questioning whether poor people in the United States or Canada would be able to help themselves with greater access to credit, he wrote: "On the surface, it appears to be too simplistic to be true." Still, he was prepared to be surprised.

In the developing world, where investment barriers are low and millions of microentrepreneurs are already supporting themselves with readily marketable skills, Grameen had demonstrated that credit is indeed a key to a door. But was credit a skeleton key? In the United States and Canada, operating a successful sole-proprietorship means getting through a series of doors with different locks: meeting government regulations, dealing with tax laws, competing with big business, maintaining ongoing access to suppliers, responding to rapidly changing markets, and so on. And if the first "door" represents "self-employment," only a minority of Americans or Canadians ever try to open it in the first place.

"What Yunus plugged into in Bangladesh is a very long tradition of people being self-employed," explained Ron Grzywinski, one of the founders of the South Shore Bank in Chicago. "In the United States, there's a romantic notion attached to being self-employed, but it isn't what everybody on your block does. Here, it's more the uncommon thing." Less than 10 percent of Americans are self-employed, with another 5 or 6 percent self-employed part-time.

My guess is that, given these statistics, Yunus would simply flip them over to suggest the great potential for credit programs in the United States and Canada: If 10 percent of Americans and Canadians were currently self-employed, then 90 percent of them were candidates to *become* self-employed. What an enormous market to capture!

And, if so, he may have been right. For years, social commentators have been arguing that small business and self-employment will continue to play increasingly important roles in the American and Canadian economies.

In *The Third Wave,* Alvin Toffler predicted that the "decentralization and deurbanization of production" would shift millions of jobs from factories back to the home. "[I]f individuals came to own their electronic terminals and equipment, purchased perhaps on credit," he wrote, "they would become, in effect, independent entrepreneurs rather than classical employees."

Toffler was writing way back in another epoch, in 1980, before millions owned personal computers. And even he may have been surprised by how quickly the change has come. In a September 1994 article, headlined "More and More People Are Making a Living in the Dining Room," the *New York Times* reported that more than 43 million Americans (roughly one third of the workforce) worked at least part-time at home, a 73 percent increase over 1988. The article noted that the figure was predicted to grow by 15 percent a year, and would hit 56 million by 1997.

Clearly, technology was making it possible for many Americans to "telecommute" from their "electronic cottages," but did this mean that they were prepared to take the risk to create their own jobs?

Some argued that they soon might have no other choice. According to census data compiled by the U.S. Small Business Administration, between 1989 and 1991, firms with fewer than four employees hired 2.6 million people, while larger businesses cut 2 million jobs. In a *New York Times* op-ed piece in September 1995, Michael Lind, a senior editor of *The New Republic,* reported that over the next decade the number of new entrants to the workforce would "outstrip the number of jobs created by more than a million and a half."

In a 1993 essay in *Harper's Magazine* entitled "The End of Jobs," Richard J. Barnet, a senior fellow at the Institute for Policy Studies, in Washington, D.C., argued that unless the idea of "work" was reimagined, neither the American nor the global economies would be capable of generating jobs to keep pace with the growing labor force.

"The problem is starkly simple," he wrote. "[A]n astonishingly large and increasing number of human beings are not needed or wanted to make the goods or to provide the services that the paying customers of the world can afford." Due to "automation, the increasing use of subcontractors, suppliers, and temporary workers," steady, well-paying jobs were fast becoming "poignant memories or just dreams" for more and more Americans. One "sensible" response, Barnet noted, were the (then) one hundred microcredit programs in the United States modeled after the Grameen Bank.

A year later, *Fortune* magazine published a cover story by William Bridges under the headline "The End of the Job." The recession was over; corporations had trimmed, reengineered, flattened, and automated, and still, each day, more jobs were lost. It wasn't the fault of the politicians, wrote Bridges, and it wasn't global competition. "The reality we face is much more troubling, for what is disappearing is not just a certain number of jobs. What is disappearing is the very thing itself: the job."

The job, as a means of organizing work, was a "social artifact," he wrote, and American corporations were already, if unknowingly, shifting away from it. Taking this trend to its logical conclusion, Bridges envisioned a "de-jobbed" world—a world beyond "flex-time, job sharing and telecommuting" where issues such as leaves of absence, vacations, and retirement would be "insignificant" because each employee would behave like an "independent business." In a "de-jobbed" world, millions of people would manage themselves within, and across, corporations and, in all likelihood, a great many of them would create their own employment.

But if these writers were correct and, in the coming decades, more Americans would support themselves through self-employment, did this imply that self-employment was equally viable for the American affluent, middle-class, and *poor*? It's one thing for a former marketing manager, a victim of "downsizing," to switch to free-lance consulting; it's quite another for someone with a high school education on welfare or earning minimum wage to open a business selling homemade clothes.

The two oldest Grameen replication programs in the United States —the Good Faith Fund, in Pine Bluff, Arkansas, and the Women's Self-Employment Project, on the South Side of Chicago—have been grappling with this question since the late 1980s. Both programs operate under the auspices of the Chicago-based Shorebank Corporation. I first met Mary Houghton and Ron Grzywinski, president and chairman, respectively, of Shorebank, in 1992 in Bangladesh, when they participated in the midterm review mission organized by Grameen's donors. At the time, their microenterprise programs were struggling to adapt the Grameen model to impoverished rural and urban areas. Mary seemed hopeful; Ron was more skeptical. When I spoke with them three years later in Chicago, Mary was still hopeful and Ron was still skeptical.

Bankers in the United States who attempt to tackle poverty with credit, explained Ron, quickly discover that low-income Americans who have never been self-employed require training and counseling before they can run businesses. "These programs said, 'Oh, here's a good idea —small amounts of short-term credit. Let's get it to the poorest people.' And then, low and behold, the information you need to compete in this society is different, the competition is different. Maybe the idea is good, but it doesn't all hang together."

The Women's Self-Employment Project (WSEP), one of the larger microenterprise programs in the country, had, by 1995, extended close to $1 million in loans to more than three hundred businesses and provided business counseling services to 5,000 women. The Good Faith Fund had extended a half million dollars to a few hundred low-income people. Both programs enjoyed repayment rates above 90 percent.

"The Women's Self-Employment Project has demonstrated that there is a big market in Chicago for self-employment among single women who are either very low income or on welfare," explained Mary. Although no microbanker had yet developed a systematic, self-sustaining methodology for turning low-income Americans into successful entrepreneurs, many had discovered "a fair number of ways by which poor people can add to their incomes by two or five or ten thousand dollars a year."

Steven Balkin, a professor of economics at Roosevelt University in Chicago, and author of the book *Self-Employment for Low-Income People,* had worked closely with the poor vendors in one of the oldest and largest open-air markets in the United States—the Maxwell Street Market—until the city of Chicago shut it down in 1994. A number of WSEP's borrowers were vendors at the Maxwell Street Market. Balkin felt that its closing was a perfect example of the policy contradictions inherent in politicians telling poor citizens to "get to work" or "get out of the wagon and help the rest of us pull" while simultaneously erecting barriers to self-employment.

"Governments like to spend money on expensive classroom-based self-employment training, yet at the same time they're squashing these markets," he told me. "Street markets offer a low-cost way to start a business, interact with other vendors and customers, and build up trust in a community. And once you have trust, information flows, money flows, and deals can be made." Markets were stepping stones, he added. People learn about business through access to social networks and exposure to other entrepreneurs. "Observe immigrants and see how they start businesses," he said. In America's poorest communities, these networks are badly lacking.

When jobs are scarce, Balkin suggested that governments exhibit a little "benign neglect" toward these markets and other often "extra-legal" business activities. In cases where conflicts arise with established small businesses, the solution lay in mediation. But simply shutting down informal markets (as was done in Chicago and New York City) was "bad policy." "Certainly, going to New York University is a better route to economic mobility than peddling irregular shoes on 125th Street in Harlem," he added. "But markets are a poor man's NYU."

Collectively, the hundreds of microcredit programs in the United States were said to comprise a "movement," and yet, within that movement, there was little agreement on strategy or policy or what constituted "success," and how to measure it. Some programs concentrated on training, others on credit services; some operated in sparsely populated rural areas, others in urban centers; some used borrowing groups; others provided loans to individuals; some targeted the "poorest of the poor"

—single women on welfare; others aimed at the "entrepreneurial" or "working" poor; some called themselves Grameen replications; others adamantly rejected the label.

Amidst the diverse voices, in what has been dubbed the "micromaze," one comment that seemed to capture the movement's ethos came from Julia Vindasius, the former director of the Good Faith Fund: "There is a great need not only for credit," she explained, "but for support to spark latent entrepreneurial energy, to create an investment orientation instead of a *spending* orientation among our low-income citizens."

Here, there were no arguments. The central thrust of U.S. poverty programs had to change. People did not eat their way out of poverty; they had to accumulate assets. Welfare didn't promote this, nor did low-wage employment. Thomas Jefferson believed small property ownership to be essential to the success of a participatory democracy. But it was precisely in this area that American society displayed the greatest disparity. In *The Politics of Rich and Poor,* political analyst Kevin Phillips noted that, in 1986, while the richest 20 percent of Americans earned almost 44 percent of all income, the top 10 percent controlled 68 percent of the nation's wealth. The bottom 10 percent owned almost nothing. There was also a great disparity in the way Americans and Canadians acquired financial resources. The poor received wages and government payments, while the wealthy and middle class received wages and government payments, as well as inheritances, investments, and borrowings.

The microcredit movement hoped to alter this imbalance. It was a daunting task, but most practitioners seemed to approach it with the gumption of small entrepreneurs. Like Yunus, many saw themselves as pioneers, striving to build sustainable institutions that demonstrated faith and respect in poor Americans. And they spoke proudly of their borrowers, poor people who now supported themselves as beauticians, caterers, carpenters, word processors, painters, mechanics, shoemakers, street vendors, landscapers, masons, printers, junk dealers, quilters, florists, jewelry manufacturers, house cleaners, knife sharpeners, locksmiths, land cultivators, poultry raisers, and barbers. In *Systems of Survival,* Jane Jacobs wrote of microcredit programs: "Mavericks thought them up . . . mavericks who were tired of seeing things not work out." And Mary Houghton called America's microbankers "merciless innovators."

They had to be. Without exception, they faced a serious problem: making their programs sustainable. Because they provided training, technical assistance, and access to business networks, in addition to credit, their operational costs remained high—well above revenues. They were forced to subsist on donor funds, primarily from private sources. Nobody knew how long the private support would continue; at the same time, government funding was shrinking at all levels.

By 1995, none of the microenterprise lenders in the United States and Canada came close to breaking even, and only a few had more than a few hundred clients. Most of these bankers felt that it was far too premature to discuss financial performance. The "product"—the mix of services and credit that would yield optimal results—was still in development. Many shunned comparisons with the Grameen Bank, arguing that microenterprise in Bangladesh and the United States had almost nothing in common. A focus on profitability only created false expectations among donors and placed an undue burden on practitioners and their clients. "Microcredit is still in its embryonic stage," commented Sam Daley-Harris, of Results, a Washington-based "citizens' lobby" that was organizing an "International Micro-Credit Summit," to be held in early 1997.

Instead, microbankers defended their program costs by (1) framing the issue in terms of social justice, and (2) posing the question, What is the cost of not providing these services?

In the absence of these relatively small investments in poor people today, society will pay a high price down the road, they argued. With the job market for unskilled labor shrinking, or, at best, stagnating, disadvantaged Americans would continue to fall behind, even as newspapers reported that the distribution of wealth in the United States was already the most skewed of any industrialized nation on earth. Given that the climb out of poverty is often an intergenerational process, what was the likelihood that the children of the poor would be properly equipped to fulfill Jefferson's hopes for democracy tomorrow, if their parents' "latent entrepreneurial energy" was not sparked today?

Microbankers were on strongest ground when they appealed to Americans' notions of fairness, arguing that every American, rich or poor, should be entitled to a limited quantity of resources on loan, at the commercial rate or higher, provided that he or she demonstrated commitment, a desire to work, and what appeared to be a viable business plan.

In his book *The End of Equality,* Mickey Kaus makes a strong case that the best prospect in the foreseeable future to make American society more egalitarian is to strengthen the public sphere. Why should a low income consign an individual or a family to a third-class existence—to third-rate schools, day care, and health care and to a disproportionately weak voice in politics? he asked. "[E]veryone, even the economy's losers, should be able to pass the test necessary for equal dignity in the public sphere," Kaus wrote. But how could Americans be motivated to rebuild the public sphere? "We're looking for a value, shared by rich and poor alike, on which to build an egalitarian life," Kaus noted. "It seems to me there is only one real candidate: work."

Americans do honor hard work. Is it conceivable, then, that the "public sphere" could be enlarged so as to encompass the idea that all citizens are entitled to an allotment of credit for self-employment regardless of their ability to furnish collateral or a guarantor? Would society be willing to accept the costs of administering these loans? It is an attractive idea, but is it politically feasible? One of those who think not is Jeffrey Ashe, director of Working Capital, based in Cambridge, Massachusetts. Ashe, a former Peace Corps volunteer, had worked in microenterprise in South America, Africa, and Asia for more than a decade before he founded Working Capital in late 1990, today the largest microcredit program in the United States. "There was total and utter skepticism," he told me. "Everybody said, 'People won't repay you, their businesses won't progress and the banks won't cooperate.' "

Working Capital provides group-based support, credit, training, and technical assistance to low-income people throughout New England. Unlike the Grameen Bank and other microenterprise programs, Working Capital does not target the poorest of the poor. Its market, best described as the "entrepreneurial poor," is made up of people already involved in income-generating activities who lack access to financial resources and other support services.

However, like Yunus, Ashe does not attempt to turn poor people into entrepreneurs; he supports people who are already entrepreneurs, or at least show promising signs of soon becoming entrepreneurs. In this sense he is, in his approach, closer to Yunus's pragmatic spirit than are microlenders who target poorer clients. Writing in the July, 1994, issue of *The Atlantic Monthly,* Amitai Etzioni argued that it is "wise policy" for social programs to seek early success by starting with a "realistic notion of human transformation"—in this case, not expecting poor people just to go out and start viable businesses.

Ashe agrees. By 1995, Working Capital had extended $1.6 million in loans, of amounts ranging from $500 to $5,000, to close to 1,500 businesses, and was training hundreds more; its repayment rate was 98 percent. Today, Ashe remains unique among his colleagues in his determination to demonstrate that it is possible to be a banker for poor Americans (although not the poorest) and still cover costs. "Almost everybody has rejected this out of hand," he told me. "But the truth is, for these programs to reach any appreciable scale, we have to show that they can be self-sustaining. And if we can prove that, we can blow this whole movement to another level."

"I figure that microenterprise in this country has a window of opportunity for the next four or five years," he told me in late 1995. "Right now there's interest among funders, but already major questions about cost-effectiveness are being raised."

Ashe has plans to franchise his operation, to support as many as 4,000 businesses by the end of 1997, and has started franchises in Delaware and South Miami. His cost per borrower continues to drop; it is somewhere between 10 and 20 percent of the cost in other programs; and he is looking for new ways to increase revenues, including raising the loan ceiling to $10,000 and charging membership fees to groups. He projects that with an investment of $5 million over five years, Working Capital could generate $60 million in new jobs by the end of the sixth year and could break even in the seventh year.

"People latch onto the concept of microenterprise pretty fast," Ashe said, "but the trick is actually designing a structure that will produce sustainable results. More and more, as I slog through this on a day-to-day basis, I appreciate what Yunus has accomplished."

49

Socially Conscious Capitalism

While U.S. microbankers continue to refine their "product," many face an inherent limitation in their approach. In accepting credit as a development tool, most did not duplicate the process Yunus undertook to *arrive* at credit. Indeed, the importance of credit as a development tool is only one of many lessons to be drawn from the experience of the Grameen Bank, and, I would argue, in the U.S. context, not the most important one.

What the Grameen Bank has demonstrated is far more universal: namely, how to (1) identify solutions to complex social problems, (2) build an institution to implement those solutions, and (3) implement them in a commercially oriented, cost-effective manner. These processes are equally applicable to Bangladesh and the United States.

We can begin by recalling how Yunus got started. After seven years away from home, he arrived at Chittagong University in 1972, twenty miles from where he grew up, and proceeded to spend four years listening to villagers, trying a number of different experiments, before he stumbled upon "credit" in 1976. Next, he developed his system with the help of inexperienced but highly committed student volunteers for three years before testing it in a new location. Another five years elapsed before Grameen sharply expanded. That's *twelve* years of incubation—the equivalent of three U.S. presidential terms. It's also important to note that as Grameen was preparing to expand across the country, it was experiencing serious repayment problems in Tangail, which it downplayed. If Grameen's donors had been fully apprised of the situation in Tangail, one has to ask, would they still have come forward with $38 million?

Regarding U.S. replication, one must also ask: If Yunus had an American counterpart who spent four years walking around a poor urban neighborhood in the United States (presumably close to where he grew up), asking people what they needed to solve their problems, what would have emerged? Would people have talked about credit? Or vocational services? Or improved public schools? Or locally based policemen? Or better political representation? The answer remains open to speculation. But one thing is certain: It cannot be ascertained from a distance.

Later, as Grameen recruited thousands of employees, Yunus instituted a rigorous training program to weed out the least enthusiastic third of each class. Grameen recruits were fresh out of school; they had never held previous jobs; none came from elite families. Just as well. Grameen had little use for "stars"; it needed locally based, reliable people who were willing to work under difficult conditions and accept modest salaries. To compensate, the bank offered staff members steady work, and the opportunity to manage others and bring about positive changes in their lives. Yunus's leadership qualities and Grameen's corporate style helped cultivate an esprit de corps based on pride and difference.

Along the way, Yunus built a new type of institution—a "socially conscious capitalist enterprise"—an institution capable of addressing an urgent social need through the format of a vital and competitive business. "The world has always visualized capitalism by saying that the driving force is greed," Yunus told me. "But Grameen is a capitalist institution. Make no mistake. We're gung-ho to maximize profits. We want to pay dividends to the shareholders. Now, you cannot say greed is moving this bank, so your theory will have a shock coming."

"It's not just Grameen Bank," he added. "We want to operate the health program on a cost-recovery basis. Look at the Fisheries. There's a business producing high-quality food at a cheap price addressing a market where people remain hungry. And it makes money!"

"I say it's possible," declared Yunus. "But only if we imagine that capitalism can be practiced this way. In the past, we didn't—and we create the world the way we imagine it."

Balancing seemingly incompatible objectives is the hallmark of the "socially conscious capitalist enterprise." "Sometimes you're pulled by viability considerations," Yunus explained, "sometimes by human considerations. It's like a pendulum. You swing this way and that way and hope that the swing becomes shorter and shorter."

To be sure, there is little similarity between the Grameen Bank and new-age companies like Ben and Jerry's or The Body Shop, which promote themselves as "caring capitalists" because they champion popular causes such as protecting the environment and opposing cosmetics testing on animals. This is all very well. But such business practices are nothing new. Philip Morris, the giant cigarette manufacturer, has long supported museums and theaters across the United States. Does that make it a "caring capitalist"?

This last point is not to equate ice cream and cosmetics with cigarettes, but to illustrate that, as an institution, the Grameen Bank is a different species altogether. For Grameen, "social consciousness" is not a by-product of the business; it *is* the business. Lending money to landless women in Bangladesh *is* Grameen's business. And within its mandate, it does everything possible to maximize profits. It is different from a conventional firm in two significant ways; (1) the business is not profitable in the short run and, at face value, may not *appear* to be profitable in the long run, and (2) if management discovers a more lucrative business, it cannot switch.

In development circles, it is now generally accepted that successful development programs must grow under the leadership of a locally based "organizational entrepreneur"—someone like Yunus, who has good instincts, is not afraid to take risks, and brings a competitive edge to the task at hand.

This can only be good news for Americans and Canadians interested in addressing their own social problems. Here you find "organizational entrepreneurs" in all walks: They run charitable foundations, theater troupes, drug-dealing operations, and bowling leagues. And, of course, they run businesses—no less than 21 million of them. But of course, they don't run them all the same way. Some entrepreneurs sell X-rated videos while others sell child-safety devices.

Yunus believes that many would-be socially conscious entrepreneurs turn away from business because they fail to see the transformative potential in it. "They should jump in and design their own things," he says. "Look at a social problem and see if you can find a commercially oriented approach to solve it. And once you do that, make a network of these organizations and support one another."

Can institutions like the Grameen Bank be legislated? The experience of the bank suggests that while governments can, and should, play a supporting role, they cannot play the leading role. Like successful businesses, these institutions must evolve out of the efforts of talented individuals. The government can help by subsidizing the costs of institutional development; Grameen was heavily subsidized for its first seventeen years. The subsidy, however, should not be indefinite. The goal is to help socially conscious businesses aiming at long-term profitability—like Working Capital—cover their costs in the short run. In the long run, they must stand on their own. Of course, what constitutes "short run" and "long run" will depend on the particular industry and the difficulty of the undertaking.

But government help will not be enough. In *Dead Right,* David Frum makes the point that politicians are often motivated less by the "material temptations" of office than by the "desire to please"—to hear the crowd's applause. Similarly, it may not be the drive for wealth and power that animates an entrepreneur but the desire for the status and recognition associated with these things. But status can come many ways, and here the media can help the most. All the praise Yunus has received over the years—most of it from the United States and Canada—has not only made it easier for him to raise funds but has made him one of the most highly respected figures in international development and in his country.

How far could socially conscious capitalism go? In a 1995 speech, Yunus suggested that social sector investments in education, research, training, health, and the environment, as well as in poverty alleviation, could be well-managed by such businesses. Here his idea is likely to run into a great deal of ideological opposition in the United States. As Nicholas Lemann notes in *The Promised Land,* transforming America's poorest communities is a massive job: "For both practical and moral reasons, the institution by far best suited to the task is the federal government."

But America's millions of "organizational entrepreneurs" cannot be overlooked as potential instruments for social change (beyond the employment opportunities their businesses generate). They are a national resource and their talents should be directed accordingly. No doubt, many Americans and Canadians would be excited to see businesses like the Grameen Bank crop up to address social problems. If so, they will have to create the conditions where organizational entrepreneurs like Muhammad Yunus and Jeffrey Ashe will be motivated to build them. With appropriate support and incentives—and some hearty applause— perhaps a few would be willing to exchange the "material temptations" of ordinary business for the challenge and prestige of creating socially conscious capitalist enterprises. And, perhaps, as in the case of the Grameen Bank, a few of them will exceed our expectations by a country mile.

50

Everywhere You Look

Khalid Shams reclined in his chair and brought his hands together under his chin. I had inquired about a program everybody in the head office was talking about: Grameen Check. "Ahh, that's my favorite," he replied, rubbing his palms together. "You know, the whole thing was an accidental discovery—it started with just one telephone call."

What Khalid learned in that phone conversation was that Bangladesh had one million weavers and 500,000 handlooms, and half the looms were currently unused. This, at a time when garment manufacturing was Bangladesh's fastest-growing industry. Why did so much cloth have to be imported while so many local weavers remained idle? One particular type of cloth known as Madras check was very similar to a common Bangladeshi weave, and yet local manufacturers imported $50 million worth of it each year.

Khalid contacted Masud; he wanted to know how many of Grameen's 2 million borrowers were weavers or owned hand looms. Soon the tally worked its way up to the head office: 50,000 members (or their husbands) were weavers. But many had switched to other activities because local market prices for cloth were too low for them to support themselves this way.

Khalid set up a meeting with several garment manufacturers to inquire if and how they might be able to do business with Grameen's weavers. "These weavers are all scattered," he was told. "How will you deal with them? They're illiterate. They'll cheat you."

"Let's have a look at this check," he said to the manufacturers, and was surprised when no one would even offer him a sample. A short time later, he ran into a former student at the airport who had recently opened a factory to manufacture clothes for export, and happened to have several samples of Madras check on him, which he was pleased to lend to Khalid. Back at the office, he laid them on Yunus's desk.

"They look just like *lungis* to me," Yunus said.

They called in Daiyan, then in charge of Grameen's Technology Department. Could Grameen's weavers reproduce these samples? Daiyan said he would see. He left Dhaka for Serajganj, a district near Tangail. "We picked Serajganj because that's where they weave the *lungis*," explained Khalid, "and they have been weaving them for hundreds of years."

In Serajganj, Daiyan spoke with several weavers who said they could reproduce the samples provided they had access to quality yarn and dyes. He arranged for the supplies and soon returned to Dhaka with the check samples.

Khalid arranged a second meeting with the garment manufacturers. "This is very good cloth," he was told.

Within two years, Grameen had mobilized more than 1,000 weavers and sold more than one million yards of Grameen Check to local garment manufacturers producing clothes for export. The villagers had demonstrated the ability to produce cloth that met international standards; they were reliable and their price was competitive. Soon short-sleeve shirts made from cloth woven by villagers in Serajganj could be found in Wal-Mart stores, selling for $13.94. The following year, Grameen opened another division—Grameen Flannel—to compete with imports from Pakistan and China. Two thousand more weavers were being organized; the production targets for 1996 and 1997 were 6 and 10 million yards.

But how should the cloth be marketed? Khalid was wondering one evening, when his wife brought to his attention a feature story in *The Daily Star*, a local English-language newspaper, headlined, "Bibi Is Back." Bibi Russell, Bangladesh's most famous international fashion model, was back in the country after having lived in Italy and England for more than a decade. "My God," he exclaimed. "This is exactly the sort of person we need to promote our check."

Khalid contacted Bibi. After a meeting at the head office, Bibi traveled to Serajganj with Daiyan, and spent a few days observing village weavers dyeing, spinning, weaving, and transporting fabrics, synchronizing activities, standardizing quality, and meeting production schedules. "It was absolutely amazing," she said. "I had heard about it, but until I saw it, I didn't believe it could be done."

"Of course, technically they'll improve," she added. "But they are making wonderful fabrics right now. And what I'm hoping to do is create a market for them—like Benetton. All their colors. You saw all their colors! And, of course, all we have to do to export Grameen Check is tell the story behind it."

"Once manufacturers see the comparative advantage of getting fabrics locally, they will come," explained Khalid. "And then the weavers will start to think in terms of upgrading technology, using power looms. That will be the next step."

"Today we have started with Grameen Check," Yunus declared. "Tomorrow we can talk about making popcorn for you, or cereal, or raising orchids, or making shoes. We're building a highway. And tomorrow you'll have a telephone and I'll have a telephone—you, in Washington, D.C., talking to someone in Serajganj, Bangladesh."

In fact, Yunus had already proposed to the government that Grameen take over the rural cellular phone implementation in Bangladesh. With a network extending into 35,000 villages, Grameen was a natural choice.

Among Grameen's other enterprises, the Fisheries were by far the most promising. Productivity had soared. Yunus commented that Bangladesh had nearly 2 *million* unutilized or underutilized ponds. The DTWs were another story. "We have not yet accomplished anything in sustainable terms," Khalid told me. Recently, a new manager had been deployed, however. After three years in Rangpur, Shah Alam had set the zone on the path to recovery. Now, Yunus challenged him to tackle the problems of the Krishi Foundation.

Shah Alam accepted.

Shortly before my departure, the big news at the head office was that Mortuza had returned after a two-year leave of absence and had immediately reapplied for an additional leave. Mortuza had accepted a position with a foreign development agency where his salary was rumored to be twenty times that of Yunus's. (Yunus received 10,000 takas or about $250 per month, plus a housing allowance.)

The older managers were touchy about staff leaving Grameen for opportunities abroad. "We created the conditions so that Mortuza could become an international consultant," Daiyan told me. "It's because *we* have sacrificed." With the bank regarded by many as the world's preeminent development organization, its top managers were in demand. Dipal had recently turned down a consultancy offer at fifteen times his salary.

Typically, a staff member who leaves the bank is treated as a "deserter" and never rehired. Mortuza was a special case. He had sought, and received, a leave of absence. And of course, many remembered him as the individual who had carried the bank through the crisis in Tangail. Even so, Yunus would not grant the second leave. This time, when Mortuza left, he left for good.

The old-timers felt that Yunus had made the correct decision. Nurjahan, for one, was troubled about a general change in attitude among the staff. "Today, people come in expecting travel and food allowances, even bonuses," she said. Dipal was still looking for ways to replace older staff members with "fresh blood." However, his cousin Priti, in Jobra, did not plan to take the option for early retirement; she wanted to complete her twenty years to become the bank's first full pensioner.

Muzammel had pulled back from his duties and Masud had taken over the dealings with Grameen's donors. Muzammel wasn't sure what the future held. "When I see that I'm no longer needed," he told me, "I'll do something else. Maybe write down what I have learned from the poor."

"What have you learned?" I asked.

"The poor have tremendous management capability," he replied. "They know exactly what they want to do and how they want to do it. They only lack the resources." And the resources, he added, were available in abundance, if people only cared to look. The cost of providing employment opportunities to 2 million families, observed Muzammel, was less than the price of two F-16 fighter planes.

When I dropped in to say good-bye to Khalid he had just gotten off the phone with the zonal manager from Bogra. Religious fundamentalists in the area had recently mobilized against the bank. "This time they've made a well-coordinated assault," he explained. "They're being used by the landlords. I think the sudden expansion of the seasonal loan must have threatened quite a few of them."

"We'll let the local offices discuss this among themselves and mobilize opinion in their favor," he added. "You have to be patient in this sort of situation."

After so many years, were fundamentalists still a threat? I asked. Khalid said no. Grameen was a powerful institution; the only major external threat could come from the government. "The biggest danger remains the lack of appreciation at the political level as to what Grameen is doing," he explained. "Without that, we will face too many risks, like when this government decided to forgive all its loans under 5,000 takas."

As I was preparing to leave, Khalid stopped me to ask if I had heard about the bank's new Nutrition Program. I told him I hadn't. "I'm looking to see if we can now connect the Krishi Foundation with the

Health Program," he explained, "so that the maize, soybean, and wheat we grow can provide a nutrition supplement for children and their mothers in areas where there is acute malnourishment." He added: "We need the right kind of food at a price that people can afford."

Muzammel had suggested that before I leave I ask Yunus what he thought about Bangladesh's population. He said I would receive an interesting reply. The population of Bangladesh has quadrupled during the twentieth century. Every development worker I met spoke about the country's population growth in cataclysmic terms. Grameen strongly advised its borrowers to have small families. Nonetheless, Yunus felt that international agencies or programs whose main objective was "population control" were ill-conceived.

"Population is not the problem," he told me. "If you had a lot of *land,* would you worry? No, you wouldn't. You'd think it was a source of income. If you had a lot of *trees,* you wouldn't worry. So why worry if there are a lot of *people*? Because they eat. They take away resources. But you're only looking at one side of the picture; you forget that they also *produce.* You're not seeing that part of it and that's why you worry. I see the other part. I see that people are creative. You worry because you don't promote that creativity. You don't allow them to produce things."

The solution, as he saw it, was clear as day: Make it possible for each individual to contribute his or her fair share. "If we provide opportunities for people, we don't have to worry about them," he said.

"Then what do *you* worry about?" I asked.

"Is it an efficient process?" he replied. "Can we find a newer way, a better way, a faster way? We're still in the horse-and-buggy days. We have to move to cars and planes."

In a 1992 speech to a delegation of Grameen replicators, Yunus had commented: "There are a billion people on the earth who are extremely poor, and every minute the number is increasing because the world system creates poor people, but it does nothing to reduce their numbers. So here we are talking about a system that will stop it. Then, we'll track them back gradually from a billion to less than a billion to less than a million and so on." Three years later, he told another audience: "Hunger can be turned into a matter of the distant past." Now he told me: "I'm saying, 'Let's give the responsibility back to the poor people and create an environment where they can take control of their own lives. And let's do it well.' "

• • •

A few weeks earlier, Yunus had attended a ceremony in his honor at Chittagong University, where he had spoken of his experiences in Jobra two decades before. He spoke about Grameen's beginnings, but he also related another story—about when he first arrived at the university and was told that the campus spanned 2,200 acres, and he discovered that the university occupied only a tiny fragment of this land. Most of it was bare hills.

Bangladesh had just won its independence. The country had been ravaged by war. There was an infinite amount of work to be done. And here were bare hills! Hills are rare things in Bangladesh. Yunus could not fathom why nobody made use of these valuable resources. "If we grow these hills, this university wouldn't have to accept any money from the government," he told his colleagues. "We could build a forest. The university could generate its own money."

He spoke to his colleagues and approached the university administrators. "I wanted to walk along the campus borderline," he recalled. "But nobody knew where it was; and nobody wanted to see where it was. Everybody just said, 'We don't know.' They didn't even realize that the land was all hills and there were no trees on the hills. Then they told me that it wasn't really 2,200 acres, it was actually 1,600 acres. I said, 'That's good enough.' But when I started looking deeper, they said, 'No, no, it's not 1,600 acres, it's 1,400.' Then they said 1,200, and finally 1,100."

"Look," Yunus said to them. "I'll walk along the boundary line. Don't you have boundary posts?"

"No, we just have it on paper."

"We could raise a million takas!" he exclaimed. "Two million takas—for a start! We could earn it all back."

"This isn't our job," his colleagues replied. "Our job is to teach. We don't know anything about forestry."

Yunus brought his hands together near his chest, palms up, as if he were cradling a small bird and beseeching someone "Look! Take it!" His hands fell. His tone shifted. "So now those hills remain the same barren hills as before. Nothing has happened. In the meantime, we've tried to get a forestry institute on campus." He paused, and then with a note of certainty, added: "Some day those forestry students will afforest the whole place."

"Opportunities," he said. "Everywhere you look there are opportunities."

Interest

Six months after I left Bangladesh, I received a letter from Oirashi. It was handwritten in Bangla, perhaps by Monohor, the schoolteacher. Maheen Sultan translated it.

David,

I send you greetings. Give your mother, your father, your brother, and your sister my greetings. I hope that God has kept you well.

After you left, I was very worried wondering if you had reached your own country safely. I was very happy to receive your letter and the seven photographs you sent.

I still don't go to the center and in the future I won't go anymore. Some of the people who have gone against me are not paying their installments.

Some people in my old center have asked me to return, but I'll never go back. Because they'll cause trouble for me again.

The manager wants me to pay back everything I owe. Then he wants me to set up a new center and take more loans. I will, if it is possible.

You had wanted to know how my business is doing. With Nonie's salary, I manage to pay my installments. And with what's left over, I buy merchandise. I'm managing, with difficulty, to get by.

I haven't been able to build my new house and I haven't yet managed to marry off Nonie. Unless I build the house, I won't be able to find a son-in-law.

If you get married, you must send me photographs. And if you ever return to Bangladesh, you must come visit me.

If I have offended you in any way, please forgive me.

Yours,
Oirashibala Dhor

Acknowledgments

I wish to express my sincere gratitude to The Explorations Program of the Canada Council and to The Ford Foundation for their generous support during the writing of this book. I would also like to thank C. Michael Curtis, of *The Atlantic Monthly,* who acquired and edited the magazine article from which this book grew.

I am deeply indebted to Sadia Hamid Kazi and S. Arifa Hafiz (Miti), my translators, whose ability to put people at ease and whose deep respect for the villagers we interviewed are felt in each line of this book. I am indebted as well to dozens of Grameen Bank staff members posted in the Patuakhali, Tangail, Chittagong, Rajshahi, Rangpur, and Dhaka zones. Although the list of their names is too long to include here, I would like to thank five individuals in particular: Sabina Yasmin in the Dibuapur branch, Rezaul Islam in Patharghata, Saleha Begum in Fathyabad, Nurul Huda in Paira Banth, and Priti Rani Barua in Jobra.

A great number of people helped me to understand the inner workings of the Grameen Bank and international aid and a number of important things about life in Bangladesh. First, I would like to thank Muhammad Yunus, for allowing me virtually unlimited access to the bank. I am grateful to Nasreen Khundker, Syed M. Hashemi, Muzammel Huq, Khalid Shams, Dipal Chandra Barua, Shaikh Abdud Daiyan, Nurjahan Begum, S. M. Shamim Anwar, M. Masud Isa, Zubairul Hoque, H. I. Latifee, Jannat Quanine, Maheen Sultan, Mir Akhtar Hossain, the staff of the International Training Unit, particularly Chitta Ranjan Chaki, Mir Hossain Chowdhury, and Mohammed Abul Hossain, Afrozi Begum, Atiur Rahman, Muhammad Mortuza, Firoza Begum, Mohammad Shah Alam, A. K. M. Golam Mowla, Farah Ghuznavi, A. M. A. Muhith, Anthony Knowles, Randi Davis, Jennifer A. Topping, Richard Holloway, Brian Proskurniak, Joan Hubbard, Claudio Barcelo, David Gibbons,

Humaira Islam, Humaira Mahmud, Suhaila Khan, Bibi Russell, Rebecca Davey, Razia Quadir, Ruby Q. Noble, Shireen Quadir, and Jigdish Dutt.

I would also like to thank the following individuals based in the United States and Canada who offered their assistance and shared their ideas with me: Jeffrey Ashe, Christine Benuzzi, Henry Jackelen, Susan Gibson, Nina Nayer, Anita Jahan Bose, Tony Sheldon, Kim Wilson, Steven Balkin, Mary Houghton, Rob Rooy, Adrienne Germaine, Janet Dunnett, Martin Connell, Doug Salloum, Julia Vindasius, Ron Grzywinski, and Sam Daley-Harris.

Because they read all or part of the book before publication and offered comments or suggestions, I am deeply grateful to Lisa Silver, L. Rex Kay, Ted Riccardi, Susan Davis, Patricia Rodriguez, Diana Cohn, Mitchell Stephens, Chris Gampel, Annette Hunt, Rebecca Mead, Ellen Rozman, Gary Mart, Lloyd Fischler, Limor Tomer, Steven Wetta, Timothy A. Brown, and, especially, Ellen Coon, whose wisdom was indispensable to me at every stage of this project (and still is). I am grateful to Jack Hitt, Guy Gavriel Kay, Mark Segal, and Gary Taubes for their advice and support. My thanks also to Katy McLaughlin, Kathleen Barnes, Lisa Lazarus, Mitchell Kotansky, Rosemary Warnock, Christina Laurin, Mitchell Stotland, and Stuart J. Servetar, all of whom offered comments on the article that later became the book. I am indebted to the late Jack Robertson, executive producer of the Quiet Revolution documentary series, who got me interested in sustainable development, and to my friend Barbara Zahm, who gave me the idea of writing about the Grameen Bank.

I would like to thank my two editors, Mitch Horowitz, who signed me up for Simon & Schuster, and Mary Ann Naples, who inherited the book and brought it all together. Many thanks also to Laurie Chittenden, who was a delight to work with. I am extremely fortunate to be associated with Mildred Marmur, my literary agent, adviser, and friend, who knows more about the publishing world than just about anyone alive, and who is never anything less than the consummate professional. Thanks also to her associate, Jane Lebowitz, for handling so many requests with patience and efficiency.

This book was made possible through the combined participation of two groups of people who have never met each other and never will. I am indebted to those who shared their stories, hopes, and frustrations with me: Oirashi, Nonie, the two Aleyas, Ansar, Rani, Sahera, Rokeya, Alum, Taslima, Amena, Parveen, Manjira, Irani, Fotorani, Minara, Hajera, Putulrani, Ferdozi, Masuda, Jebal Hossain, Monwara, and others.

I could not have stuck it out for the four years it took to complete this project if not for the love and encouragement of my family: my parents,

Barbara and Robert, my brother, Garner, and sister-in-law, Jane, my sister Lisa, my extraordinary aunts, Selma and Susan, and my dear friend Felicia.

Above all, this book belongs to Abigail. There is not a single page which does not bear the imprint of her thinking on mine: her merciless honesty and her ferocious kindness. Once I asked her to briefly sum up Yunus's accomplishment in creating the Grameen Bank, and she wrote to me: "It is a rarity when a human being has the ability to see truth clearly and acts on it, creating the visibility of the truth for others." This, Abigail has done for me.

Author's Note

Much of the research for this book was conducted during two visits to Bangladesh: from January to May, 1992, and from February to June, 1994. During my stays in rural Bangladesh I relied extensively on the assistance and guidance of translators.

A number of friends and colleagues who read early versions of this book expressed curiosity about how I conducted my research in villages. It took me a couple of months to work out a system for interviewing villagers. In the beginning, I felt awkward. In a few cases, shortly after meeting a villager, I clumsily pulled out my tape recorder and began asking direct questions. When these interviews were later transcribed they invariably came out wooden and dull. The villagers were guarded; I had done nothing to gain their trust.

Later, I tried on-the-spot note-taking, which seemed less intrusive, but, eventually, I abandoned note-taking on visits with villagers. This allowed me to relax and listen and observe. Afterward, back at the branch office where my translator and I stayed, we would discuss our work and write everything down. This method had its limitations, however. For example, we would not have been able to recall in its entirety Rokeya's moving account of the death of her son.

Everything was made easier with time. After a number of visits, villagers usually got accustomed to my questions, and I felt comfortable asking them if I could take notes or use a tape recorder. At this point, villagers often responded by going to the opposite extreme—rather than stiffen up, they would embellish their stories for my benefit (and for the benefit of their neighbors and relatives). One woman's account of her battles with a brother who had stolen her land and burned down her house was particularly riveting. I spent two days getting it down before I learned from other villagers that little of it was true. This was only one of a number of instances (that I know of) when I was taken in.

In the end, the stories and words in this book were selected from more than a thouand pages of notes as those I believe to be most faithful to the experiences of Grameen Bank borrowers.

Afterword

Since this book was published, I haven't had the opportunity to return to Bangladesh. Late last year, I received a letter from Oirashi. She wrote that she was still experiencing difficulties with her former center members. Nonie, her daughter, was still unmarried. Oirashi hoped to have enough money to build her house in a few more years.

I often see Yunus on his visits to the United States. He is always filled with fresh enthusiasm. Grameen has diversified into a number of new areas in the past few years. The organization now has so much momentum that ideas seem to become reality overnight. Grameen Telecom already has 4,000 cellular phone subscribers in Dhaka and will be operating in 150 villages by December 1997. Grameen Cybernet—currently the largest internet provider in Bangladesh—is exploring new ways to make use of the Internet in poverty-alleviation efforts. Grameen Energy has launched pilot projects to test solar, wind, and bio-gas energy in villages throughout the country. Grameen Check now employs 15,000 village-based, hand-loom weavers and has exported 20 million yards of cloth to Europe and North America.

Grameen's momentum reaches far beyond Bangladesh as micro-credit continues to spread around the world. Earlier this year, more than 2,600 people from 137 countries gathered in Washington, D.C., for the world's first "International Micro-Credit Summit." Organized by the Washington-based Results Educational Fund, the Micro-Credit Summit brought together representatives from microenterprise organizations, governments, multilateral agencies, banks, corporations, and a wide array of NGOs. A number of heads of state attended, as well as U.S. First Lady Hillary Rodham Clinton. Their goal was to launch a global movement to "reach 100 million of the world's poorest families, especially the women of those families, with credit for self-employment and other financial and business services by the year 2005." The estimated cost of achieving this goal: $21.6 billion.

I attended the summit and found the event quite moving. The evening before the opening plenary session, I looked in on the ball-room at the Sheraton Washington Hotel. The room contained 2,500 chairs; it seemed amazing to me that so many people had traveled from around the world, on the strength of an idea and a vision, to fill those seats. I thought of Yunus's struggle over the past two decades to get others to share his vision, and I imagined what an emotional day it would be for him.

In his opening speech, Yunus said, "I wish to take this opportunity to thank millions of micro-borrowers and thousands of staff who worked very hard to right a wrong which has caused so much avoidable human misery." He added, "This summit is about setting the stage to unleash human creativity and the endeavor of the poor. This summit is about creating a process which will send poverty to the museum."

I listened as Yunus compared the microcredit movement today to the Wright Brothers' first flight, which lasted twelve seconds. "At that moment the seed of a new world was planted," he said. Only sixty-five years later, he added, men walked on the moon. In another half century, Yunus told the gathering, "we'll also go to our moon—we'll create a poverty-free world."

Looking around at the sea of very different faces, I thought of how such a gathering would have been inconceivable just five years earlier. I recalled Muzammel telling me how, in the early 1980s, the bankers had predicted that Grameen would soon "burst like a balloon." Listening to Yunus in that hall, I felt a great sense of possibility. I pictured the thousands of people around me returning to their countries, energized and inspired and full of new ideas. I imagined them working in their villages and cities, forging ahead steadily, relentlessly, over the years, the way Grameen had done. And for a moment, I could see how Yunus's vision would come to be.

June 1997

New York

For those interested in learning more about the Grameen Bank, contact the Grameen Foundation (tel: 202-543-2636; fax: 202-546-7512; e-mail: grameen_foundation@ msn.com). For inquiries relating to the Microcredit Summit, contact the Results Educational Fund (tel: 202-546-1900; fax: 202-546-3228; e-mail: microcredit@igc.apc.org; Web: http://www.igc.org/MicrocreditSummit). Both the Grameen Foundation and the Results Educational Fund can be reached at the following address: 236 Massachusetts Avenue, NE, Suite 300, Washington, D.C., 20002.

The Grameen Foundation has recently launched a campaign called the People's Fund. The goal is to raise $100 million for microenterprise development through one million individual "commitments" of $100. Only contributions of $100 are accepted.

Those who cannot donate $100 may sign a "Note of Confidence." Donors who seek to give more than $100 may do so, but only on behalf of individuals who have previously signed notes of confidence. The purpose is to raise funds for microenterprise while educating one million people about the work of the Grameen Bank. One hundred percent of proceeds will be used for Grameen replication projects. Funding for administrative costs will be raised separately. (tel: 800-587-3252; Web: http://www.peoplesfund.com.)

Other publications on the Grameen Bank include: *Give Us Credit: How Muhammad Yunus's Micro-Credit Revolution is Empowering Women from Bangladesh to Chicago,* by Alex Counts (Random House, 1996); *Women at the Center: Grameen Bank Borrowers After One Decade,* by Helen Todd (Westview Press, 1996, tel: 800-822-4090); *Managing to Empower: The Grameen Bank's Experience of Poverty Alleviation,* by Susan Holcombe (Zed Books, 1995, available from Humanities Press International: 908-872-1441); *The Grameen Reader,* edited by David S. Gibbons (Grameen Bank, 1994); *Jorimon and Others: Faces of Poverty,* edited by Muhammad Yunus (Grameen Bank, 1991); and *Participation as Process—Process as Growth,* by Andreas Fuglesang and Dale Chandler (Grameen Trust, 1993). The Grameen Trust also publishes a quarterly newsletter, *Grameen Dialogue.* All Grameen publications are available from the Grameen Foundation.

Credit for the Poor, a newsletter focusing on Grameen replications in Asia, is available from CASHPOR Technical Services, in Malaysia (fax: 606-764-2307, e-mail: gibbons@pc.jaring.my). CASHPOR has several other excellent publications for microcredit researchers and practitioners.

A fast growing body of information about microenterprise is available on the Internet, most of which is easily found using major Web search engines. A few starting points are: The Grameen Bank Homepage (http://www.citechco.net/grameen); the Informal Credit Homepage (http://titsoc.soc.titech.ac.jp/titsoc/higuchi-lab/icm); the Accion International Homepage (http://www.accion.org); the Grameen Bank Support Group of Australia (http://www.rdc.com.au/grameen).

Each year, the Grameen Trust organizes several week-and-a-half-long Grameen International Dialogue Programmes, designed to assist those who have launched, or are planning to launch, credit programs for poor people based on the Grameen Bank approach. In addition, students, journalists, and researchers at all levels of study are welcomed by Grameen for extended visits. Requests should be directed to the Managing Director of the Grameen Trust. The Grameen Bank and Grameen Trust have the same address: Mirpur Two, Dhaka 1216, Bangladesh (fax: 880-2-803-559 or 880-2-806-319; e-mail: grameen.bank@citechco.net or grameen.trust@citechco.net).

For information on microenterprise organizations in the United States and Canada, contact the Association for Enterprise Opportunity at 70 East Lake Street, Suite 620, Chicago 60601; tel: 312-357-0177; fax: 312-357-0180. The Aspen Institute's Self-Employment Learning Project has conducted extensive research on domestic microenterprise programs. Write to: The Aspen Institute, SELP, 1333 New Hampshire Ave. NW, Suite 1070, Washington 20036; or tel: 202-736-5800. In Canada, information on the Grameen Bank and other microenterprise programs can be obtained from Calmeadow at 4 King Street West, Suite 300, Toronto, Ontario, Canada M5H 1B6; tel: 416-362-9670; fax: 416-362-0769.

Index

(Page numbers in *italics* refer to illustrations.)

immunizations, 33, 298
Independence Day Award, 218
India, 31, 64, 278
industrial development banks, 177
industrialization, 23–24
infant mortality, 233–34, 312
"informal" economy, 229
infrastructure, 26, 227, 241–42, 249, 332
inheritance, 152–53, 159, 202, 278
Inquilab, The (newspaper), 156
Institute of Policy Studies, Washington, D.C., 334
insurance, 20, 139, 300; health, 154, 300; life, 52
Integrated Rural Development Program, 228, 244
interest rates, 21, 26, 45, 61, 80, 99, 104, 120, 143, 153, 154, 170, 171, 290, 293–95, 311
International Dialogue Conference, 273
International Fund for Agricultural Development (IFAD), 119–24, 127–28, 140, 176–78
International Monetary Fund, 234
International Peace Research Institute, 121–22
International Training Unit, 71–73, 171
"irregular loanee," 222
irrigation, 34–37, 215, 216, 254–56, 266
Isa, M. Masud, *see* Masud Isa, M.
Islam, 31, 78, 142, 161, 183, 220, 222; law, 139–40

Jackelen, Henry, 255
Jacobs, Jane, *Systems of Survival,* 337
Jamuna River, 213–14
Janata Bank, 36, 40, 42, 44, 47, 50, 61, 105, 110, 114
Japan, 23, 295
jaundice, 299

Jobra, 32–67, 109, 114, 167, 171, 216, 217, 265, 350
Jobra Landless Association, 41
Johnson, Samuel, 117
joint enterprises, 219
Joysagar Fish Farm, 219, 254, 295, 299, 342
Jugis, 325

Kaplan, Robert, 22–23
Kaus, Mickey, *The End of Equality,* 338–39
Kenyan Rural Enterprise Program, 228
Keynes, John Maynard, 239
Khalid Shams, 260–63, 266, 274–75, 296, *298,* 299, 345–49
Khatun, Manjira, *see* Manjira Khatun
Khundker, Nasreen, 125
King Baudouin International Development Prize, 301–7, 331
kinship clans, 96, 216, 319–21, 324–325
Knowles, Anthony, 243–47
Koran, 214
Kreditanstalt für Wiederaufbau (KfW), 250, 252
Krishi (Agricultural) Foundation, 299, 347, 348
Krishi Bank, 48–51, 61, 105, 220, 223

land inheritance, 152–53, 159, 202, 278–79
landlessness, 38, 41, 53–54, 55, 62, 125, 128–29, 139, 140, 143, 145, 148–49, 152, 181, 183–84, 190, 197, 211, 234, 258, 279, 280, 291, 297–98; *see also* poverty
land purchase loans, 289
land reform, 38, 53–54, 152
language, 31, 304
Latin America, 228, 294, 332
law, Islamic, 139–40
"left-hand practices," 171–73